BODIES THAT MATTER

BODIES THAT MATTER

ON THE

DISCURSIVE

LIMITS

OF

"SEX"

JUDITH BUTLER

Routledge ▪ New York & London

Published in 1993 by

Routledge
29 West 35 Street
New York, NY 10001

Published in Great Britain by

Routledge
11 New Fetter Lane
London EC4P 4EE

Copyright © 1993 by Routledge

Printed in the United States on acid free paper.

Library of Congress Cataloging-in-Publication Data
Butler, Judith P.
    Bodies that matter: on the discursive limits of "sex" /
Judith Butler.
        p.   cm.
    Includes index (p.   ).
    ISBN 0-415-90365-3 (CL). — ISBN 0-415-90366-1 (PB)
    1. Feminist theory.   2. Sex role—Philosophy.   3. Sex differ-
    ences (Psychology)   4. Sexual orientation—Philosophy.   5.
    Identity (Psychology)   6. Femininity (Psychology)   I. Title.
HQ1190.B88   1993
305.3—dc20
                                                    93-7667
                                                    CIP

British Library Cataloguing-in-Publication Data also available.

CONTENTS

Acknowledgments *vii*

Preface *ix*

Introduction *1*

PART ONE

1 Bodies that Matter *27*

2 The Lesbian Phallus and the Morphological Imaginary *57*

3 Phantasmatic Identification and the Assumption of Sex *93*

4 Gender Is Burning: Questions of Appropriation and Subversion *121*

PART TWO

5 "Dangerous Crossing": Willa Cather's Masculine Names *143*

6 Passing, Queering: Nella Larsen's Psychoanalytic Challenge *167*

7 Arguing with the Real *187*

8 Critically Queer *223*

Notes *243*

Index *285*

ACKNOWLEDGMENTS

I thank Maureen MacGrogan once again for soliciting and sustaining this book with her characteristic generosity and intelligence. My enduring appreciation also goes to Joan W. Scott for the incisive way she grasps the project first, for her excellent reading of the entire text, and for her fine friendship. I have been very lucky to have excellent readers in Drucilla Cornell, Elizabeth Grosz, and Margaret Whitford; their criticisms of earlier drafts were enormously useful. I thank as well my seminar at Cornell University for engaging conversations in the fall of 1991 when this project began to take shape. The production staff at Routledge was also enormously helpful throughout this process. A number of colleagues and students have helped in thinking about the text, sometimes reading drafts and offering excellent criticism or helping with the production of the manuscript: Elizabeth Abel, Bice Benvenuto, Teresa Brennan, Alexandra Chasin, William Connolly, Karin Cope, Peter Euben, Carla Freccero, Nelly Furman, Jonathan Goldberg, Simon Goldhill, Donna Haraway, Susan Harding, Gail Hershatter, Morris Kaplan, Debra Keates, Biddy Martin, Bridget McDonald, Mandy Merck, Michael Moon, Naomi Schor, Eve Kosofsky Sedgwick, Josh Shapiro, James Swenson, Jen Thomas, Tim Walters, Dave Wittenberg, and Elizabeth Weed. I thank Eloise Moore Agger, for her disarming ways; Linda L. Anderson, Inès Azar, Fran Bartkowski, Robert Gooding-Williams, Jeff Nunokawa, Mary Poovey, and Eszti Votaw for their indispensable friendship; and Wendy Brown for engaging my thinking thoroughly and critically, and for the careful persuasion which helped me to see how revisions of some of my earlier positions might better suit and clarify my aims.

This project was assisted through various highly appreciated forms of institutional support. Three of these chapters were presented in shorter versions as the Beckman Lectures for the Department of English at the University of California at Berkeley during the spring of 1992. I am very glad to have had such an opportunity to learn from colleagues and students at UC-Berkeley. As a senior fellow at the Society for the Humanities at Cornell University in the fall of 1991, I gained invaluable commentary on the project from faculty and students alike. I thank Jonathan Culler for supporting my research in various ways, including his invitation to the Humanities Research Institute at the University of California at Irvine in April of 1992.

My students at Johns Hopkins University have been invaluable inter-locutors. And my colleagues at the Humanities Center at Johns Hopkins University not only supported my research, but provided a rich, interdis-ciplinary intellectual life for which I am most grateful.

This book is written in the memory of those friends and family I have lost in recent years: my father, Dan Butler; my grandmother, Helen Greenberger Lefkowich; my friends, Linda Singer and Kathy Natanson. And it is written for the company of colleagues who inform, sustain, and receive this labor, such as it is.

PREFACE

I began writing this book by trying to consider the materiality of the body only to find that the thought of materiality invariably moved me into other domains. I tried to discipline myself to stay on the subject, but found that I could not fix bodies as simple objects of thought. Not only did bodies tend to indicate a world beyond themselves, but this movement beyond their own boundaries, a movement of boundary itself, appeared to be quite central to what bodies "are." I kept losing track of the subject. I proved resistant to discipline. Inevitably, I began to consider that perhaps this resistance to fixing the subject was essential to the matter at hand.

Still doubtful, though, I reflected that this wavering might be the vocational difficulty of those trained in philosophy, always at some distance from corporeal matters, who try in that disembodied way to demarcate bodily terrains: they invariably miss the body or, worse, write against it. Sometimes they forget that "the" body comes in genders. But perhaps there is now another difficulty after a generation of feminist writing which tried, with varying degrees of success, to bring the feminine body into writing, to write the feminine proximately or directly, sometimes without even the hint of a preposition or marker of linguistic distance between the writing and the written. It may be only a question of learning how to read those troubled translations, but some of us nevertheless found ourselves returning to pillage the Logos for its useful remains.

Theorizing from the ruins of the Logos invites the following question: "What about the materiality of the body?" Actually, in the recent past, the question was repeatedly formulated to me this way: "What about the materiality of the body, *Judy*?" I took it that the addition of "Judy" was an effort to dislodge me from the more formal "Judith" and to recall me to a bodily life that could not be theorized away. There was a certain exasperation in the delivery of that final diminutive, a certain patronizing quality which (re)constituted me as an unruly child, one who needed to be brought to task, restored to that bodily being which is, after all, considered to be most real, most pressing, most undeniable. Perhaps this was an effort to recall me to an apparently evacuated femininity, the one that was constituted at that moment in the mid-'50s when the figure of Judy Garland inadvertently produced a string of "Judys" whose later appropriations and derailments could not have been predicted. Or perhaps someone forgot to teach me "the facts of life"? Was I lost to my own imaginary musings as that vital conversation was taking place? And if I persisted in this notion that bodies were in some way *constructed*, perhaps I really thought that words alone had the power to craft bodies from their own linguistic substance?

Couldn't someone simply take me aside?

Matters have been made even worse, if not more remote, by the questions raised by the notion of gender performativity introduced in *Gender Trouble*.[1] For if I were to argue that genders are performative, that could mean that I thought that one woke in the morning, perused the closet or some more open space for the gender of choice, donned that gender for the day, and then restored the garment to its place at night. Such a willful and instrumental subject, one who decides *on* its gender, is clearly not its gender from the start and fails to realize that its existence is already decided *by* gender. Certainly, such a theory would restore a figure of a choosing subject—humanist—at the center of a project whose emphasis on construction seems to be quite opposed to such a notion.

But if there is no subject who decides on its gender, and if, on the contrary, gender is part of what decides the subject, how might one formulate a project that preserves gender practices as sites of critical agency? If gender is constructed through relations of power and, specifically, normative constraints that not only produce but also regulate various bodily beings, how might agency be derived from this notion of gender as the effect of productive constraint? If gender is not an artifice to be taken on or taken off at will and, hence, not an effect of choice, how are we to understand the constitutive and compelling status of gender norms without falling into the trap of cultural determinism? How precisely are we to understand the ritualized repetition by which such norms produce and stabilize not only the effects of gender but the materiality of sex? And can this repetition, this rearticulation, also constitute the occasion for a critical reworking of apparently constitutive gender norms?

To claim that the materiality of sex is constructed through a ritualized repetition of norms is hardly a self-evident claim. Indeed, our customary notions of "construction" seem to get in the way of understanding such a claim. For surely bodies live and die; eat and sleep; feel pain, pleasure; endure illness and violence; and these "facts," one might skeptically proclaim, cannot be dismissed as mere construction. Surely there must be some kind of necessity that accompanies these primary and irrefutable experiences. And surely there is. But their irrefutability in no way implies what it might mean to affirm them and through what discursive means. Moreover, why is it that what is constructed is understood as an artificial and dispensable character? What are we to make of constructions without which we would not be able to think, to live, to make sense at all, those which have acquired for us a kind of necessity? Are certain constructions of the body constitutive in this sense: that we could not operate without them, that without them there would be no "I," no "we"? Thinking the body as constructed demands a rethinking of the meaning of construction itself. And if certain constructions appear constitutive, that is, have this character of being that "without which" we could not think at all, we might suggest that bodies only appear, only endure, only live within the productive constraints of certain highly gendered regulatory schemas.

Given this understanding of construction as constitutive constraint, is it still possible to raise the critical question of how such constraints not only produce the domain of intelligible bodies, but produce as well a domain of unthinkable, abject, unlivable bodies? This latter domain is not the opposite of the former, for oppositions are, after all, part of intelligibility; the latter is the excluded and illegible domain that haunts the former domain as the spectre of its own impossibility, the very limit to intelligibility, its constitutive outside. How, then, might one alter the very terms that constitute the "necessary" domain of bodies through rendering unthinkable and unlivable another domain of bodies, those that do not matter in the same way.

The discourse of "construction" that has for the most part circulated in feminist theory is perhaps not quite adequate to the task at hand. It is not enough to argue that there is no prediscursive "sex" that acts as the stable point of reference on which, or in relation to which, the cultural construction of gender proceeds. To claim that sex is already gendered, already constructed, is not yet to explain in which way the "materiality" of sex is forcibly produced. What are the constraints by which bodies are materialized as "sexed," and how are we to understand the "matter" of sex, and of bodies more generally, as the repeated and violent circumscription of cultural intelligibility? Which bodies come to matter—and why?

This text is offered, then, in part as a rethinking of some parts of *Gender Trouble* that have caused confusion, but also as an effort to think further about the workings of heterosexual hegemony in the crafting of matters sexual and political. As a critical rearticulation of various theoretical practices, including feminist and queer studies, this text is not intended to be programmatic. And yet, as an attempt to clarify my "intentions," it appears destined to produce a new set of misapprehensions. I hope that they prove, at least, to be productive ones.

INTRODUCTION

> Why should our bodies end at the skin, or include at best other beings encapsulated by skin?
>
> —Donna Haraway, *A Manifesto for Cyborgs*

> If one really thinks about the body as such, there is no possible outline of the body as such. There are thinkings of the systematicity of the body, there are value codings of the body. The body, as such, cannot be thought, and I certainly cannot approach it.
>
> —Gayatri Chakravorty Spivak, "In a Word," interview with Ellen Rooney

> There is no nature, only the effects of nature: denaturalization or naturalization.
>
> —Jacques Derrida, *Donner le Temps*

Is there a way to link the question of the materiality of the body to the performativity of gender? And how does the category of "sex" figure within such a relationship? Consider first that sexual difference is often invoked as an issue of material differences. Sexual difference, however, is never simply a function of material differences which are not in some way both marked and formed by discursive practices. Further, to claim that sexual differences are indissociable from discursive demarcations is not the same as claiming that discourse causes sexual difference. The category of "sex" is, from the start, normative; it is what Foucault has called a "regulatory ideal." In this sense, then, "sex" not only functions as a norm, but is part of a regulatory practice that produces the bodies it governs, that is, whose regulatory force is made clear as a kind of productive power, the power to produce—demarcate, circulate, differentiate—the bodies it controls. Thus, "sex" is a regulatory ideal whose materialization is compelled, and this materialization takes place (or fails to take place) through certain highly regulated practices. In other words, "sex" is an ideal construct which is forcibly materialized through time. It is not a simple fact or static condition of a body, but a process whereby regulatory norms materialize "sex" and achieve this materialization through a forcible reiteration of those norms. That this reiteration is necessary is a sign that materialization is never quite complete, that bodies never quite comply with the norms by which their materialization is impelled. Indeed, it is the instabilities, the possibilities for rematerialization, opened up by this process that mark one domain in which the force of the regulatory law can be turned against itself to spawn rearticulations that call into question the hegemonic force of that very regulatory law.

But how, then, does the notion of gender performativity relate to this conception of materialization? In the first instance, performativity must be understood not as a singular or deliberate "act," but, rather, as the reiterative and citational practice by which discourse produces the effects that it names. What will, I hope, become clear in what follows is that the regulatory norms of "sex" work in a performative fashion to constitute the materiality of bodies and, more specifically, to materialize the body's sex, to materialize sexual difference in the service of the consolidation of the heterosexual imperative.

In this sense, what constitutes the fixity of the body, its contours, its movements, will be fully material, but materiality will be rethought as the effect of power, as power's most productive effect. And there will be no way to understand "gender" as a cultural construct which is imposed upon the surface of matter, understood either as "the body" or its given sex. Rather, once "sex" itself is understood in its normativity, the materiality of the body will not be thinkable apart from the materialization of that regulatory norm. "Sex" is, thus, not simply what one has, or a static description of what one is: it will be one of the norms by which the "one" becomes viable at all, that which qualifies a body for life within the domain of cultural intelligibility.[1]

At stake in such a reformulation of the materiality of bodies will be the following: (1) the recasting of the matter of bodies as the effect of a dynamic of power, such that the matter of bodies will be indissociable from the regulatory norms that govern their materialization and the signification of those material effects; (2) the understanding of performativity not as the act by which a subject brings into being what she/he names, but, rather, as that reiterative power of discourse to produce the phenomena that it regulates and constrains; (3) the construal of "sex" no longer as a bodily given on which the construct of gender is artificially imposed, but as a cultural norm which governs the materialization of bodies; (4) a rethinking of the process by which a bodily norm is assumed, appropriated, taken on as not, strictly speaking, undergone *by a subject*, but rather that the subject, the speaking "I," is formed by virtue of having gone through such a process of assuming a sex; and (5) a linking of this process of "assuming" a sex with the question of *identification*, and with the discursive means by which the heterosexual imperative enables certain sexed identifications and forecloses and/or disavows other identifications. This exclusionary matrix by which subjects are formed thus requires the simultaneous production of a domain of abject beings, those who are not yet "subjects," but who form the constitutive outside to the domain of the subject. The abject[2] designates here precisely those "unlivable" and "uninhabitable" zones of social life which are nevertheless densely populated by those who do not enjoy the status of the subject, but whose living under the sign of the "unlivable" is required to circumscribe the domain of the subject. This zone of uninhabitability will constitute the defining limit of the subject's domain; it will constitute that site of dreaded identification against which—and by virtue of which—the domain of the subject will circumscribe its own claim to autonomy and to life. In this sense, then, the subject is constituted through the force of exclusion and abjection, one which produces a constitutive outside to the subject, an abjected outside, which is, after all, "inside" the subject as its own founding repudiation.

The forming of a subject requires an identification with the normative phantasm of "sex," and this identification takes place through a repudiation which produces a domain of abjection, a repudiation without which the subject cannot emerge. This is a repudiation which creates the valence of "abjection" and its status for the subject as a threatening spectre. Further, the materialization of a given sex will centrally concern *the regulation of identificatory practices* such that the identification with the abjection of sex will be persistently disavowed. And yet, this disavowed abjection will threaten to expose the self-grounding presumptions of the sexed subject, grounded as that subject is in a repudiation whose consequences it cannot fully control. The task will be to consider this threat and disruption not as a permanent contestation of social norms condemned to the pathos of perpetual failure, but rather as a critical resource in the struggle to rearticulate the very terms of symbolic legitimacy and intelligibility.

Lastly, the mobilization of the categories of sex within political discourse will be haunted in some ways by the very instabilities that the categories effectively produce and foreclose. Although the political discourses that mobilize identity categories tend to cultivate identifications in the service of a political goal, it may be that the persistence of *dis*identification is equally crucial to the rearticulation of democratic contestation. Indeed, it may be precisely through practices which underscore disidentification with those regulatory norms by which sexual difference is materialized that both feminist and queer politics are mobilized. Such collective disidentifications can facilitate a reconceptualization of which bodies matter, and which bodies are yet to emerge as critical matters of concern.

FROM CONSTRUCTION TO MATERIALIZATION

The relation between culture and nature presupposed by some models of gender "construction" implies a culture or an agency of the social which acts upon a nature, which is itself presupposed as a passive surface, outside the social and yet its necessary counterpart. One question that feminists have raised, then, is whether the discourse which figures the action of construction as a kind of imprinting or imposition is not tacitly masculinist, whereas the figure of the passive surface, awaiting that penetrating act whereby meaning is endowed, is not tacitly or—perhaps—quite obviously feminine. Is sex to gender as feminine is to masculine?[3]

Other feminist scholars have argued that the very concept of nature needs to rethought, for the concept of nature has a history, and the figuring of nature as the blank and lifeless page, as that which is, as it were, always already dead, is decidedly modern, linked perhaps to the emergence of technological means of domination. Indeed, some have argued that a rethinking of "nature" as a set of dynamic interrelations suits both feminist and ecological aims (and has for some produced an otherwise unlikely alliance with the work of Gilles Deleuze). This rethinking also calls into question the model of construction whereby the social unilaterally acts on the natural and invests it with its parameters and its meanings. Indeed, as much as the radical distinction between sex and gender has been crucial to the de Beauvoirian version of feminism, it has come under criticism in more recent years for degrading the natural as that which is "before" intelligibility, in need of the mark, if not the mar, of the social to signify, to be known, to acquire value. This misses the point that nature has a history, and not merely a social one, but, also, that sex is positioned ambiguously in relation to that concept and its history. The concept of "sex" is itself troubled terrain, formed through a series of contestations over what ought to be decisive criterion for distinguishing between the two sexes; the concept of sex has a history that is covered over by the figure of the site or surface of inscription. Figured as such a site or surface, however, the natural is construed as that which is also without value; moreover, it assumes its value at the same time that it assumes its social character, that is, at the same time that nature relinquishes itself as the natural. According to this view, then, the social construction of the natural presupposes the cancellation of the natural by the social. Insofar as it relies on this construal, the sex/gender distinction founders along parallel lines; if gender is the social significance that sex assumes within a given culture—and for the sake of argument we will let "social" and "cultural" stand in an uneasy interchangeability—then what, if anything, is left of "sex" once it has assumed its social character as gender? At issue is the meaning of "assumption," where to be "assumed" is to be taken up into a more elevated sphere, as in "the Assumption of the Virgin." If gender consists of the social meanings that sex assumes, then sex does not *accrue* social meanings as additive properties but, rather, *is replaced by* the social meanings it takes on; sex is relinquished in the course of that assumption, and gender emerges, not as a term in a continued relationship of opposition to sex, but as the term which absorbs and displaces "sex," the mark of its full substantiation into gender or what, from a materialist point of view, might constitute a full *de*substantiation.

When the sex/gender distinction is joined with a notion of radical linguistic constructivism, the problem becomes even worse, for the "sex" which is referred to as prior to gender will itself be a postulation, a construction, offered within language, as that which is prior to language, prior to construction. But this sex posited as prior to construction will, by virtue of being posited, become the effect of that very positing, the construction of construction. If gender is the social construction of sex, and if there is no access to this "sex" except by means of its construction, then it appears not only that sex is absorbed by gender, but that "sex" becomes something like a fiction, perhaps a fantasy, retroactively installed at a prelinguistic site to which there is no direct access.

But is it right to claim that "sex" vanishes altogether, that it is a fiction over and against what is true, that it is a fantasy over and against what is reality? Or do these very oppositions need to be rethought such that if "sex" is a fiction, it is one within whose necessities we live, without which life itself would be unthinkable? And if "sex" is a fantasy, is it perhaps a phantasmatic field that constitutes the very terrain of cultural intelligibility? Would such a rethinking of such conventional oppositions entail a rethinking of "constructivism" in its usual sense?

The radical constructivist position has tended to produce the premise that both refutes and confirms its own enterprise. If such a theory cannot take account of sex as the site or surface on which it acts, then it ends up presuming sex as the unconstructed, and so concedes the limits of linguistic constructivism, inadvertently circumscribing that which remains unaccountable within the terms of construction. If, on the other hand, sex is a contrived premise, a fiction, then gender does not presume a sex which it acts upon, but rather, gender produces the misnomer of a prediscursive "sex," and the meaning of construction becomes that of linguistic monism, whereby everything is only and always language. Then, what ensues is an exasperated debate which many of us have tired of hearing: Either (1) constructivism is reduced to a position of linguistic monism, whereby linguistic construction is understood to be generative and deterministic. Critics making that presumption can be heard to say, "If everything is discourse, what about the body?" or (2) when construction is figuratively reduced to a verbal action which appears to presuppose a subject, critics working within such a presumption can be heard to say, "If gender is constructed, then who is doing the constructing?"; though, of course, (3) the most pertinent formulation of this question is the following: "If the subject is constructed, then who is constructing the subject?" In the first case, construction has taken the place of a godlike agency which not only causes but composes everything which is its object; it is the divine performative, bringing into being and exhaustively constituting that which it names, or, rather, it is that kind of transitive referring which names and inaugurates at once. For something to be constructed, according to this view of construction, is for it to be created and determined through that process.

In the second and third cases, the seductions of grammar appear to hold sway; the critic asks, Must there not be a human agent, a subject, if you will, who guides the course of construction? If the first version of constructivism presumes that construction operates deterministically, making a mockery of human agency, the second understands constructivism as presupposing a voluntarist subject who makes its gender through an instrumental action. A construction is understood in this latter case to be a kind of manipulable artifice, a conception that not only presupposes a subject, but rehabilitates precisely the voluntarist subject of humanism that constructivism has, on occasion, sought to put into question.

If gender is a construction, must there be an "I" or a "we" who enacts or performs that construction? How can there be an activity, a constructing, without presupposing an agent who precedes and performs that activity? How would we account for the motivation and direction of construction without such a subject? As a rejoinder, I would suggest that it takes a certain suspicion toward grammar to reconceive the matter in a different light. For if gender is constructed, it is not necessarily constructed by an "I" or a "we" who stands before that construction in any spatial or temporal sense of "before." Indeed, it is unclear that there can be an "I" or a "we" who has not been submitted, subjected to gender, where gendering is, among other things, the differentiating relations by which speaking subjects come into being. Subjected to gender, but subjectivated by gender, the "I" neither precedes nor follows the process of this gendering, but emerges only within and as the matrix of gender relations themselves.

This then returns us to the second objection, the one which claims that constructivism forecloses agency, preempts the agency of the subject, and finds itself presupposing the subject that it calls into question. To claim that the subject is itself produced in and as a gendered matrix of relations is not to do away with the subject, but only to ask after the conditions of its emergence and operation. The "activity" of this gendering cannot, strictly speaking, be a human act or expression, a willful appropriation, and it is certainly *not* a question of taking on a mask; it is the matrix through which all willing first becomes possible, its enabling cultural condition. In this sense, the matrix of gender relations is prior to the emergence of the "human". Consider the medical interpellation which (the recent emergence of the sonogram notwithstanding) shifts an infant from an "it" to a "she" or a "he," and in that naming, the girl is "girled," brought into the domain of language and kinship through the interpellation of gender. But that "girling" of the girl does not end there; on the contrary, that founding interpellation is reiterated by various authorities and throughout various intervals of time to reenforce or contest this naturalized effect. The naming is at once the setting of a boundary, and also the repeated inculcation of a norm.

Such attributions or interpellations contribute to that field of discourse and power that orchestrates, delimits, and sustains that which qualifies as "the human." We see this most clearly in the examples of those abjected beings who do not appear properly gendered; it is their very humanness that comes into question. Indeed, the construction of gender operates through *exclusionary* means, such that the human is not only produced over and against the inhuman, but through a set of foreclosures, radical erasures, that are, strictly speaking, refused the possibility of cultural articulation. Hence, it is not enough to claim that human subjects are constructed, for the construction of the human is a differential operation that produces the more and the less "human," the inhuman, the humanly unthinkable. These excluded sites come to bound the "human" as its constitutive outside, and to haunt those boundaries as the persistent possibility of their disruption and rearticulation.[4]

Paradoxically, the inquiry into the kinds of erasures and exclusions by which the construction of the subject operates is no longer constructivism, but neither is it essentialism. For there is an "outside" to what is constructed by discourse, but this is not an absolute "outside," an ontological thereness that exceeds or counters the boundaries of discourse;[5] as a constitutive "outside," it is that which can only be thought—when it can—in relation to that discourse, at and as its most tenuous borders. The debate between constructivism and essentialism thus misses the point of deconstruction altogether, for the point has never been that "everything is discursively constructed"; that point, when and where it is made, belongs to a kind of discursive monism or linguisticism that refuses the constitutive force of exclusion, erasure, violent foreclosure, abjection and its disruptive return within the very terms of discursive legitimacy.

And to say that there is a matrix of gender relations that institutes and sustains the subject is not to claim that there is a singular matrix that acts in a singular and deterministic way to produce a subject as its effect. That is to install the "matrix" in the subject-position within a grammatical formulation which itself needs to be rethought. Indeed, the propositional form "Discourse constructs the subject" retains the subject-position of the grammatical formulation even as it reverses the place of subject and discourse. Construction must mean more than such a simple reversal of terms.

There are defenders and critics of construction, who construe that position along structuralist lines. They often claim that there are structures that construct the subject, impersonal forces, such as Culture or Discourse or Power, where these terms occupy the grammatical site of the subject after the "human" has been dislodged from its place. In such a view, the grammatical and metaphysical place of the subject is retained even as the candidate that occupies that place appears to rotate. As a result, construction is still understood as a unilateral process initiated by a prior subject, fortifying that presumption of the metaphysics of the subject that where there is activity, there lurks behind it an initiating and willful subject. On such a view, discourse or language or the social becomes personified, and in the personification the metaphysics of the subject is reconsolidated.

In this second view, construction is not an activity, but an act, one which happens once and whose effects are firmly fixed. Thus, constructivism is reduced to determinism and implies the evacuation or displacement of human agency.

This view informs the misreading by which Foucault is criticized for "personifying" power: if power is misconstrued as a grammatical and metaphysical subject, and if that metaphysical site within humanist discourse has been the privileged site of the human, then power appears to have displaced the human as the origin of activity. But if Foucault's view of power is understood as the disruption and subversion of this grammar and metaphysics of the subject, if power orchestrates the formation and sustenance of subjects, then it cannot be accounted for in terms of the "subject" which is its effect. And here it would be no more right to claim that the term "construction" belongs at the grammatical site of subject, for construction is neither a subject nor its act, but a process of reiteration by which both "subjects" and "acts" come to appear at all. There is no power that acts, but only a reiterated acting that is power in its persistence and instability.

What I would propose in place of these conceptions of construction is a return to the notion of matter, not as site or surface, but as *a process of materialization that stabilizes over time to produce the effect of boundary, fixity, and surface we call matter.* That matter is always materialized has, I think, to be thought in relation to the productive and, indeed, materializing effects of regulatory power in the Foucaultian sense.[6] Thus, the question is no longer, How is gender constituted as and through a certain interpretation of sex? (a question that leaves the "matter" of sex untheorized), but rather, Through what regulatory norms is sex itself materialized? And how is it that treating the materiality of sex as a given presupposes and consolidates the normative conditions of its own emergence?

Crucially, then, construction is neither a single act nor a causal process initiated by a subject and culminating in a set of fixed effects. Construction not only takes place *in* time, but is itself a temporal process which operates through the reiteration of norms; sex is both produced and destabilized in the course of this reiteration.[7] As a sedimented effect of a reiterative or ritual practice, sex acquires its naturalized effect, and, yet, it is also by virtue of this reiteration that gaps and fissures are opened up as the constitutive instabilities in such constructions, as that which escapes or exceeds the norm, as that which cannot be wholly defined or fixed by the repetitive labor of that norm. This instability is the *de*constituting possibility in the very process of repetition, the power that undoes the very effects by which "sex" is stabilized, the possibility to put the consolidation of the norms of "sex" into a potentially productive crisis.[8]

Certain formulations of the radical constructivist position appear almost compulsively to produce a moment of recurrent exasperation, for it seems that when the constructivist is construed as a linguistic idealist, the constructivist refutes the reality of bodies, the relevance of science, the alleged facts of birth, aging, illness, and death. The critic might also suspect the constructivist of a certain somatophobia and seek assurances that this abstracted theorist will admit that there are, minimally, sexually differentiated parts, activities, capacities, hormonal and chromosomal differences that can be conceded without reference to "construction." Although at this moment I want to offer an absolute reassurance to my interlocutor, some anxiety prevails. To "concede" the undeniability of "sex" or its "materiality" is always to concede some version of "sex," some formation of "materiality." Is the discourse in and through which that concession occurs—and, yes, that concession invariably does occur—not itself formative of the very phenomenon that it concedes? To claim that discourse is formative is not to claim that it originates, causes, or exhaustively composes that which it concedes; rather, it is to claim that there is no reference to a pure body which is not at the same time a further formation of that body. In this sense, the linguistic capacity to refer to sexed bodies is not denied, but the very meaning of "referentiality" is altered. In philosophical terms, the constative claim is always to some degree performative.

In relation to sex, then, if one concedes the materiality of sex or of the body, does that very conceding operate—performatively—to materialize that sex? And further, how is it that the reiterated concession of that sex— one which need not take place in speech or writing but might be "signaled" in a much more inchoate way—constitutes the sedimentation and production of that material effect?

The moderate critic might concede that *some part* of "sex" is constructed, but some other is certainly not, and then, of course, find him or herself not only under some obligation to draw the line between what is and is not constructed, but to explain how it is that "sex" comes in parts whose differentiation is not a matter of construction. But as that line of demarcation between such ostensible parts gets drawn, the "unconstructed" becomes bounded once again through a signifying practice, and the very boundary which is meant to protect some part of sex from the taint of constructivism is now defined by the anti-constructivist's own construction. Is construction something which happens to a ready-made object, a pregiven thing, and does it happen *in degrees*? Or are we perhaps referring on both sides of the debate to an inevitable practice of signification, of demarcating and delimiting that to which we then "refer," such that our "references" always presuppose—and often conceal—this prior delimitation? Indeed, to "refer" naively or directly to such an extra-discursive object will always require the prior delimitation of the extra-discursive. And insofar as the extra-discursive is delimited, it is formed by the very discourse from which it seeks to free itself. This delimitation, which often is enacted as an untheorized presupposition in any act of description, marks a boundary that includes and excludes, that decides, as it were, what will and will not be the stuff of the object to which we then refer. This marking off will have some normative force and, indeed, some violence, for it can construct only through erasing; it can bound a thing only through enforcing a certain criterion, a principle of selectivity.

What will and will not be included within the boundaries of "sex" will be set by a more or less tacit operation of exclusion. If we call into question the fixity of the structuralist law that divides and bounds the "sexes" by virtue of their dyadic differentiation within the heterosexual matrix, it will be from the exterior regions of that boundary (not from a "position," but from the discursive possibilities opened up by the constitutive outside of hegemonic positions), and it will constitute the disruptive return of the excluded from within the very logic of the heterosexual symbolic.

The trajectory of this text, then, will pursue the possibility of such disruption, but proceed indirectly by responding to two interrelated questions that have been posed to constructivist accounts of gender, not to defend constructivism per se, but to interrogate the erasures and exclusions that constitute its limits. These criticisms presuppose a set of metaphysical oppositions between materialism and idealism embedded in received grammar which, I will argue, are critically redefined by a poststructuralist rewriting of discursive performativity as it operates in the materialization of sex.

PERFORMATIVITY AS CITATIONALITY

When, in Lacanian parlance, one is said to assume a "sex," the grammar of the phrase creates the expectation that there is a "one" who, upon waking, looks up and deliberates on which "sex" it will assume today, a grammar in which "assumption" is quickly assimilated to the notion of a highly reflective choice. But if this "assumption" is *compelled* by a regulatory apparatus of heterosexuality, one which reiterates itself through the forcible production of "sex," then the "assumption" of sex is constrained from the start. And if there is *agency*, it is to be found, paradoxically, in the possibilities opened up in and by that constrained appropriation of the regulatory law, by the materialization of that law, the compulsory appropriation and identification with those normative demands. The forming, crafting, bearing, circulation, signification of that sexed body will not be a set of actions performed in compliance with the law; on the contrary, they will be a set of actions mobilized by the law, the citational accumulation and dissimulation of the law that produces material effects, the lived necessity of those effects as well as the lived contestation of that necessity.

Performativity is thus not a singular "act," for it is always a reiteration of a norm or set of norms, and to the extent that it acquires an act-like status in the present, it conceals or dissimulates the conventions of which it is a repetition. Moreover, this act is not primarily theatrical; indeed, its apparent theatricality is produced to the extent that its historicity remains dissimulated (and, conversely, its theatricality gains a certain inevitability given the impossibility of a full disclosure of its historicity). Within speech act theory, a performative is that discursive practice that enacts or produces that which it names.[9] According to the biblical rendition of the performative, i.e., "Let there be light!," it appears that it is by virtue of *the power of a subject or its will* that a phenomenon is named into being. In a critical reformulation of the performative, Derrida makes clear that this power is not the function of an originating will, but is always derivative:

> Could a performative utterance succeed if its formulation did not repeat a "coded" or iterable utterance, or in other words, if the formula I pronounce in order to open a meeting, launch a ship or a marriage were not identifiable as conforming with an iterable model, if it were not then identifiable in some way as a "citation"?...in such a typology, the category of intention will not disappear; it will have its place, but from that place it will no longer be able to govern the entire scene and system of utterance [*l'énonciation*].[10]

To what extent does discourse gain the authority to bring about what it names through citing the conventions of authority? And does a subject appear as the author of its discursive effects to the extent that the citational practice by which he/she is conditioned and mobilized remains unmarked? Indeed, could it be that the production of the subject as originator of his/her effects is precisely a consequence of this dissimulated citationality? Further, if a subject comes to be through a subjection to the norms of sex, a subjection which requires an assumption of the norms of sex, can we read that "assumption" as precisely a modality of this kind of citationality? In other words, the norm of sex takes hold to the extent that it is "cited" as such a norm, but it also derives its power through the citations that it compels. And how it is that we might read the "citing" of the norms of sex as the process of approximating or "identifying with" such norms?

Further, to what extent within psychoanalysis is the sexed body secured through identificatory practices governed by regulatory schemas? Identification is used here not as an imitative activity by which a conscious being models itself after another; on the contrary, identification is the assimilating passion by which an ego first emerges.[11] Freud argues that "the ego is first and foremost a bodily ego," that this ego is, further, "a projection of a surface,"[12] what we might redescribe as an imaginary morphology. Moreover, I would argue, this imaginary morphology is not a presocial or presymbolic operation, but is itself orchestrated through regulatory schemas that produce intelligible morphological possibilities. These regulatory schemas are not timeless structures, but historically revisable criteria of intelligibility which produce and vanquish bodies that matter.

If the formulation of a bodily ego, a sense of stable contour, and the fixing of spatial boundary is achieved through identificatory practices, and if psychoanalysis documents the hegemonic workings of those identifications, can we then read psychoanalysis for the inculcation of the heterosexual matrix at the level of bodily morphogenesis? What Lacan calls the "assumption" or "accession" to the symbolic law can be read as a kind of *citing* of the law, and so offers an opportunity to link the question of the materialization of "sex" with the reworking of performativity as citationality. Although Lacan claims that the symbolic law has a semi-autonomous status prior to the assumption of sexed positions by a subject, these normative positions, i.e., the "sexes," are only known through the approximations that they occasion. The force and necessity of these norms ("sex" as a symbolic function is to be understood as a kind of command-ment or injunction) is thus functionally *dependent on* the approximation and citation of the law; the law without its approximation is no law or, rather, it remains a governing law only for those who would affirm it on the basis of religious faith. If "sex" is assumed in the same way that a law is cited—an analogy which will be supported later in this text—then "the law of sex" is repeatedly fortified and idealized as the law only to the extent that it is reiterated as the law, produced as the law, the anterior and inapproximable ideal, by the very citations it is said to command. Reading the meaning of "assumption" in Lacan as citation, the law is no longer given in a fixed form *prior* to its citation, but is produced through citation as that which precedes and exceeds the mortal approximations enacted by the subject.

In this way, the symbolic law in Lacan can be subject to the same kind of critique that Nietzsche formulated of the notion of God: the power attributed to this prior and ideal power is derived and deflected from the attribution itself.[13] It is this insight into the illegitimacy of the symbolic law of sex that is dramatized to a certain degree in the contemporary film *Paris Is Burning*: the ideal that is mirrored depends on that very mirroring to be sustained as an ideal. And though the symbolic appears to be a force that cannot be contravened without psychosis, the symbolic ought to be rethought as a series of normativizing injunctions that secure the borders of sex through the threat of psychosis, abjection, psychic unlivability. And further, that this "law" can only remain a law to the extent that it compels the differentiated citations and approximations called "feminine" and "masculine." The presumption that the symbolic law of sex enjoys a separable ontology prior and autonomous to its assumption is contravened by the notion that the citation of the law is the very mechanism of its production and articulation. What is "forced" by the symbolic, then, is a citation of its law that reiterates and consolidates the ruse of its own force. What would it mean to "cite" the law to produce it differently, to "cite" the law in order to reiterate and coopt its power, to expose the heterosexual matrix and to displace the effect of its necessity?

The process of that sedimentation or what we might call *materialization* will be a kind of citationality, the acquisition of being through the citing of power, a citing that establishes an originary complicity with power in the formation of the "I."

In this sense, the agency denoted by the performativity of "sex" will be directly counter to any notion of a voluntarist subject who exists quite apart from the regulatory norms which she/he opposes. The paradox of subjectivation (*assujetissement*) is precisely that the subject who would resist such norms is itself enabled, if not produced, by such norms. Although this constitutive constraint does not foreclose the possibility of agency, it does locate agency as a reiterative or rearticulatory practice, immanent to power, and not a relation of external opposition to power.

As a result of this reformulation of performativity, (a) gender performativity cannot be theorized apart from the forcible and reiterative practice of regulatory sexual regimes; (b) the account of agency conditioned by those very regimes of discourse/power cannot be conflated with voluntarism or individualism, much less with consumerism, and in no way presupposes a choosing subject; (c) the regime of heterosexuality operates to circumscribe and contour the "materiality" of sex, and that "materiality" is formed and sustained through and as a materialization of regulatory norms that are in part those of heterosexual hegemony; (d) the materialization of norms requires those identificatory processes by which norms are assumed or appropriated, and these identifications precede and enable the formation of a subject, but are not, strictly speaking, performed by a subject; and (e) the limits of constructivism are exposed at those boundaries of bodily life where abjected or delegitimated bodies fail to count as "bodies." If the materiality of sex is demarcated in discourse, then this demarcation will produce a domain of excluded and delegitimated "sex." Hence, it will be as important to think about how and to what end bodies are constructed as is it will be to think about how and to what end bodies are *not* constructed and, further, to ask after how bodies which fail to materialize provide the necessary "outside," if not the necessary support, for the bodies which, in materializing the norm, qualify as bodies that matter.

How, then, can one think through the matter of bodies as a kind of materialization governed by regulatory norms in order to ascertain the workings of heterosexual hegemony in the formation of what qualifies as a viable body? How does that materialization of the norm in bodily formation produce a domain of abjected bodies, a field of deformation, which, in failing to qualify as the fully human, fortifies those regulatory norms? What challenge does that excluded and abjected realm produce to a symbolic hegemony that might force a radical rearticulation of what qualifies as bodies that matter, ways of living that count as "life," lives worth protecting, lives worth saving, lives worth grieving?

TRAJECTORY OF THE TEXT

The texts that form the focus of this inquiry come from diverse traditions of writing: Plato's Timaeus, Freud's "On Narcissism," writings by Jacques Lacan, stories by Willa Cather, Nella Larsen's novella *Passing*, Jennie Livingston's film *Paris Is Burning*, and essays in recent sexual theory and politics, as well as texts in radical democratic theory. The historical range of materials is not meant to suggest that a single heterosexualizing imperative persists in each of these contexts, but only that the instability produced by the effort to fix the site of the sexed body challenges the boundaries of discursive intelligibility in each of these contexts. The point here is not only to remark upon the difficulty of delivering through discourse the uncontested site of sex. Rather, the point is to show that the uncontested status of "sex" within the heterosexual dyad secures the workings of certain symbolic orders, and that its contestation calls into question where and how the limits of symbolic intelligibility are set.

Part One of the text centrally concerns the production of sexed morphologies through regulatory schemas. Throughout these chapters I seek to show how power relations work in the very formation of "sex" and its "materiality." The first two essays are different genealogical efforts to trace the power relations that contour bodies: "Bodies That Matter" suggests how certain classical tensions are taken up in contemporary theoretical positions. The essay briefly considers Aristotle and Foucault, but then offers a revision of Irigaray's reading of Plato through a consideration of the *chora* in Plato's *Timaeus*. The *chora* is that site where materiality and femininity appear to merge to form a materiality prior to and formative of any notion of the empirical. In "The Lesbian Phallus and the Morphological Imaginary" I attempt to show how normative heterosexuality shapes a bodily contour that vacillates between materiality and the imaginary, indeed, that is that very vacillation. Neither of these essays is meant to dispute the materiality of the body; on the contrary, together they constitute partial and overlapping genealogical efforts to establish the normative conditions under which the materiality of the body is framed and formed, and, in particular, how it is formed through differential categories of sex.

In the course of the second essay, another set of questions emerges concerning the problematic of morphogenesis: how do identifications function to produce and contest what Freud has called "the bodily ego"? As a projected phenomenon, the body is not merely the source from which projection issues, but is also always a phenomenon in the world, an estrangement from the very "I" who claims it. Indeed, the assumption of "sex," the assumption of a certain contoured materiality, is itself a giving form to that body, a morphogenesis that takes place through a set of identificatory projections. That the body which one "is" is to some degree a body which gains its sexed contours in part under specular and exteriorizing conditions suggests that identificatory processes are crucial to the forming of sexed materiality.[14]

This revision of Freud and Lacan continues in the third chapter, "Phantasmatic Identification and the Assumption of Sex." Here, two concerns of social and political significance emerge: (1) if identificatory projections are regulated by social norms, and if those norms are construed as heterosexual imperatives, then it appears that normative heterosexuality is partially responsible for the kind of form that contours the bodily matter of sex; and (2) given that normative heterosexuality is clearly not the only regulatory regime operative in the production of bodily contours or setting the limits to bodily intelligibility, it makes sense to ask what other regimes of regulatory production contour the materiality of bodies.

Here it seems that the social regulation of race emerges not simply as another, fully separable, domain of power from sexual difference or sexuality, but that its "addition" subverts the monolithic workings of the heterosexual imperative as I have described it so far. The symbolic—that register of regulatory ideality—is also and always a racial industry, indeed, the reiterated practice of *racializing* interpellations. Rather than accept a model which understands racism as discrimination on the basis of a pre-given race, I follow those recent theories which have made the argument that the "race" is partially produced as an effect of the history of racism, that its boundaries and meanings are constructed over time not only in the service of racism, but also in the service of the contestation of racism.[15] Rejecting those models of power which would reduce racial differences to the derivative effects of sexual difference (as if sexual difference were not only autonomous in relation to racial articulation but somehow more prior, in a temporal or ontological sense), it seems crucial to rethink the scenes of reproduction and, hence, of sexing practices not only as ones through which a heterosexual imperative is inculcated, but as ones through which boundaries of racial distinction are secured as well as contested. Especially at those junctures in which a compulsory heterosexuality works in the service of maintaining hegemonic forms of racial purity, the "threat" of homosexuality takes on a distinctive complexity.

It seems crucial to resist the model of power that would set up racism and homophobia and misogyny as parallel or analogical relations. The assertion of their abstract or structural equivalence not only misses the specific histories of their construction and elaboration, but also delays the important work of thinking through the ways in which these vectors of power require and deploy each other for the purpose of their own articulation. Indeed, it may not be possible to think any of these notions or their interrelations without a substantially revised conception of power in both its geopolitical dimensions and in the contemporary tributaries of its intersecting circulation.[16] On the one hand, any analysis which foregrounds one vector of power over another will doubtless become vulnerable to criticisms that it not only ignores or devalues the others, but that its own constructions depend on the exclusion of the others in order to proceed. On the other hand, any analysis which pretends to be able to encompass every vector of power runs the risk of a certain epistemological imperialism which consists in the presupposition that any given writer might fully stand for and explain the complexities of contemporary power. No author or text can offer such a reflection of the world, and those who claim to offer such pictures become suspect by virtue of that very claim. The failure of the mimetic function, however, has its own political uses, for the production of texts can be one way of reconfiguring what will count as the world. Because texts do not reflect the entirety of their authors or their worlds, they enter a field of reading as partial provocations, not only requiring a set of prior texts in order to gain legibility, but—at best—initiating a set of appropriations and criticisms that call into question their fundamental premises.

This demand to think contemporary power in its complexity and interarticulations remains incontrovertibly important even in its impossibility. And yet it would be a mistake to impose the same criteria on every cultural product, for it may be precisely the partiality of a text which conditions the radical character of its insights. Taking the heterosexual matrix or heterosexual hegemony as a point of departure will run the risk of narrowness, but it will run it in order, finally, to cede its apparent priority and autonomy as a form of power. This will happen within the text, but perhaps most successfully in its various appropriations. Indeed, it seems to me that one writes into a field of writing that is invariably and promisingly larger and less masterable than the one over which one maintains a provisional authority, and that the unanticipated reappropriations of a given work in areas for which it was never consciously intended are some of the most useful. The political problematic of operating within the complexities of power is raised toward the end of "Phantasmatic Identification and the Assumption of Sex," and further pursued in the reading of the film *Paris Is Burning* in the fourth chapter, "Gender Is Burning: Questions of Appropiation and Subversion," and again in chapter six, "Passing, Queering: Nella Larsen's Psychoanalytic Challenge."

In Part Two of the text, I turn first to selections from Willa Cather's fiction, where I consider how the paternal symbolic permits subversive reterritorializations of both gender and sexuality. Over and against the view that sexuality might be fully disjoined from gender, I suggest that Cather's fiction enacts a certain gender trespass in order to facilitate an otherwise unspeakable desire. The brief readings of Cather's fiction, in particular "Tommy the Unsentimental," "Paul's Case," and portions of *My Ántonia*, take up the question of the resignifiability of the paternal law as it destabilizes the operation of names and body parts as sites of crossed identification and desire. In Cather, the name effects a destabilization of conventional notions of gender and bodily integrity that simultaneously deflect and expose homosexuality. This kind of textual cunning can be read as a further instance of what Eve Kosofsky Sedgwick has deftly analyzed as "the epistemology of the closet."[17] In Cather, however, the discursive articulation of gender is linked to the narration and narrativizability of lesbian desire such that her fiction implicitly calls into question the specific ways in which Sedgwick, in relation to Cather, has suggested a disjoining of sexuality from gender.[18]

The reading of Nella Larsen's *Passing* considers how a redescription of the symbolic as a vector of gendered and racial imperatives calls into question the assertion that sexual difference is in some sense prior to racial differences. The term "queering" in Larsen's text rallies both racial and sexual anxieties, and compels a reading which asks how sexual regulation operates through the regulation of racial boundaries, and how racial distinctions operate to defend against certain socially endangering sexual transgressions. Larsen's novella offers a way to retheorize the symbolic as a racially articulated set of sexual norms, and to consider both the historicity of such norms, their sites of conflict and convergence, and the limits on their rearticulation.

If performativity is construed as that power of discourse to produce effects through reiteration, how are we to understand the limits of such production, the constraints under which such production occurs? Are these social and political limits on the resignifiability of gender and race, or are these limits that are, strictly speaking, outside the social? Are we to understand this "outside" as that which permanently resists discursive elaboration, or is it a variable boundary set and reset by specific political investments?

The innovative theory of political discourse offered by Slavoj Žižek in *The Sublime Object of Ideology* takes up the question of sexual difference in Lacan in relation to the performative character of political signifiers. The reading of his work, and the subsequent essay on the resignification of "queer" are inquiries into the uses and limits of a psychoanalytic perspective for a theory of political performatives and democratic contestation. Žižek develops a theory of political signifiers as performatives which, through becoming sites of phantasmatic investment, effect the power to mobilize constituencies politically. Central to Žižek's formulation of the political performative is a critique of discourse analysis for its failure to mark that which resists symbolization, what he variously calls a "trauma" and "the real." An instructive and innovative theory, it nevertheless tends to rely on an unproblematized sexual antagonism that unwittingly installs a heterosexual matrix as a permanent and incontestable structure of culture in which women operate as a "stain" in discourse. Those who try to call this structure into question are thus arguing with the real, with what is outside all argumentation, the trauma and the necessity of oedipalization that conditions and limits all discourse.

Žižek's efforts to link the performative character of discourse to the power of political mobilization are nevertheless quite valuable. His explicit linking of the theory of performativity to that of hegemony as it is articulated in the radical democratic theory of Ernesto Laclau and Chantal Mouffe offers insights into political mobilization through recourse to a psychoanalytically informed theory of ideological fantasy. Through a critical engagement with his theory, then, I consider how performativity might be rethought as citationality and resignification, and where psychoanalysis might retain its explanatory force in a theory of hegemony which reifies neither the heterosexual norm nor its misogynist consequence.

In the final chapter, then, I suggest that the contentious practices of "queerness" might be understood not only as an example of citational politics, but as a specific reworking of abjection into political agency that might explain why "citationality" has contemporary political promise. The public assertion of "queerness" enacts performativity as citationality for the purposes of resignifying the abjection of homosexuality into defiance and legitimacy. I argue that this does not have to be a "reverse-discourse" in which the defiant affirmation of queer dialectically reinstalls the version it seeks to overcome. Rather, this is the politicization of abjection in an effort to rewrite the history of the term, and to force it into a demanding resignification. Such a strategy, I suggest, is crucial to creating the kind of community in which surviving with AIDS becomes more possible, in which queer lives become legible, valuable, worthy of support, in which passion, injury, grief, aspiration become recognized without fixing the terms of that recognition in yet another conceptual order of lifelessness and rigid exclusion. If there is a "normative" dimension to this work, it consists precisely in assisting a radical resignification of the symbolic domain, deviating the citational chain toward a more possible future to expand the very meaning of what counts as a valued and valuable body in the world.

To recast the symbolic as capable of this kind of resignification, it will be necessary to think of the symbolic as the temporalized regulation of signification, and not as a quasi-permanent structure. This rethinking of the symbolic in terms of the temporal dynamics of regulatory discourse will take seriously the Lacanian challenge to Anglo-American accounts of gender, to consider the status of "sex" as a linguistic norm, but will recast that normativity in Foucaultian terms as a "regulatory ideal." Drawing from the Anglo-American accounts of gender as well, this project seeks to challenge the structural stasis of the heterosexualizing norm within the psychoanalytic account without dispensing with what is clearly valuable in psychoanalytic perspectives. Indeed, "sex" is a regulatory ideal, a forcible and differential materialization of bodies, that will produce its remainder, its outside, what one might call its "unconscious." This insistence that every formative movement requires and institutes its exclusions takes seriously the psychoanalytic vocabulary of both repression and foreclosure.

In this sense, I take issue with Foucault's account of the repressive hypothesis as merely an instance of juridical power, and argue that such an account does not address the ways in which "repression" operates as a modality of productive power. There may be a way to subject psycho-analysis to a Foucaultian redescription even as Foucault himself refused that possibility.[19] This text accepts as a point of departure Foucault's notion that regulatory power produces the subjects it controls, that power is not only imposed externally, but works as the regulatory and normative means by which subjects are formed. The return to psychoanalysis, then, is guided by the question of how certain regulatory norms form a "sexed" subject in terms that establish the indistinguishability of psychic and bod-ily formation. And where some psychoanalytic perspectives locate the constitution of "sex" at a developmental moment or as an effect of a quasi-permanent symbolic structure, I understand this constituting effect of regulatory power as reiterated and reiterable. To this understanding of power as a constrained and reiterative production it is crucial to add that power also works through the foreclosure of effects, the production of an "outside," a domain of unlivability and unintelligibility that bounds the domain of intelligible effects.

To what extent is "sex" a constrained production, a forcible effect, one which sets the limits to what will qualify as a body by regulating the terms by which bodies are and are not sustained? My purpose here is to understand how what has been foreclosed or banished from the proper domain of "sex"—where that domain is secured through a heterosexualizing imperative—might at once be produced as a troubling return, not only as an *imaginary* contestation that effects a failure in the workings of the inevitable law, but as an enabling disruption, the occasion for a radical rearticulation of the symbolic horizon in which bodies come to matter at all.

PART *one*

1

BODIES THAT MATTER

If I understand deconstruction, deconstruction is not an exposure of error, certainly not other people's error. The critique in deconstruction, the most serious critique in deconstruction, is the critique of something that is extremely useful, something without which we cannot do anything.

> —Gayatri Chakravorty Spivak, "In a Word,"
> interview with Ellen Rooney

...the necessity of "reopening" the figures of philosophical discourse...One way is to interrogate the conditions under which systematicity itself is possible: what the coherence of the discursive utterance conceals of the conditions under which it is produced, whatever it may say about these conditions in discourse. For example the "matter" from which the speaking subject draws nourishment in order to produce itself, to reproduce itself; the *scenography* that makes representation feasible, representation as defined in philosophy, that is, the architectonics of its theatre, its framing in space-time, its geometric organization, its props, its actors, their respective positions, their dialogues, indeed their tragic relations, without overlooking the *mirror*, most often hidden, that allows the logos, the subject, to reduplicate itself, to reflect itself by itself. All these are interventions on the scene; they ensure its coherence so long as they remain uninterpreted. Thus they have to be reenacted, in each figure of discourse away from its mooring in the value of "presence." For each philosopher, beginning with those whose names define some age in the history of philosophy, we have to point out how the break with material contiguity is made (il faut repérer comment s'opère la coupure d'avec la contiguité materielle), how the system is put together, how the specular economy works.

> —Luce Irigaray, "The Power of Discourse"

Within some quarters of feminist theory in recent years, there have been calls to retrieve the body from what is often characterized as the linguistic idealism of poststructuralism. In another quarter, philosopher Gianni Vattimo has argued that poststructuralism, understood as textual play, marks the dissolution of *matter* as a contemporary category. And it is this lost matter, he argues, which must now be reformulated in order for poststructuralism to give way to a project of greater ethical and political value.[1] The terms of these debates are difficult and unstable ones, for it is difficult to know in either case who or what is designated by the term "poststructuralism," and perhaps even more difficult to know what to retrieve under the sign of "the body." And yet these two signifiers have for some feminists and critical theorists seemed fundamentally antagonistic. One hears warnings like the following: If everything is discourse, what happens to the body? If everything is a text, what about violence and bodily injury? Does anything *matter* in or for poststructuralism?

It has seemed to many, I think, that in order for feminism to proceed as a critical practice, it must ground itself in the sexed specificity of the female body. Even as the category of sex is always reinscribed as gender, that sex must still be presumed as the irreducible point of departure for the various cultural constructions it has come to bear. And this presumption of the material irreducibility of sex has seemed to ground and to authorize feminist epistemologies and ethics, as well as gendered analyses of various kinds. In an effort to displace the terms of this debate, I want to ask how and why "materiality" has become a sign of irreducibility, that is, how is it that the materiality of sex is understood as that which only bears cultural constructions and, therefore, cannot be a construction? What is the status of this exclusion? Is materiality a site or surface that is excluded from the process of construction, as that through which and on which construction works? Is this perhaps an enabling or constitutive exclusion, one without which construction cannot operate? What occupies this site of unconstructed materiality? And what kinds of constructions are foreclosed through the figuring of this site as outside or beneath construction itself?

In what follows, what is at stake is less a theory of cultural construction than a consideration of the scenography and topography of construction. This scenography is orchestrated by and as a matrix of power that remains disarticulated if we presume constructedness and materiality as necessarily oppositional notions.

In the place of materiality, one might inquire into other foundationalist premises that operate as political "irreducibles." Instead of rehearsing the theoretical difficulties that emerge by presuming the notion of the subject as a foundational premise or by trying to maintain a stable distinction between sex and gender, I would like to raise the question of whether recourse to matter and to the materiality of sex is necessary in order to establish that irreducible specificity that is said to ground feminist practice. And here the question is not whether or not there ought to be reference to matter, just as the question never has been whether or not there ought to be speaking about women. This speaking will occur, and for feminist reasons, it must; the category of women does not become useless through deconstruction, but becomes one whose uses are no longer reified as "referents," and which stand a chance of being opened up, indeed, of coming to signify in ways that none of us can predict in advance. Surely, it must be possible both to use the term, to use it tactically even as one is, as it were, used and positioned by it, and also to subject the term to a critique which interrogates the exclusionary operations and differential power-relations that construct and delimit feminist invocations of "women." This is, to paraphrase the citation from Spivak above, the critique of something useful, the critique of something we cannot do without. Indeed, I would argue that it is a critique without which feminism loses its democratizing potential through refusing to engage—take stock of, and become transformed by—the exclusions which put it into play.

Something similar is at work with the concept of materiality, which may well be "something without which we cannot do anything." What does it mean to have recourse to materiality, since it is clear from the start that matter has a history (indeed, more than one) and that the history of matter is in part determined by the negotiation of sexual difference. We may seek to return to matter as prior to discourse to ground our claims about sexual difference only to discover that matter is fully sedimented with discourses on sex and sexuality that prefigure and constrain the uses to which that term can be put. Moreover, we may seek recourse to matter in order to ground or to verify a set of injuries or violations only to find that *matter itself is founded through a set of violations*, ones which are unwittingly repeated in the contemporary invocation.

Indeed, if it can be shown that in its constitutive history this "irreducible" materiality is constructed through a problematic gendered matrix, then the discursive practice by which matter is rendered irreducible simultaneously ontologizes and fixes that gendered matrix in its place. And if the constituted effect of that matrix is taken to be the indisputable ground of bodily life, then it seems that a genealogy of that matrix is foreclosed from critical inquiry. Against the claim that poststructuralism reduces all

materiality to linguistic stuff, an argument is needed to show that to deconstruct matter is not to negate or do away with the usefulness of the term.
And against those who would claim that the body's irreducible materiality is a necessary precondition for feminist practice, I suggest that that
prized materiality may well be constituted through an exclusion and
degradation of the feminine that is profoundly problematic for feminism.

Here it is of course necessary to state quite plainly that the options for
theory are not exhausted by *presuming* materiality, on the one hand, and
negating materiality, on the other. It is my purpose to do precisely neither of
these. To call a presupposition into question is not the same as doing away
with it; rather, it is to free it from its metaphysical lodgings in order to
understand what political interests were secured in and by that metaphysical placing, and thereby to permit the term to occupy and to serve
very different political aims. To problematize the matter of bodies may
entail an initial loss of epistemological certainty, but a loss of certainty is not
the same as political nihilism. On the contrary, such a loss may well indicate
a significant and promising shift in political thinking. This unsettling of
"matter" can be understood as initiating new possibilities, new ways for
bodies to matter.

The body posited as prior to the sign, is always *posited* or *signified* as *prior*.
This signification produces as an *effect* of its own procedure the very body
that it nevertheless and simultaneously claims to discover as that which
precedes its own action. If the body signified as prior to signification is an
effect of signification, then the mimetic or representational status of language, which claims that signs follow bodies as their necessary mirrors, is
not mimetic at all. On the contrary, it is productive, constitutive, one might
even argue *performative*, inasmuch as this signifying act delimits and contours the body that it then claims to find prior to any and all signification.[2]

This is not to say that the materiality of bodies is simply and only a linguistic effect which is reducible to a set of signifiers. Such a distinction
overlooks the materiality of the signifier itself. Such an account also fails to
understand materiality as that which is bound up with signification from
the start; to think through the indissolubility of materiality and signification is no easy matter. To posit by way of language a materiality outside
of language is still to posit that materiality, and the materiality so posited
will retain that positing as its constitutive condition. Derrida negotiates
the question of matter's radical alterity with the following remark: "I am

not even sure that there can be a 'concept' of an absolute exterior."[3] To have the concept of matter is to lose the exteriority that the concept is suppose to secure. Can language simply refer to materiality, or is language also the very condition under which materiality may be said to appear?

If matter ceases to be matter once it becomes a concept, and if a concept of matter's exteriority to language is always something less than absolute, what is the status of this "outside"? Is it produced by philosophical discourse in order to effect the appearance of its own exhaustive and coherent systematicity? What is cast out from philosophical propriety in order to sustain and secure the borders of philosophy? And how might this repudiation return?

MATTERS OF FEMININITY

The classical association of femininity with materiality can be traced to a set of etymologies which link matter with *mater* and *matrix* (or the womb) and, hence, with a problematic of reproduction. The classical configuration of matter as a site of *generation* or *origination* becomes especially significant when the account of what an object is and means requires recourse to its originating principle. When not explicitly associated with reproduction, matter is generalized as a principle of origination and causality. In Greek, *hyle* is the wood or timber out of which various cultural constructions are made, but also a principle of origin, development, and teleology which is at once causal and explanatory. This link between matter, origin, and significance suggests the indissolubility of classical Greek notions of materiality and signification. That which matters about an object is its matter.[4]

In both the Latin and the Greek, matter (*materia* and *hyle*) is neither a simple, brute positivity or referent nor a blank surface or slate awaiting an external signification, but is always in some sense temporalized. This is true for Marx as well, when "matter" is understood as a principle of *transformation*, presuming and inducing a future.[5] The matrix is an originating and formative principle which inaugurates and informs a development of some organism or object. Hence, for Aristotle, "matter is potentiality [*dynameos*], form actuality."[6] In reproduction, women are said to contribute the matter; men, the form.[7] The Greek *hyle* is wood that already has been cut from trees, instrumentalized and instrumentalizable, artifactual, on the way to being put to use. *Materia* in Latin denotes the stuff out of which things are made, not only the timber for houses and ships but whatever serves as nourishment for infants: nutrients that act as extensions of the mother's body. Insofar as matter appears in these cases to be invested with a certain capacity to originate and to compose that for which it also supplies the principle of intelligibility, then matter is clearly defined by a certain power of creation and rationality that is for the most part divested from the more modern empirical deployments of the term. To speak within these classical contexts of *bodies that matter* is not an idle pun, for to be material means to materialize, where the principle of that materialization is precisely what "matters" about that body, its very intelligibility. In this sense, to know the significance of something is to know how and why it matters, where "to matter" means at once "to materialize" and "to mean."

Obviously, no feminist would encourage a simple return to Aristotle's natural teleologies in order to rethink the "materiality" of bodies. I want to consider, however, Aristotle's distinction between body and soul to effect a brief comparison between Aristotle and Foucault in order to suggest a possible contemporary redeployment of Aristotelian terminology. At the end of this brief comparison, I will offer a limited criticism of Foucault, which will then lead to a longer discussion of Irigaray's deconstruction of materiality in Plato's *Timaeus*. It is in the context of this second analysis that I hope to make clear how a gendered matrix is at work in the constitution of materiality (although it is obviously present in Aristotle as well), and why feminists ought to be interested, not in taking materiality as an irreducible, but in conducting a critical genealogy of its formulation.

ARISTOTLE/FOUCAULT

For Aristotle the soul designates the actualization of matter, where matter is understood as fully potential and unactualized. As a result, he maintains in *de Anima* that the soul is "the first grade of actuality of a naturally organized body." He continues, "That is why we can wholly dismiss as unnecessary the question whether the soul and the body are one: it is as meaningless to ask whether the wax and the shape given to it by the stamp are one, or generally the matter [*hyle*] of a thing and that of which it is the matter [*hyle*]."[8] In the Greek, there is no reference to "stamps," but the phrase, "the shape given by the stamp" is contained in the single term, "*schema.*" *Schema* means form, shape, figure, appearance, dress, gesture, figure of a syllogism, and grammatical form. If matter never appears without its *schema*, that means that it only appears under a certain grammatical form and that the principle of its recognizability, its characteristic gesture or usual dress, is indissoluble from what constitutes its matter.

In Aristotle, we find no clear phenomenal distinction between materiality and intelligibility, and yet for other reasons Aristotle does not supply us with the kind of "body" that feminism seeks to retrieve. To install the principle of intelligibility in the very development of a body is precisely the strategy of a natural teleology that accounts for female development through the rationale of biology. On this basis, it has been argued that women ought to perform certain social functions and not others, indeed, that women ought to be fully restricted to the reproductive domain.

We might historicize the Aristotelian notion of the *schema* in terms of culturally variable principles of formativity and intelligibility. To understand the *schema* of bodies as a historically contingent nexus of power/discourse is to arrive at something similar to what Foucault describes in *Discipline and Punish* as the "materialization" of the prisoner's body. This process of materialization is at stake as well in the final chapter of the first volume of *The History of Sexuality* when Foucault calls for a "history of bodies" that would inquire into "the manner in which what is most material and vital in them has been invested."[9]

At times it appears that for Foucault the body has a materiality that is ontologically distinct from the power relations that take that body as a site of investments. And yet, in *Discipline and Punish*, we have a different configuration of the relation between materiality and investment. There the soul is taken as an instrument of power through which the body is cultivated and formed. In a sense, it acts as a power-laden schema that produces and actualizes the body itself.

We can understand Foucault's references to the "soul" as an implicit reworking of the Aristotelian formulation. Foucault argues in *Discipline and Punish* that the "soul" becomes a normative and normalizing ideal according to which the body is trained, shaped, cultivated, and invested; it is an historically specific imaginary ideal (*idéal speculatif*) under which the body is effectively materialized. Considering the science of prison reform, Foucault writes, "The man described for us, whom we are invited to free, is already in himself the effect of a subjection [*assujettissement*] much more profound than himself. A 'soul' inhabits him and brings him to existence, which is itself a factor in the mastery that power exercises over the body. The soul is the effect and instrument of a political anatomy; the soul is the prison of the body."[10]

This "subjection," or *assujettissement,* is not only a subordination but a securing and maintaining, a putting into place of a subject, a subjectiva-tion. The "soul brings [the prisoner] to existence"; and not fully unlike Aristotle, the soul described by Foucault as an instrument of power, forms and frames the body, stamps it, and in stamping it, brings it into being. Here "being" belongs in quotation marks, for ontological weight is not presumed, but always conferred. For Foucault, this conferral can take place only within and by an operation of power. This operation produces the subjects that it subjects; that is, it subjects them in and through the compulsory power relations effective as their formative principle. But power is that which forms, maintains, sustains, and regulates bodies at once, so that, strictly speaking, power is not a subject who acts on bodies as its distinct objects. The grammar which compels us to speak that way enforces a metaphysics of external relations, whereby power acts on bod-ies but is not understood to form them. This is a view of power as an external relation that Foucault himself calls into question.

Power operates for Foucault in the *constitution* of the very materiality of the subject, in the principle which simultaneously forms and regulates the "subject" of subjectivation. Foucault refers not only to the materiality of the body of the prisoner but to the materiality of the body of the prison. The materiality of the prison, he writes, is established to the extent that [*dans la mesure où*] it is a vector and instrument of power.[11] Hence, the prison is *materialized* to the extent that it is *invested with power,* or, to be grammatically accurate, there is no prison prior to its materialization. Its materialization is coextensive with its investiture with power relations, and materiality is the effect and gauge of this investment. The prison comes to be only within the field of power relations, but more specifically, only to the extent that it is invested or saturated with such relations, that such a saturation is itself formative of its very being. Here the body is not an independent materiality that is invested by power relations external to it, but it is that for which materialization and investiture are coextensive.

"Materiality" designates a certain effect of power or, rather, *is* power in its formative or constituting effects. Insofar as power operates successfully by constituting an object domain, a field of intelligibility, as a taken-for-granted ontology, its material effects are taken as material data or primary givens. These material positivities appear *outside* discourse and power, as its incontestable referents, its transcendental signifieds. But this appearance is precisely the moment in which the power/discourse regime is most fully dissimulated and most insidiously effective. When this material effect is taken as an epistemological point of departure, a *sine qua non* of some political argumentation, this is a move of empiricist foundationalism that, in accepting this constituted effect as a primary given, successfully buries and masks the genealogy of power relations by which it is constituted.[12]

Insofar as Foucault traces the process of materialization as an investiture of discourse and power, he focuses on that dimension of power that is productive and formative. But we need to ask what constrains the domain of what is materializable, and whether there are *modalities* of materialization—as Aristotle suggests, and Althusser is quick to cite.[13] To what extent is materialization governed by principles of intelligibility that require and institute a domain of radical *unintelligibility* that resists materialization altogether or that remains radically dematerialized? Does Foucault's effort to work the notions of discourse and materiality through one another fail to account for not only what is *excluded* from the economies of discursive intelligibility that he describes, but what *has to be excluded* for those economies to function as self-sustaining systems?

This is the question implicitly raised by Luce Irigaray's analysis of the form/matter distinction in Plato. This argument is perhaps best known from the essay "Plato's Hystera," in *Speculum of the Other Woman*, but is trenchantly articulated as well in the less well-known essay, "Une Mère de Glace," also in *Speculum*.

Irigaray's task is to reconcile neither the form/matter distinction nor the distinctions between bodies and souls or matter and meaning. Rather, her effort is to show that those binary oppositions are formulated through the exclusion of a field of disruptive possibilities. Her speculative thesis is that those binaries, even in their reconciled mode, are part of a phallogocentric economy that produces the "feminine" as its constitutive outside. Irigaray's intervention in the history of the form/matter distinction underscores "matter" as the site at which the feminine is excluded from philosophical binaries. Inasmuch as certain phantasmatic notions of the feminine are traditionally associated with materiality, these are specular effects which confirm a phallogocentric project of autogenesis. And when those specular (and spectral) feminine figures are taken to be the feminine, the feminine is, she argues, fully erased by its very representation. The economy that claims to include the feminine as the subordinate term in a binary opposition of masculine/feminine excludes the feminine, produces the feminine as that which must be excluded for that economy to operate. In what follows, I will consider first Irigaray's speculative mode of engaging with philosophical texts and then turn to her rude and provocative reading of Plato's discussion of the receptacle in the *Timaeus*. In the final section of this essay, I will offer my own rude and provocative reading of the same passage.

IRIGARAY/PLATO

The largeness and speculative character of Irigaray's claims have always put me a bit on edge, and I confess in advance that although I can think of no feminist who has read and reread the history of philosophy with the kind of detailed and critical attention that she has,[14] her terms tend to mime the grandiosity of the philosophical errors that she underscores. This miming is, of course, tactical, and her reenactment of philosophical error requires that we learn how to read her for the difference that her reading performs. Does the voice of the philosophical father echo in her, or has she occupied that voice, insinuated herself into the voice of the father? If she is "in" that voice for either reason, is she also at the same time "outside" it? How do we understand the being "between," the two possibilities as something other than a spatialized *entre* that leaves the phallogocentric binary opposition intact?[15] How does the difference from the philosophical father resound in the mime which appears to replicate his strategy so faithfully? This is, clearly, no place between "his" language and "hers," but only a disruptive *movement* which unsettles the topographical claim.[16] This is a taking of his place, not to assume it, but to show that it is *occupiable*, to raise the question of the cost and movement of that assumption.[17] Where and how is the critical departure from that patrilineage performed in the course of the recitation of his terms? If the task is not a loyal or proper "reading" of Plato, then perhaps it is a kind of overreading which mimes and exposes the speculative excess in Plato. To the extent that I replicate that speculative excess here, I apologize, but only half-heartedly, for sometimes a hyperbolic rejoinder is necessary when a given injury has remained unspoken for too long.

When Irigaray sets out to reread the history of philosophy, she asks how its borders are secured: what must be excluded from the domain of philosophy for philosophy itself to proceed, and how is it that the excluded comes to constitute negatively a philosophical enterprise that takes itself to be self-grounding and self-constituting? Irigaray then isolates the feminine as precisely this constitutive exclusion, whereupon she is compelled to find a way of reading a philosophical text for what it refuses to include. This is no easy matter. For how can one read a text for what does *not* appear within its own terms, but which nevertheless constitutes the illegible conditions of its own legibility? Indeed, how can one read a text for the movement of that disappearing by which the textual "inside" and "outside" are constituted?

Although feminist philosophers have traditionally sought to show how the body is figured as feminine, or how women have been associated with materiality (whether inert—always already dead—or fecund—ever-living and procreative) where men have been associated with the principle of rational mastery,[18] Irigaray wants to argue that in fact the feminine is precisely what is excluded in and by such a binary opposition. In this sense, when and where women are represented within this economy is precisely the site of their erasure. Moreover, when matter is described within philosophical descriptions, she argues, it is at once a substitution for and displacement of the feminine. One cannot interpret the philosophical relation to the feminine through the figures that philosophy provides, but, rather, she argues, through siting the feminine as the unspeakable condition of figuration, as that which, in fact, can *never be* figured within the terms of philosophy proper, but whose exclusion from that propriety is its enabling condition.

No wonder then that the feminine appears for Irigaray only in *catachresis*, that is, in those figures that function improperly, as an improper transfer of sense, the use of a proper name to describe that which does not properly belong to it, and that return to haunt and coopt the very language from which the feminine is excluded. This explains in part the radical citational practice of Irigaray, the catachrestic usurpation of the "proper" for fully improper purposes.[19] For she mimes philosophy—as well as psychoanalysis—and, in the mime, takes on a language that effectively cannot belong to her, only to call into question the exclusionary rules of proprietariness that govern the use of that discourse. This contestation of propriety and property is precisely the option open to the feminine when it has been constituted as an excluded impropriety, as the improper, the propertyless. Indeed, as Irigaray argues in *Marine Lover [Amante marine]*, her work on Nietzsche, "woman neither is nor has an essence," and this is the case for her precisely because "woman" is what is excluded from the discourse of metaphysics.[20] If she takes on a proper name, even the proper name of "woman" in the singular, that can only be a kind of radical mime that seeks to jar the term from its ontological presuppositions. Jane Gallop makes this brilliantly clear in her reading of the two lips as both synecdoche and catachresis, a reading which offers an interpretation of Irigaray's language of biological essentialism as rhetorical strategy. Gallop shows that Irigaray's figural language constitutes the feminine in language as a persistent linguistic impropriety.[21]

This exclusion of the feminine from the proprietary discourse of metaphysics takes place, Irigaray argues, in and through the formulation of "matter." Inasmuch as a distinction between form and matter is offered within phallogocentrism, it is articulated through a further materiality. In other words, every explicit distinction takes place in an inscriptional space that the distinction itself cannot accommodate. Matter as a *site* of inscription cannot be explicitly thematized. And this inscriptional site or space is, for Irigaray, a *materiality* that is not the same as the category of "matter" whose articulation it conditions and enables. It is this unthematizable materiality that Irigaray claims becomes the site, the repository, indeed, the receptacle of and for the feminine *within* a phallogocentric economy. In an important sense, this second inarticulate "matter" designates the constitutive outside of the Platonic economy; it is what must be excluded for that economy to posture as internally coherent.[22]

This excessive matter that cannot be contained within the form/matter distinction operates like the supplement in Derrida's analysis of philosophical oppositions. In Derrida's consideration of the form/matter distinction in *Positions*, he suggests as well that matter must be redoubled, at once as a pole within a binary opposition, and as that which exceeds that binary coupling, as a figure for its nonsystematizability.

Consider Derrida's remark in response to the critic who wants to claim that matter denotes the radical outside to language: "It follows that if, and in the extent to which, *matter* in this general economy designates, as you said, radical alterity (I will specify: in relation to philosophical oppositions), then what I write can be considered 'materialist.'"[23] For both Derrida and Irigaray, it seems, what is excluded from this binary is also *produced* by it in the mode of exclusion and has no separable or fully independent existence as an absolute outside. A constitutive or relative outside is, of course, composed of a set of exclusions that are nevertheless *internal* to that system as its own nonthematizable necessity. It emerges within the system as incoherence, disruption, a threat to its own systematicity.

Irigaray insists that this exclusion that mobilizes the form/matter binary is the differentiating relation between masculine and feminine, where the masculine occupies both terms of binary opposition, and the feminine cannot be said to be an intelligible term at all. We might understand the feminine figured within the binary as the *specular* feminine and the feminine which is erased and excluded from that binary as the *excessive* feminine. And yet, such nominations cannot work, for in the latter mode, the feminine, strictly speaking, cannot be named at all and, indeed, is not a mode.

For Irigaray, the "feminine" which cannot be said to *be* anything, to participate in ontology at all, is—and here grammar fails us—set under erasure as the impossible necessity that enables any ontology. The feminine, to use a catachresis, is domesticated and rendered unintelligible within a phallogocentrism that claims to be self-constituting. Disavowed, the remnant of the feminine survives as the *inscriptional space* of that phallogocentrism, the specular surface which receives the marks of a masculine signifying act only to give back a (false) reflection and guarantee of phallogocentric self-sufficiency, without making any contribution of its own. As a topos of the metaphysical tradition, this inscriptional space makes its appearance in Plato's *Timaeus* as the receptacle (*hypodoche*), which is also described as the *chora*. Although extensive readings of the *chora* have been offered by Derrida and Irigaray, I want to refer here to only one passage which is about the very problem of passage: namely, that passage by which a form can be said to generate its own sensible representation. We know that for Plato any material object comes into being only through participating in a Form which is its necessary precondition. As a result, material objects are copies of Forms and exist only to the extent that they instantiate Forms. And yet, where does this instantiation take place? Is there a place, a site, where this reproduction occurs, a medium through which the transformation from form to sensible object occurs?

In the cosmogony offered in the *Timaeus*, Plato refers to three natures that must be taken into account: the first, which is the process of generation; the second, that in which the generation takes place; and the third, that of which the thing generated is a resemblance naturally produced. Then, in what appears to be an aside, we may "liken the receiving principle to a mother, and the source or spring to a father, and the intermediate nature to a child"(50d).[24] Prior to this passage, Plato refers to this receiving principle as a "nurse" (40b) and then as "the universal nature which receives all bodies," according to the Hamilton/Cairns translation. But this latter phrase might be better translated as "the dynamic nature (*physis*) that receives (*dechesthai*) all the bodies that there are (*ta panta somata*)" (50b).[25] Of this all-receiving function, Plato argues, she "must always be called the same, for inasmuch as she always receives all things, she never departs at all from her own nature (*dynamis*) and never, in any way or at any time, assumes a form (*eilephen*) like that of any of the things which enter into her...the forms that enter into and go out of her are the likenesses of eternal realities modeled after their own patterns (*diaschematizomenon*)..."(50c).[26] Here her proper function is to receive, *dechesthai*, to take, accept, welcome, include, and even comprehend. What enters into this *hypodoche* is a set of forms or, better, shapes (*morphe*), and yet this receiving principle, this *physis*, has no proper shape and is not a body. Like Aristotle's *hyle*, *physis* cannot be defined.[27] In effect, the receiving principle potentially includes all bodies, and so applies universally, but its universal applicability must not resemble at all, ever, those eternal realities (*eidos*) which in the *Timaeus* prefigure universal forms, and which pass into the receptacle. There is here a prohibition on resemblance (*mimeta*), which is to say that this nature cannot be said to be like either the eternal Forms or their material, sensible, or imaginary copies. But in particular, this *physis* is only to be entered, but never to enter. Here the term *eisienai* denotes a going toward or into, an approach and penetration; it also denotes going into a *place*, so that the *chora*, as an enclosure, cannot be that which enters into another enclosure; metaphorically, and perhaps coincidentally, this prohibited form of entry also means "being brought into court", i.e., subject to public norms, and "coming into mind" or "beginning to think."

Here there is also the stipulation not "to assume a form like those that enter her." Can this receptacle, then, be likened to any body, to that of the mother, or to the nurse? According to Plato's own stipulation, we cannot define this "nature," and to know it by analogy is to know it only by "bastard thinking." In this sense the human who would know this nature is dispossessed of/by the paternal principle, a son out of wedlock, a deviation from patrilineality and the analogical relation by which patronymic lineage proceeds. Hence, to offer a metaphor or analogy presupposes a likeness between that nature and a human form. It is this last point that Derrida, accepting Plato's dictum, takes as salient to the understanding of the *chora*, arguing that it can never be collapsed into any of the figures that it itself occasions. As a result, Derrida argues, it would be wrong to take the association of the chora with femininity as a decisive collapse.[28]

In a sense, Irigaray agrees with this contention: the figures of the nurse, the mother, the womb cannot be fully identified with the receptacle, for those are specular figures which displace the feminine at the moment they purport to represent the feminine. The receptacle cannot be exhaustively thematized or figured in Plato's text, precisely because it is that which conditions and escapes every figuration and thematization. *This receptacle/nurse is not a metaphor based on likeness to a human form, but a disfiguration that emerges at the boundaries of the human both as its very condition and as the insistent threat of its deformation; it cannot take a form, a morphe, and in that sense, cannot be a body.*

Insofar as Derrida argues that the receptacle cannot be identified with the figure of the feminine, Irigaray would seem to be in agreement. But she takes the analysis a step further, arguing that the feminine exceeds its figuration, just as the receptacle does, and that this unthematizability constitutes the feminine as the impossible yet necessary foundation of what can be thematized and figured. Significantly, Julia Kristeva *accepts* this collapse of the *chora* and the maternal/nurse figure, arguing in *Revolution in Poetic Language* that "Plato leads us" to this "process...[of] rhythmic space."[29] In contrast with Irigaray's refusal of this conflation of the *chora* and the feminine/maternal, Kristeva affirms this association and further asserts her notion of the semiotic as that which "precedes"(26) the symbolic law: "The mother's body is therefore what mediates the symbolic law organizing social relations and becomes the ordering principle of the semiotic *chora*"(27).

Whereas Kristeva insists upon this identification of the *chora* with the maternal body, Irigaray asks how the discourse which performs that conflation invariably produces an "outside" where the feminine which is *not* captured by the figure of the *chora* persists. Here we need to ask, How is this assignation of a feminine "outside" possible within language? And is it not the case that there is within any discourse and thus within Irigaray's as well, a set of constitutive exclusions that are inevitably produced by the circumscription of the feminine as that which monopolizes the sphere of exclusion?

In this sense, the receptacle is not simply a figure *for* the excluded, but, taken as a figure, stands for the excluded and thus performs or enacts yet another set of exclusions of all that remains unfigurable under the sign of the feminine—that in the feminine which resists the figure of the nurse-receptacle. In other words, taken as a figure, the nurse-receptacle freezes the feminine as that which is necessary for the reproduction of the human, but which itself is not human, and which is in no way to be construed as the formative principle of the human form that is, as it were, produced through it.[30]

The problem is not that the feminine is made to stand for matter or for universality; rather, the feminine is cast outside the form/matter and universal/particular binarisms. She will be neither the one nor the other, but the permanent and unchangeable condition of both—what can be construed as a nonthematizable materiality.[31] She will be entered, and will give forth a further instance of what enters her, but she will never resemble either the formative principle or that which it creates. Irigaray insists that here it is the female power of reproduction that is taken over by the phallogocentric economy and remade into its own exclusive and essential action. When *physis* is articulated as *chora*, as it is in Plato, some of the dynamism and potency included in the meaning of *physis* is suppressed. In the place of a femininity that makes a contribution to reproduction, we have a phallic Form that reproduces only and always further versions of itself, and does this through the feminine, but with no assistance from her. Significantly, this transfer of the reproductive function from the feminine to the masculine entails the topographical suppression of *physis*, the dissimulation of *physis* as *chora*, as place.

The word matter does not occur in Plato to describe this *chora* or *hypodoche*, and yet Aristotle remarks in *The Metaphysics* that this section of the *Timaeus* articulates most closely his own notion of *hyle*. Taking up this suggestion, Plotinus wrote the Sixth Tractate of the *Enneads,* "The

Impassivity of the Unembodied," an effort to account for Plato's notion of the *hypodoche* as *hyle* or matter.[32] In a twist that the history of philosophy has perhaps rarely undergone, Irigaray accepts and recites Plotinus's effort to read Plato through Aristotelian "matter" in "Une Mère de Glace."

In that essay, she writes that for Plato matter is "sterile," "female in receptivity only, not in pregnancy...castrated of that impregnating power which belongs only to the unchangeably masculine."[33] Her reading establishes the cosmogony of the Forms in the *Timaeus* as a phallic phantasy of a fully self-constituted patrilineality, and this fantasy of autogenesis or self-constitution is effected through a denial and cooptation of the female capacity for reproduction. Of course, the "she" who is the "receptacle" is neither a universal nor a particular, and because for Plato anything that can be named is either a universal or a particular, the receptacle cannot be named. Taking speculative license, and wandering into what he himself calls "a strange and unwonted inquiry" (48d), Plato nevertheless proceeds to name what cannot be properly named, invoking a catachresis in order to describe the receptacle as a universal receiver of bodies even as it cannot be a universal, for, if it were, it would participate in those eternal realities from which it is excluded.

In the cosmogony prior to the one which introduces the receptacle, Plato suggests that if the appetites, those tokens of the soul's materiality, are not successfully mastered, a soul, understood as a man's soul, risks coming back as a woman, and then as a beast. In a sense woman and beast are the very figures for unmasterable passion. And if a soul participates in such passions, it will be effectively and ontologically transformed by them and into the very signs, woman and beast, by which they are figured. In this prior cosmogony, woman represents a descent into materiality.

But this prior cosmogony calls to be rewritten, for if man is at the top of an ontological hierarchy, and woman is a poor or debased copy of man, and beast is a poor or debased copy of both woman and of man, then there is still a *resemblance* between these three beings, even as that resemblance is hierarchically distributed. In the following cosmogony, the one that introduces the receptacle, Plato clearly wants to disallow the possibility of a resemblance between the masculine and the feminine, and he does this through introducing a feminized receptacle that is prohibited from resembling any form. Of course, strictly speaking, the receptacle can have no ontological status, for ontology is constituted by forms, and the receptacle

cannot be one. And we cannot speak about that for which there is no ontological determination, or if we do, we use language improperly, imputing
being to that which can have no being. So, the receptacle seems from the
start to be an impossible word, a designation that cannot be designated.
Paradoxically, Plato proceeds to tell us that this very receptacle must always
be called the same.[34] Precisely because this receptacle can only occasion a
radically improper speech, that is, a speech in which all ontological claims
are suspended, the terms by which it is named must be consistently applied,
not in order to make the name fit the thing named but precisely because
that which is to be named can have no proper name, bounds and threatens
the sphere of linguistic propriety, and, therefore, must be controlled by a
forcibly imposed set of nominative rules.

How is it that Plato can concede the undesignatable status of this receptacle and prescribe for it a consistent name? Is it that the receptacle, designated as the undesignatable, *cannot* be designated, or is it rather that this
"cannot" functions as an "ought not to be"? Should this limit to what is
representable be read as a prohibition against a certain kind of representation? And since Plato does offer us a representation of the receptacle,
one that he claims ought to remain a singularly authoritative representation
(and makes this offer in the very same passage in which he claims its
radical unrepresentability), ought we not to conclude that Plato, in autho-
rizing a single representation of the feminine, means to prohibit the very
proliferation of nominative possibilities that the undesignatable might
produce? Perhaps this is a representation within discourse that functions to
prohibit from discourse any further representation, one which represents
the feminine as unrepresentable and unintelligible, but which in the
rhetoric of the constative claim defeats itself. After all, Plato *posits* that
which he claims cannot be *posited*. And he further contradicts himself when
he claims that that which cannot be posited ought to be posited in only
one way. In a sense, this authoritative naming of the receptacle as the
unnameable constitutes a primary or founding inscription that secures this
place as an inscriptional space. This naming of what cannot be named is
itself a penetration into this receptacle which is at once a violent erasure,
one which establishes it as an impossible yet necessary site for all further
inscriptions.[35] In this sense, the very *telling* of the story about the phallo-
morphic genesis of objects *enacts* that phallomorphosis and becomes an
allegory of its own procedure.

Irigaray's response to this exclusion of the feminine from the economy of representation is effectively to say, Fine, I don't want to be in your economy anyway, and I'll show you what this unintelligible receptacle can do to your system; I will not be a poor copy in your system, but I will resemble you nevertheless by *miming* the textual passages through which you construct your system and showing that what cannot enter it is already inside it (as its necessary outside), and I will mime and repeat the gestures of your operation until this emergence of the outside within the system calls into question its systematic closure and its pretension to be self-grounding.

This is part of what Naomi Schor means when she claims that Irigaray mimes mimesis itself.[36] Through miming, Irigaray transgresses the prohibition against resemblance at the same time that she refuses the notion of resemblance as copy. She cites Plato again and again, but the citations expose precisely what is excluded from them, and seek to show and to reintroduce the excluded into the system itself. In this sense, she performs a repetition and displacement of the phallic economy. *This is citation, not as enslavement or simple reiteration of the original, but as an insubordination that appears to take place within the very terms of the original, and which calls into question the power of origination that Plato appears to claim for himself.* Her miming has the effect of repeating the origin only to displace that origin *as* an origin.

And insofar as the Platonic account of the origin is itself a *displacement* of a maternal origin, Irigaray merely mimes that very act of displacement, displacing the displacement, showing that origin to be an "effect" of a certain ruse of phallogocentric power. In line with this reading of Irigaray, then, the feminine as maternal does not offer itself as an alternative origin. For if the feminine is said to be anywhere or anything, it is that which is produced through displacement and which returns as the possibility of a reverse-displacement. Indeed, one might reconsider the conventional characterization of Irigaray as an uncritical maternalist, for here it appears that the reinscription of the maternal takes place by writing with and through the language of phallic philosophemes. This textual practice is not grounded in a rival ontology, but inhabits—indeed, penetrates, occupies, and redeploys—the paternal language itself.

One might well ask whether this kind of penetrative textual strategy does not suggest a different textualization of eroticism than the rigorously anti-penetrative eros of surfaces that appears in Irigaray's "When Our

Lips Speak Together": "You are not *in me*. I do not contain you or retain you in my stomach, my arms, my head. Nor in my memory, my mind, my language. You are there, like my skin."[37] The refusal of an eroticism of entry and containment seems linked for Irigaray with an opposition to appropriation and possession as forms of erotic exchange. And yet the kind of reading that Irigaray performs requires not only that she enter the text she reads, but that she work the inadvertent uses of that containment, especially when the feminine is sustained as an internal gap or fissure in the philosophical system itself. In such appropriative readings, Irigaray appears to enact the very spectre of a penetration in reverse—or a penetration elsewhere—that Plato's economy seeks to foreclose ("the 'elsewhere' of feminine pleasure can be found only at the price of *crossing back* (*retraversée*) through the mirror that subtends all speculation"[38]). At the level of rhetoric this "crossing back" constitutes an eroticism that critically mimes the phallus—an eroticism structured by repetition and displacement, penetration and exposure—that counters the eros of surfaces that Irigaray explicitly affirms.

The opening quotation of Irigaray's essay claims that philosophical systems are built on "a break with material contiguity," and that the concept of matter constitutes and conceals that rupture or cut (*la coupure*). This argument appears to presume some order of contiguity that is prior to the concept, prior to matter, and which matter works to conceal. In Irigaray's most systematic reading of the history of ethical philosophy, *Éthique de la différence sexuelle*, she argues that ethical relations ought to be based on relations of closeness, proximity, and intimacy that reconfigure conventional notions of reciprocity and respect. Traditional conceptions of reciprocity exchange such relations of intimacy for those characterized by violent erasure, substitutability, and appropriation.[39] Psychoanalytically, that material closeness is understood as the uncertain separation of boundaries between maternal body and infant, relations that reemerge in language as the metonymic proximity of signs. Insofar as concepts, like matter and form, repudiate and conceal the metonymic signifying chains from which they are composed, they serve the phallogocentric purpose of breaking with that maternal/material contiguity. On the other hand, that contiguity confounds the phallogocentric effort to set up a series of substitutions through metaphorical equivalences or conceptual unities.[40]

This contiguity that exceeds the concept of matter is, according to

Margaret Whitford, not itself a natural relation, but a *symbolic* articulation proper to women. Whitford takes "the two lips" as a figure for metonymy,[41] "a figure for the vertical and horizontal relationships between women...women's sociality".[42] But Whitford also points out that feminine and masculine economies are never fully separable; as a result, it seems, relations of contiguity subsist *between* those economies and, hence, do not belong exclusively to the sphere of the feminine.

How, then, do we understand Irigaray's textual practice of lining up alongside Plato? To what extent does she repeat his text, not to augment its specular production, but to cross back over and through that specular mirror to a feminine "elsewhere" that must remain problematically within citation marks?

There is for Irigaray, always, a matter that exceeds matter, where the latter is disavowed for the autogenetic form/matter coupling to thrive. Matter occurs in two modalities: first, as a metaphysical concept that serves a phallogocentrism; second, as an ungrounded figure, worrisomely speculative and catachrestic, that marks for her the possible linguistic site of a critical mime.

> To play with mimesis is thus, for a woman, to try to recover the place of her exploitation by discourse, without allowing herself to be simply reduced to it. It means to resubmit herself—inasmuch as she is on the side of the "perceptible," of "matter"—to "ideas," in particular to ideas about herself, that are elaborated in/by a masculine logic, but so as to make "visible," by an effect of playful repetition, what was supposed to remain invisible: the cover up of a possible operation of the feminine in language.[43]

So perhaps here is the return of essentialism, in the notion of a "feminine in language"? And yet, she continues by suggesting that *miming* is that very operation of the feminine in language. To mime means to participate in precisely that which is mimed, and if the language mime is the language of phallogocentrism, then this is only a specifically feminine language to the extent that the feminine is radically implicated in the very terms of a phallogocentrism it seeks to rework. The quotation continues, "[to play with mimesis means] 'to unveil' the fact that, if women are such good mimics, it is because they are not simply resorbed in this function. *They also remain elsewhere*: another case of the persistence of 'matter'..."

They mime phallogocentrism, but they also expose what is covered over by the mimetic self-replication of that discourse. For Irigaray, what is broken with and covered over is the linguistic operation of metonymy, a closeness and proximity which appears to be the linguistic residue of the initial proximity of mother and infant. It is this metonymic excess in every mime, indeed, in every metaphorical substitution, that is understood to disrupt the seamless repetition of the phallogocentric norm.

To claim, though, as Irigaray does, that the logic of identity is potentially disruptible by the insurgence of metonymy, and then to identify this metonymy with the repressed and insurgent feminine is to consolidate the place of the feminine in and as the irruptive chora, that which cannot be figured, but which is necessary for any figuration. That is, of course, to figure that chora nevertheless, and in such a way that the feminine is "always" the outside, and the outside is "always" the feminine. This is a move that at once positions the feminine as the unthematizable, the non-figurable, but which, in identifying the feminine with that position, thematizes and figures, and so makes use of the phallogocentric exercise to produce this identity which "is" the non-identical.

There are good reasons, however, to reject the notion that the feminine monopolizes the sphere of the excluded here. Indeed, to enforce such a monopoly redoubles the effect of foreclosure performed by the phallogocentric discourse itself, one which "mimes" its founding violence in a way that works against the explicit claim to have found a linguistic site in metonymy that works as disruption. After all, Plato's scenography of intelligibility depends on the exclusion of women, slaves, children, and animals, where slaves are characterized as those who do not speak his language, and who, in not speaking his language, are considered diminished in their capacity for reason. This xenophobic exclusion operates through the production of racialized Others, and those whose "natures" are considered less rational by virtue of their appointed task in the process of laboring to reproduce the conditions of private life. This domain of the less than rational human bounds the figure of human reason, producing that "man" as one who is without a childhood; is not a primate and so is relieved of the necessity of eating, defecating, living and dying; one who is not a slave, but always a property holder; one whose language remains originary and untranslatable. This is a figure of disembodiment, but one which is nevertheless a figure of a body, a bodying forth of a masculinized rationality, the figure of a male body which is not a body, a figure in crisis, a figure that enacts a crisis it cannot fully control. This figuration of masculine reason as disembodied body is one whose imaginary morphology is crafted through the exclusion of other possible bodies. This is a materialization of reason which operates through the dematerialization of other bodies, for the feminine, strictly speaking, has no morphe, no morphology, no contour, for it is that which contributes to the contouring of things, but is itself undifferentiated, without boundary. The body that is reason dematerializes the bodies that may not properly stand for reason or its replicas, and yet this is a figure in crisis, for this body of reason is itself the phantasmatic dematerialization of masculinity, one which requires that women and slaves, children and animals be the body, perform the bodily functions, that it will not perform.[44]

Irigaray does not always help matters here, for she fails to follow through the metonymic link between women and these other Others, idealizing and appropriating the "elsewhere" as the feminine. But what is the "elsewhere" of Irigaray's "elsewhere"? If the feminine is not the only or primary kind of being that is excluded from the economy of masculinist reason, what and who is excluded in the course of Irigaray's analysis?

IMPROPER ENTRY: PROTOCOLS OF SEXUAL DIFFERENCE

The above analysis has considered not the materiality of sex, but the sex of materiality. In other words, it has traced materiality as the site at which a certain drama of sexual difference plays itself out. The point of such an exposition is not only to warn against an easy return to the *materiality* of the body or the materiality of sex, but to show that to invoke matter is to invoke a sedimented history of sexual hierarchy and sexual erasures which should surely be an *object* of feminist inquiry, but which would be quite problematic as a *ground* of feminist theory. To return to matter requires that we return to matter as a *sign* which in its redoublings and contradictions enacts an inchoate drama of sexual difference.

Let us then return to the passage in the *Timaeus* in which matter redoubles itself as a proper and improper term, differentially sexed, thereby conceding itself as a site of ambivalence, as a body which is no body, in its masculine form, as a matter which is no body, in its feminine.

The receptacle, she, "always receives all things, she never departs at all from her own nature and, never, in any way or any time, assumes a form like that of any of the things that enter into her" (50b). What appears to be prohibited here is partially contained by the verb *eilephen*—to assume, as in to assume a form—which is at once a continuous action, but also a kind of receptivity. The term means, among other possibilities, to gain or procure, to take, to receive hospitality, but also *to have a wife*, and *of a woman to conceive*.[45] The term suggests a procurement, but also both a capacity to conceive and to take a wife. These activities or endowments are prohibited in the passage above, thus setting limits on the kinds of "receptivity" that this receiving principle can undertake. The term for what she is never to do (i.e., "depart from her own nature") is *existhathai dynameos*. This implies that she ought never to arise out of, become separated from, or be *displaced from* her own nature; as that which is contained in itself, she is that which, quite literally, ought not to be *disordered in displacement*. The *siempre*, the "never," and the "in no way" are insistent repetitions that give this "natural impossibility" the form of an imperative, a prohibition, a legislation and allocation of proper place. What would happen if she began to resemble that which is said only and always to enter into her? Clearly, a set of positions is being secured here through the exclusive allocation of penetration to the form, and penetrability to a feminized materiality, and a full dissociation of this figure of penetrable femininity from the being resulting from reproduction.[46]

Irigaray clearly reads the "assume a form/shape" in this passage as "to conceive," and understands Plato to be prohibiting the feminine from contributing to the process of reproduction in order to credit the masculine with giving birth. But it seems that we might consider another sense of "to assume" in Greek, namely, "to have or take a wife."[47] For she will never resemble—and so never enter into—another materiality. This means that he—remember the Forms are likened to the father in this triad—will never be entered by her or, in fact, by anything. For he is the impenetrable penetrator, and she, the invariably penetrated. And "he" would not be differentiated from her were it not for this prohibition on resemblance which establishes their positions as mutually exclusive and yet complementary. In fact, if she were to penetrate in return, or penetrate elsewhere, it is unclear whether she could remain a "she" and whether "he" could preserve his own differentially established identity. For the logic of non-contradiction that conditions this distribution of pronouns is one which establishes the "he" through this exclusive position as penetrator and the "she" through this exclusive position as penetrated. As a consequence, then, without this heterosexual *matrix*, as it were, it appears that the stability of these gendered positions would be called into question.

One might read this prohibition that secures the impenetrability of the masculine as a kind of panic, a panic over becoming "like" her, effeminized, or a panic over what might happen if a masculine penetration of the masculine were authorized, or a feminine penetration of the feminine, or a feminine penetration of the masculine or a reversibility of those positions—not to mention a full-scale confusion over what qualifies as "penetration" anyway. Would the terms "masculine" and "feminine" still signify in stable ways, or would the relaxing of the taboos against stray penetration destabilize these gendered positions in serious ways? If it were possible to have a relation of penetration between two ostensibly feminine gendered positions, would this be the kind of resemblance that must be prohibited in order for Western metaphysics to get going? And would that be considered something like a cooptation and displacement of phallic autonomy that would undermine the phallic assurance over its own exclusive rights?

Is this a reverse mime that Irigaray does not consider, but which is nevertheless compatible with her strategy of a critical mime? Can we read this taboo that mobilizes the speculative and phantasmatic beginnings of Western metaphysics in terms of the spectre of sexual exchange that it produces through its own prohibition, as a panic over the lesbian or, perhaps more specifically, over the phallicization of the lesbian? Or would this kind of resemblance so disturb the compulsory gendered matrix that supports the order of things that one could not claim that these sexual exchanges that occur outside or in the interstices of the phallic economy are simply "copies" of the heterosexual origin? For clearly, this legislation of a particular version of heterosexuality attests full well to its non-originary status. Otherwise there would be no necessity to install a prohibition at the outset against rival possibilities for the organization of sexuality. In this sense, those improper resemblances or imitations that Plato rules out of the domain of intelligibility do not resemble the masculine, for that would be to privilege the masculine as origin. If a resemblance is possible, it is because the "originality" of the masculine is contestable; in other words, the miming of the masculine, which is never resorbed into it, can expose the masculine's claim to originality as suspect. Insofar as the masculine is founded here through a prohibition which outlaws the spectre of a lesbian resemblance, that masculinist institution—and the phallogocentric homophobia it encodes—is *not* an origin, but only the *effect* of that very prohibition, fundamentally dependent on that which it must exclude.[48]

Significantly, this prohibition emerges at the site where materiality is being installed as a double instance, as the copy of the Form, and as the non-contributing materiality in which and through which that self-copying mechanism works. In this sense, matter is either part of the specular scenography of phallic inscription or that which cannot be rendered intelligible within its terms. The very formulation of matter takes place in the service of an organization and denial of sexual difference, so that we are confronted with an economy of sexual difference as that which defines, instrumentalizes, and allocates matter in its own service.

The regulation of sexuality at work in the articulation of the Forms suggests that sexual difference operates in the very formulation of matter. But this is a matter that is defined not only against reason, where reason is understood as that which acts on and through a countervailing materiality, and masculine and feminine occupy these oppositional positions. Sexual difference also operates in the formulation, the staging, of what will occupy the site of inscriptional space, that is, as what must remain outside these oppositional positions as their supporting condition. There is no singular outside, for the Forms require a number of exclusions; they are and replicate themselves through what they exclude, through not being the animal, not being the woman, not being the slave, whose propriety is purchased through property, national and racial boundary, masculinism, and compulsory heterosexuality.

To the extent that a set of reverse-mimes emerge from those quarters, they will not be the same as each other; if there is an occupation and reversal of the master's discourse, it will come from many quarters, and those resignifying practices will converge in ways that scramble the self-replicating presumptions of reason's mastery. For if the copies speak, or if what is merely material begins to signify, the scenography of reason is rocked by the crisis on which it was always built. And there will be no way finally to delimit the elsewhere of Irigaray's elsewhere, for every oppositional discourse will produce its outside, an outside that risks becoming installed as its non-signifying inscriptional space.

And whereas this can appear as the necessary and founding violence of any truth-regime, it is important to resist that theoretical gesture of pathos in which exclusions are simply affirmed as sad necessities of signification. The task is to refigure this necessary "outside" as a future horizon, one in which the violence of exclusion is perpetually in the process of being over-come. But of equal importance is the preservation of the outside, the site where discourse meets its limits, where the opacity of what is not included in a given regime of truth acts as a disruptive site of linguistic impropriety and unrepresentability, illuminating the violent and contingent boundaries of that normative regime precisely through the inability of that regime to represent that which might pose a fundamental threat to its continuity. In this sense, radical and inclusive representability is not precisely the goal: to include, to speak as, to bring in every marginal and excluded position within a given discourse is to claim that a singular discourse meets its limits nowhere, that it can and will domesticate all signs of difference. If there is a violence necessary to the language of politics, then the risk of that viola-tion might well be followed by another in which we begin, without ending, without mastering, to own—and yet never fully to own—the exclusions by which we proceed.

FORMLESS FEMININITY

Awkwardly, it seems, Plato's phantasmatic economy virtually deprives the feminine of a *morphe*, a shape, for as the receptacle, the feminine is a permanent and, hence, non-living, shapeless non-thing which cannot be named. And as nurse, mother, womb, the feminine is synecdochally col-lapsed into a set of figural functions. In this sense, Plato's discourse on materiality (if we can take the discourse on the *hypodoche* to be that), is one which does not permit the notion of the female body as a human form.

How can we legitimate claims of bodily injury if we put into question the materiality of the body? What is here enacted through the Platonic text is a violation that founds the very concept of matter, a violation that mobilizes the concept and which the concept sustains. Moreover, within Plato, there is a disjunction between a materiality which is feminine and formless and, hence, without a body, and bodies which are formed through—but not of—that feminine materiality. To what extent in invok-ing received notions of materiality, indeed, in insisting that those notions function as "irreducibles," do we secure and perpetuate a constitutive violation of the feminine? When we consider that the very concept of matter preserves and recirculates a violation, and then invoke that very concept in the service of a compensation for violation, we run the risk of reproducing the very injury for which we seek redress.

The *Timaeus* does not give us bodies, but only a collapse and displacement of those figures of bodily position that secure a given fantasy of heterosexual intercourse and male autogenesis. For the receptacle is not a woman, but it is the figure that women become within the dream-world of this metaphysical cosmogony, one which remains largely inchoate in the constitution of matter. It may be, as Irigaray appears to suggest, that the entire history of matter is bound up with the problematic of receptivity. Is there a way to dissociate these implicit and disfiguring figures from the "matter" that they help to compose? And insofar as we have barely begun to discern the history of sexual difference encoded in the history of matter, it seems radically unclear whether a notion of matter or the materiality of bodies can serve as the uncontested ground of feminist practice. In this sense, the Aristotelian pun still works as a reminder of the doubleness of the matter of matter, which means that there may not be a materiality of sex that is not already burdened by the sex of materiality.

Some open-ended questions remain: How is it that the presumption of a given version of matter in the effort to describe the materiality of bodies prefigures in advance what will and will not appear as an intelligible body? How do tacit normative criteria form the matter of bodies? And can we understand such criteria not simply as epistemological impositions on bodies, but as the specific social regulatory ideals by which bodies are trained, shaped, and formed? If a bodily schema is not simply an imposition on already formed bodies, but part of the formation of bodies, how might we be able to think the production or formative power of prohibition in the process of morphogenesis?

Here the question is not simply what Plato thought bodies might be, and what of the body remained for him radically unthinkable; rather, the question is whether the forms which are said to produce bodily life operate through the production of an excluded domain that comes to bound and to haunt the field of intelligible bodily life. The logic of this operation is to a certain extent psychoanalytic inasmuch as the force of prohibition produces the spectre of a terrifying return. Can we, then, turn to psychoanalysis itself to ask how the boundaries of the body are crafted through sexual taboo?[49] To what extent does the Platonic account of the phallogenesis of bodies prefigure the Freudian and Lacanian accounts which presume the phallus as the synecdochal token of sexed positionality?

If the bounding, forming, and deforming of sexed bodies is animated by a set of founding prohibitions, a set of enforced criteria of intelligibility, then we are not merely considering how bodies appear from the vantage point of a theoretical position or epistemic location at a distance from bodies themselves. On the contrary, we are asking how the criteria of intelligible sex operates to constitute a field of bodies, and how precisely we might understand specific criteria to produce the bodies that they regulate. In what precisely does the crafting power of prohibition consist? Does it determine a psychic experience of the body which is radically separable from something that one might want to call the body itself? Or is it the case that the productive power of prohibition in morphogenesis renders the very distinction between *morphe* and *psyche* unsustainable?

2

THE LESBIAN PHALLUS AND
THE MORPHOLOGICAL IMAGINARY

> The Lacanian's desire clearly to separate *phallus* from *penis*, to
> control the meaning of the signifier *phallus*, is precisely sympto-
> matic of their desire to have the phallus, that is, their desire to be
> at the center of language, at its origin. And their inability to con-
> trol the meaning of the word *phallus* is evidence of what Lacan
> calls symbolic castration.
> —Jane Gallop, "Beyond the Phallus"

> All sorts of things in the world behave like mirrors.
> —Jacques Lacan, *Seminar II*

After such a promising title, I knew that I could not possibly offer a
satisfying essay; but perhaps the promise of the phallus is always dissatis-
fying in some way. I would like, then, to acknowledge that failure from the
start and to work that failure for its uses and to suggest that something
more interesting than satisfying the phallic ideal may come of the analysis
that I propose. Indeed, perhaps a certain wariness with respect to that
allure is a good thing. What I would like to do instead is make a critical
return to Freud, to his essay "On Narcissism: An Introduction," and consider the textual contradictions he produces as he tries to define the
boundaries of erotogenic body parts. It may not seem that the lesbian
phallus has much to do with what you are about to read, but I assure you
(promise you?) that it couldn't have been done without it.

The essay "On Narcissism: An Introduction" (1914)[1] is an effort to
explain the theory of libido in terms of those experiences which seem
at first to be most improbably conducive to its terms. Freud begins by
considering bodily pain, and he asks whether we might understand the
obsessive self-preoccupations of those who suffer physical illness or injury
to be a kind of libidinal investment in pain. And he asks further whether
this negative investment in one's own bodily discomfort can be understood
as a kind of narcissism. For the moment I want to suspend the question of

why it is that Freud chooses illness and then hypochondria as the examples of bodily experience that narcissism describes and, indeed, why it seems that narcissism seems to be negative narcissism from the start; I will, however, return to this question once the relationship between illness and erotogenicity is established. In the essay on narcissism, then, Freud first considers organic disease as that which "withdraws libido from love objects, [and] lavishes libido on itself" (82). As the first in what will become a string of examples, he cites a line of poetry from Wilhelm Busch's *Balduin Bahlamin* on the erotics of the toothache: "concentrated is his soul…in his molar's [jaw-tooth's] aching hole" (82).[2]

According to the theory of libido, the concentration eroticizes that hole in the mouth, that cavity within a cavity, redoubling the pain of the physical as and through a psychically invested pain—a pain of or from the soul, the psyche. From this example of libidinal self-investment, Freud extrapolates to other examples: sleep and then dreams, both considered as exercises in sustained self-preoccupation, and then to hypochondria. The example of physical pain thus gives way, through a textual detour through sleep, dreams, and the imaginary, to an analogy with hypochondria and finally to an argument that establishes the theoretical indissolubility of physical and imaginary injury. This position has consequences for determining what constitutes a body part at all, and, as we shall see, what constitutes an erotogenic body part in particular. In the essay on narcissism, hypochondria lavishes libido on a body part, but in a significant sense, that body part does not exist for consciousness prior to that investiture; indeed, that body part is delineated and becomes knowable for Freud only on the condition of that investiture.

Nine years later, in *The Ego and the Id* (1923)[3] Freud will state quite clearly that bodily pain is the precondition of bodily self-discovery. In this text he asks how one can account for the *formation* of the ego, that bounded sense of self, and concludes that it is differentiated from the id partially through pain:

> Pain seems to play a part in the process, and the way in which we gain new knowledge of our organs during painful illnesses is perhaps a model of the way by which in general we arrive at the idea of our own body (25-6).

In a move that prefigures Lacan's argument in "The Mirror Stage,"

Freud connects the formation of one's ego with the externalized idea one forms of one's own body. Hence, Freud's claim, "The ego is first and foremost a bodily ego; it is not merely a surface entity, but is itself the projection of a surface"(26).[4]

What is meant by the imaginary construction of body parts? Is this an idealist thesis or one which asserts the indissolubility of the psychic and physical body?[5] Curiously, Freud associates the process of erotogenicity with the consciousness of bodily pain: "Let us now, taking any part of the body, describe its activity of sending sexually exciting stimuli to the mind as its 'erotogenicity'" (Freud 1914, 84). Here, however, it is fundamentally unclear, even undecidable, whether this is a consciousness that imputes pain to the object, thereby delineating it—as is the case in hypochondria— or whether it is a pain caused by organic disease which is retrospectively registered by an attending consciousness. This ambiguity between a real and conjured pain, however, is sustained in the analogy with erotogenicity, which seems defined as the very vacillation between real and imagined body parts. If erotogenicity is produced through the conveying of a bodily activity through an idea, then the idea and the conveying are phenomenologically coincident. As a result, it would not be possible to speak about a body part that precedes and gives rise to an idea, for it is the idea that emerges simultaneously with the phenomenologically accessible body, indeed, that guarantees its accessibility. Although Freud's language engages a causal temporality that has the body part precede its "idea," he nevertheless confirms here the indissolubility of a body part and the phantasmatic partitioning that brings it into psychic experience. Later, in the first *Seminar*, Lacan will read Freud along these latter lines, arguing in his discussion on "The Two Narcissisms" that "the libidinal drive is centred on the function of the imaginary."[6]

Already in the essay on narcissism, however, we find the beginnings of this latter formulation in the discussion of the erotogenicity of body parts. Directly following his argument in favor of hypochondria as anxiety-neurosis, Freud argues that libidinal self-attention is precisely what delineates a body part as a part: "Now the familiar prototype [*Vorbild*] of an organ sensitive to pain, in some way changed and yet not diseased in the ordinary sense, is that of the genital organ in a state of excitation…" (Freud 1914, 84).

Clearly there is an assumption here of a singular genital organ, the sex which is one, but as Freud continues to write about it, it appears to lose its proper place and proliferate in unexpected locations. This example at first provides the occasion for the definition of erotogenicity I already cited, "that activity of a given bodily area which consists in conveying sexually exciting stimuli to the mind." Freud then proceeds to communicate as already accepted knowledge "that certain other areas of the body—the *erotogenic* zones—may act as substitutes for the genitals and behave analogously to them" (Freud 1914, 84). Here it seems that "the genitals," presumed to be male genitals, are at first an example of body parts delineated through anxiety-neurosis, but, as a "prototype," they are the example of examples of that process whereby body parts become epistemologically accessible through an imaginary investiture. As an exemplar or prototype, these genitals have already within Freud's text substituted not only *for* a variety of other body parts or types, but for the effects of other hypochondriacal processes as well. The gaping hole in the mouth, the panoply of organic and hypochondriacal ailments are synthesized in and summarized by the prototypical male genitals.

This collapse of substitutions performed by these genitals is, however, reversed and erased in the sentence that follows in which the erotogenic zones are said to act as substitutes *for* the genitals. In the latter case, it seems that these self-same genitals—the result or effect of a set of substitutions— are that *for which* other body parts act as substitutes. Indeed, the male genitals are suddenly themselves an originary site of erotogenization which then subsequently becomes the occasion for a set of substitutions or displacements. At first, it seems logically incompatible to assert that these genitals are at once a cumulative example *and* a prototype or originary site which occasions a process of secondary exemplifications. In the first case, they are the effect and sum of a set of substitutions, and in the second, they are an origin for which substitutions exist. But perhaps this logical problem only symptomizes a wish to understand these genitals as an originating idealization, that is, as the symbolically encoded phallus.

The phallus, which Freud invokes in *The Interpretation of Dreams*, is considered the privileged signifier by Lacan, that which originates or generates significations, but is not itself the signifying effect of a prior signifying chain. To offer a definition of the phallus—indeed, to attempt denotatively to fix its meaning—is to posture as if one *has* the phallus and, hence, to presume and enact precisely what remains to be explained.[7] In a sense, Freud's essay enacts the paradoxical process by which the phallus as the

privileged and generative signifier is itself generated *by* a string of examples
of erotogenic body parts. The phallus is then set up as that which confers
erotogenicity and signification on these body parts, although we have seen
through the metonymic slide of Freud's text the way in which the phallus
is installed as an "origin" precisely to suppress the ambivalence produced
in the course of that slide.

If Freud is here endeavoring to circumscribe the phallic function and
proposing a conflation of the penis and the phallus, then the genitals
would necessarily function in a double way: as the (symbolic) ideal that
offers an impossible and originary measure for the genitals to approximate, and as the (imaginary) anatomy which is marked by the failure to
accomplish that return to that symbolic ideal. Insofar as the male genitals
become the site of a textual vacillation, they enact the impossibility of
collapsing the distinction between penis and phallus. (Note that I have
consigned the penis, conventionally described as "real anatomy" to the
domain of the imaginary.[8] I will pursue the consequences of this consign-
ment [or liberation] toward the end of this essay.)

As if foundering amid a set of constitutive ambivalences out of his
control, Freud follows his paradoxical articulation of the male genitals as
prototype and origin by adding yet another inconsistent claim to the list:
"We can decide to regard," he claims, "erotogenicity as a general characteristic of all organs and may then speak of an increase or decrease of it in
a particular part of the body" (Freud 1914, 84).

In this last remark, which, it seems, Freud must force himself to make—
as if pure conviction will issue forth its own truth—reference to the temporal or ontological primacy of any given body part is suspended. To be a
property of all organs is to be a property necessary to *no* organ, a property
defined by its very *plasticity, transferability*, and *expropriability*. In a sense, we
have been following the metonymic chain of this roving property from
the start. Freud's discussion began with the line from Wilhelm Busch, "the
jaw-tooth's aching hole," a figure that stages a certain collision of figures, a
punctured instrument of penetration, an inverted vagina dentata, anus,
mouth, orifice in general, the spectre of the penetrating instrument penetrated.[9] Insofar as the tooth, as that which bites, cuts, breaks through, and
enters is that which is itself already entered, broken into, it figures an
ambivalence that, it seems, becomes the source of pain analogized with the
male genitals a few pages later. This figure is immediately likened to other

body parts in real or imagined pain, and is then replaced and erased by the prototypical genitals. This wounded instrument of penetration can only suffer under the ideal of its own invulnerability, and Freud attempts to restore its imaginary power by installing it first as prototype and then as originary site of erotogenization.

In the course of restoring this phallic property to the penis, however, Freud enumerates a set of analogies and substitutions that rhetorically affirm the fundamental transferability of that property. Indeed, the phallus is neither the imaginary construction of the penis nor the symbolic valence for which the penis is a partial approximation. For that formulation is still to affirm the phallus as the prototype or idealized property of the penis. And yet it is clear from the metonymic trajectory of Freud's own text, the ambivalence at the center of any construction of the phallus belongs to no body part, but is fundamentally transferable and is, at least within his text, the very principle of erotogenic transferability. Moreover, it is through this transfer, understood as a substitution of the psychical for the physical or the metaphorizing logic of hypochondria, that body parts become phenomenologically accessible at all. Here we might understand the pain/pleasure nexus that conditions erotogenicity as partially constituted by the very idealization of anatomy designated by the phallus.

On this reading, then, Freud's textualized effort to resolve the figure of the jaw-tooth's aching hole into the penis as prototype and then as phallus rhetorically enacts the very process of narcissistic investment and idealization that he seeks to document, overcoming that ambivalence through the conjuring of an ideal. One might want to read the psychic idealization of body parts as an effort to resolve a prior, physical pain. It may be, however, that the idealization produces erotogenicity as a scene of necessary failure and ambivalence, one that then prompts a return to that idealization in a vain effort to escape that conflicted condition. To what extent is this conflicted condition precisely the repetitive propulsionality of sexuality? And what does "failure to approximate" mean in the context in which every body does precisely that?

One might also argue that to continue to use the term "phallus" for this symbolic or idealizing function is to prefigure and valorize which body part will be the site of erotogenization; this is an argument that deserves a serious response. To insist, on the contrary, on the transferability of the phallus, the phallus as transferable or plastic property, is to destabilize the distinction between *being* and *having* the phallus, and to suggest that a logic of non-contradiction does not necessarily hold between those two positions. In effect, the "having" is a symbolic position which, for Lacan, institutes the masculine position within a heterosexual matrix, and which presumes an idealized relation of property which is then only partially and vainly approximated by those marked masculine beings who vainly and partially occupy that position within language. But if this attribution of property is itself improperly attributed, if it rests on a denial of that property's transferability (i.e., if this is a transfer into a non-transferable site or a site which occasions other transfers, but which is itself not transferred from anywhere), then the repression of that denial will constitute that system internally and, therefore, pose as the promising spectre of its destabilization.

Insofar as any reference to a lesbian phallus appears to be a spectral representation of a masculine original, we might well question the spectral production of the putative "originality" of the masculine. In this sense, Freud's text might be read as the forcible production of a masculinist "original" in much the same way as Plato's *Timaeus* was read. In Freud's text, this claim to originality is constituted through a reversal and erasure of a set of substitutions produced in ambivalence.

It seems that this imaginary valorization of body parts is to be derived from a kind of eroticized hypochondria. Hypochondria is an imaginary investment which, according to the early theory, constitutes a libidinal projection of the body-surface which in turn establishes its epistemological accessibility. Hypochondria here denotes something like a *theatrical* delineation or production of the body, one which gives imaginary contours to the ego itself, projecting a body which becomes the occasion of an identification which in its imaginary or projected status is fully tenuous.

But something is clearly awry in Freud's analysis from the start. For how is it that the self-preoccupation with bodily suffering or illness becomes the analogy for the erotogenic discovery and conjuring of body parts? In *The Ego and the Id*, Freud himself suggests that to figure sexuality *as* illness is symptomatic of the structuring presence of a moralistic framework of guilt. In this text, Freud argues that narcissism must give way to objects, and that one must finally love in order not to fall ill. Insofar as there is a *prohibition on love* accompanied by threats of imagined death, there is a great temptation to refuse to love, and so to be taken in by that prohibition and contract neurotic illness. Once this prohibition is installed, then, body parts emerge as sites of punishable pleasure and, hence, of pleasure and pain. In this kind of neurotic illness, then, guilt is manifest as pain that suffuses the bodily surface, and can appear as physical illness. What follows, then, if it is *this* kind of guilt-induced bodily suffering which is, as Freud claimed of other kinds of pain, analogous to the way in which we achieve an "idea" of our own body?

If prohibitions in some sense constitute projected morphologies, then reworking the terms of those prohibitions suggests the possibility of variable projections, variable modes of delineating and theatricalizing body surfaces. These would be "ideas" of the body without which there could be no ego, no temporary centering of experience. To the extent that such supporting "ideas" are regulated by prohibition and pain, they can be understood as the forcible and materialized effects of regulatory power. But precisely because prohibitions do not always "work," that is, do not always produce the docile body that fully conforms to the social ideal, they may delineate body surfaces that do not signify conventional heterosexual polarities. These variable body surfaces or bodily egos may thus become sites of transfer for properties that no longer belong properly to any anatomy. I'll make almost clear what this means for thinking through alternative imaginaries and the lesbian phallus, but first a cautionary note on Freud.

The pathologization of erotogenic parts in Freud calls to be read as a discourse produced in guilt, and although the imaginary and projective possibilities of hypochondria are useful, they call to be dissociated from the metaphorics of illness that pervade the description of sexuality. This is especially urgent now that the pathologization of sexuality generally, and the specific description of homosexuality as the paradigm for the pathological as such, are symptomatic of homophobic discourse on AIDS.

Insofar as Freud accepts the analogy between erotogenicity and illness, he produces a pathological discourse on sexuality that allows figures for organic disease to construct figures for erotogenic body parts. This conflation has a long history, no doubt, but it finds one of its contemporary permutations in the homophobic construction of male homosexuality as always already pathological—an argument recently made by Jeff Nunokawa[10]—such that AIDS is phantasmatically construed as the pathology of homosexuality itself. Clearly, the point is to read Freud not for the moments in which illness and sexuality are conflated, but, rather, for the moments in which that conflation fails to sustain itself, and where he fails to read himself in precisely the ways he teaches us to read ("Commenting on a text is like doing an analysis" [Lacan, *I*, 73]).

Prohibitions, which include the prohibition on homosexuality, work through the pain of guilt. Freud offers this link at the end of his essay when he accounts for the genesis of conscience, and its self-policing possibilities, as the introjection of the homosexual cathexis. In other words, the ego-ideal which governs what Freud calls the ego's "self-respect" requires the prohibition on homosexuality. This prohibition against homosexuality *is* homosexual desire turned back upon itself; the self-beratement of conscience *is* the reflexive rerouting of homosexual desire. If, then, as Freud contends, pain has a delineating effect, i.e., may be one way in which we come to have an idea of our body at all, it may also be that gender-instituting prohibitions work through suffusing the body with a pain that culminates in the projection of a surface, that is, a sexed morphology which is at once a compensatory fantasy and a fetishistic mask. And if one must either love or fall ill, then perhaps the sexuality that appears as illness is the insidious effect of a such a censoring of love. Can the very production of the *morphe* be read as an allegory of prohibited love, the *incorporation* of loss?

The relation between incorporation and melancholy is a complicated one to which we will return in the final chapter. Suffice it to say that the boundaries of the body are the lived experience of differentiation, where that differentiation is never neutral to the question of gender difference or the heterosexual matrix. What is excluded from the body for the body's boundary to form? And how does that exclusion haunt that boundary as an internal ghost of sorts, the incorporation of loss as melancholia? To what extent is the body surface the dissimulated effect of that loss? Freud offers something like a map of this problematic without following through on the analysis that it requires.

If this effort to rethink the physical and the psychical works well, then it is no longer possible to take anatomy as a stable referent that is somehow valorized or signified through being subjected to an imaginary schema. On the contrary, the very accessibility of anatomy is in some sense dependent on this schema and coincident with it. As a result of this coincidence, it is unclear to me that lesbians can be said to be "of" the same sex or that homosexuality in general ought to be construed as love of the same. If sex is always schematized in this sense, then there is no necessary reason for it to remain the same for all women. The indissolubility of the psychic and the corporeal suggests that any description of the body, including those that are deemed conventional within scientific discourse, takes place through the circulation and validation of such an imaginary schema.

But if the descriptions of the body take place in and through an imaginary schema, that is, if these descriptions are psychically and phantasmatically invested, is there still something we might call the body itself which escapes this schematization? At least two responses can be offered to this question. First, psychic projection confers boundaries and, hence, unity on the body, so that the very contours of the body are sites that vacillate between the psychic and the material. Bodily contours and morphology are not merely implicated in an irreducible tension between the psychic and the material but *are* that tension. Hence, the psyche is not a grid through which a pregiven body appears. That formulation would figure the body as an ontological in-itself which only becomes available through a psyche which establishes its mode of appearance as an epistemological object. In other words, the psyche would be an epistemic grid through which the body is known, but the sense in which the psyche is formative of morphology, that is, is somaticizing, would be lost.[11]

That Kantian formulation of the body requires to be reworked, first, in a more phenomenological register as an imaginary formation and, second, through a theory of signification as an effect and token of sexual difference. As for the phenomenological sense, which is sustained in the second, we might understand the psyche in this context as that which constitutes the mode by which that body is given, the condition and contour of that givenness. Here the materiality of the body ought not to be conceptualized as a unilateral or causal *effect* of the psyche in any sense that would reduce that materiality to the psyche or make of the psyche the monistic stuff out of which that materiality is produced and/or derived. This latter alternative would constitute a clearly untenable form of idealism. It must be possible to concede and affirm an array of "materialities" that pertain to the body, that which is signified by the domains of biology, anatomy, physiology, hormonal and chemical composition, illness, age, weight, metabolism, life and death. None of this can be denied.

But the undeniability of these "materialities" in no way implies what it means to affirm them, indeed, what interpretive matrices condition, enable and limit that necessary affirmation. That each of those categories have a history and a historicity, that each of them is constituted through the boundary lines that distinguish them and, hence, by what they exclude, that relations of discourse and power produce hierarchies and overlappings among them and challenge those boundaries, implies that these are *both* persistent and contested regions.

We might want to claim that what persists within these contested domains is the "materiality" of the body. But perhaps we will have fulfilled the same function, and opened up some others, if we claim that what persists here is *a demand in and for language*, a "that which" which prompts and occasions, say, within the domain of science, calls to be explained, described, diagnosed, altered or within the cultural fabric of lived experience, fed, exercised, mobilized, put to sleep, a site of enactments and passions of various kinds. To insist upon this demand, this site, as the "that without which" no psychic operation can proceed, but also as that on which and through which the psyche also operates, is to begin to circumscribe that which is invariably and persistently the psyche's site of operation; not the blank slate or passive medium upon which the psyche acts, but, rather, the constitutive demand that mobilizes psychic action from the start, that is that very mobilization, and, in its transmuted and projected bodily form, remains that psyche.

How, then, to answer the second requirement to cast the notion of "bodies" as a matter of signification?

"ARE BODIES PURELY DISCURSIVE?"

The linguistic categories that are understood to "denote" the materiality of the body are themselves troubled by a referent that is never fully or permanently resolved or contained by any given signified. Indeed, that referent persists only as a kind of absence or loss, that which language does not capture, but, instead, that which impels language repeatedly to attempt that capture, that circumscription—and to fail. This loss takes its place in language as an insistent call or demand that, while *in* language, is never fully *of* language. To posit a materiality outside of language is still to posit that materiality, and the materiality so posited will retain that positing as its constitutive condition. To posit a materiality outside of language, where that materiality is considered ontologically distinct from language, is to undermine the possibility that language might be able to indicate or correspond to that domain of radical alterity. Hence, the absolute distinction between language and materiality which was to secure the referential function of language undermines that function radically.

This is not to say that, on the one hand, the body is simply linguistic stuff or, on the other, that it has no bearing on language. It bears on language all the time. The materiality of language, indeed, of the very sign that attempts to denote "materiality," suggests that it is not the case that everything, including materiality, is always already language. On the contrary, the materiality of the signifier (a "materiality" that comprises both signs and their significatory efficacy) implies that there can be no reference to a pure materiality except via materiality. Hence, it is not that one cannot get outside of language in order to grasp materiality in and of itself; rather, every effort to refer to materiality takes place through a signifying process which, in its phenomenality, is always already material. In this sense, then, language and materiality are not opposed, for language both is and refers to that which is material, and what is material never fully escapes from the process by which it is signified.

But if language is not opposed to materiality, neither can materiality be summarily collapsed into an identity with language. On the one hand, the process of signification is always material; signs work *by appearing* (visibly, aurally), and appearing through material means, although what appears only signifies by virtue of those non-phenomenal relations, i.e., relations of differentiation, that tacitly structure and propel signification itself. Relations, even the notion of différance, institute and require relata, terms, phenomenal signifiers. And yet what allows for a signifier to signify will never be its materiality alone; that materiality will be at once an instrumentality and deployment of a set of larger linguistic relations.

The materiality of the signifier will signify only to the extent that it is impure, contaminated by the ideality of differentiating relations, the tacit structurings of a linguistic context that is illimitable in principle. Conversely, the signifier will work to the extent that it is also contaminated constitutively by the very materiality that the ideality of sense purports to overcome. Apart from and yet related to the materiality of the signifier is the materiality of the signified as well as the referent approached through the signified, but which remains irreducible to the signified. This radical difference between *referent* and *signified* is the site where the materiality of language and that of the world which it seeks to signify are perpetually negotiated. This might usefully be compared with Merleau-Ponty's notion of the flesh of the world.[12] Although the referent cannot be said to exist apart from the signified, it nevertheless cannot be reduced to it. That referent, that abiding function of the world, is to persist as the horizon and the "that which" which makes its demand in and to language. Language and materiality are fully embedded in each other, chiasmic in their interdependency, but never fully collapsed into one another, i.e., reduced to one another, and yet neither fully ever exceeds the other. Always already implicated in each other, always already exceeding one another, language and materiality are never fully identical nor fully different.

But what then do we make of the kind of materiality that is associated with the body, its physicality as well as its location, including its social and political locatedness, and that materiality that characterizes language? Do we mean "materiality" in a common sense, or are these usages examples of what Althusser refers to as modalities of matter?[13]

To answer the question of the relation between the materiality of bodies and that of language requires first that we offer an account of how it is that bodies materialize, that is, how they come to assume the *morphe*, the shape by which their material discreteness is marked. The materiality of the body is not to be taken for granted, for in some sense it is acquired, constituted, through the development of morphology. And within the Lacanian view, language, understood as rules of differentiation based on idealized kinship relations, is essential to the development of morphology. Before we consider one account of the development of linguistic and corporeal morphology, let us turn briefly to Kristeva, to provide a contrast with Lacan, and a critical introduction.

Insofar as language might be understood to emerge from the materiality of bodily life, that is, as the reiteration and extension of a material set of relations, language is a substitute satisfaction, a primary act of displacement and condensation. Kristeva argues that the materiality of the spoken signifier, the vocalization of sound, is already a psychic effort to reinstall and recapture a lost maternal body; hence, these vocalizations are temporarily recaptured in sonorous poetry which works language for its most material possibilities.[14] Even here, however, those material sputterings are already psychically invested, deployed in the service of a fantasy of mastery and restoration. Here the materiality of bodily relations, prior to any individuation into a separable body or, rather, simultaneous with it, is displaced onto the materiality of linguistic relations. The language that is the effect of this displacement nevertheless carries the trace of that loss precisely in the phantasmatic aim of recovery that mobilizes vocalization itself. Here, then, it is the materiality of that (other) body which is phantasmatically reinvoked in the materiality of signifying sounds. Indeed, what gives those sounds the power to signify is that phantasmatic structure. The materiality of the signifier is thus the displaced repetition of the materiality of the lost maternal body. In this sense, materiality is constituted in and through iterability. And to the extent that the referential impulse of language is to return to that lost originary presence, the maternal body becomes, as it were, the paradigm or figure for any subsequent referent. This is in part the function of the Real in its convergence with the unthematizable maternal body in Lacanian discourse. The Real is that which resists and compels symbolization. Whereas the "real" remains unrepresentable within Lacanian doctrine, and the spectre of its representability is the spectre of psychosis, Kristeva redescribes and reinterprets what is "outside" the symbolic as the semiotic, that is, as a poetic mode of signifying that, although dependent on the symbolic, can neither be reduced to it nor figured as its unthematizable Other.

For Kristeva, the materiality of language is in some sense derived from the materiality of infantile bodily relations; language becomes something like the infinite displacement of that *jouissance* that is phantasmatically identified with the maternal body. Every effort to signify encodes and repeats this loss. Moreover, it is only on the condition of this primary loss of the referent, the Real, understood as the maternal presence, that signification—and the materialization of language—can take place. The materiality of the maternal body is only figurable within language (a set of already differentiated relations) as the phantasmatic site of a deindividuated fusion, a *jouissance* prior to the differentiation and emergence of the subject.[15] But insofar as this loss is figured *within language* (i.e., appears as a figure in language), that loss is also denied, for language both performs and defends against the separation that it figures; as a result, any figuration of that loss will both repeat and refuse the loss itself. The relations of differentiation between parts of speech which produce signification are

themselves the *reiteration* and extension of the primary acts of differentiation and separation from the maternal body by which a speaking subject
comes into being. Insofar as language appears to be motivated by a loss it
cannot grieve, and to repeat the very loss that it refuses to recognize, we
might regard this ambivalence at the heart of linguistic iterability as the
melancholy recesses of signification.

The postulation of the primacy of the maternal body in the genesis of
signification is clearly questionable, for it cannot be shown that a differentiation from such a body is that which primarily or exclusively inaugurates the relation to speech. The maternal body prior to the formation of the
subject is always and only known by a subject who by definition postdates
that hypothetical scene. Lacan's effort to offer an account of the genesis
of bodily boundaries in "The Mirror Stage" (1949) takes the narcissistic
relation as primary, and so displaces the maternal body as a site of primary identification. This happens within the essay itself when the infant is
understood to overcome with jubilation the obstruction of the support
which presumably holds the infant in place before the mirror. The
reification of maternal dependency as a "support" and an "obstruction"
signified primarily as that which, in the overcoming, occasions jubilation,
suggests that there is a discourse on the differentiation from the maternal
in the mirror stage. The maternal is, as it were, already put under erasure
by the theoretical language which reifies her function and enacts the very
overcoming that it seeks to document.

Insofar as the mirror stage involves an *imaginary* relation, it is that of
psychic projection, but not, strictly speaking, in the register of the Symbolic, i.e., in language, the differentiated/ing use of speech. The mirror stage
is not a *developmental* account of how the idea of one's own body comes
into being. It does suggest, however, that the capacity to project a *morphe*, a
shape, onto a surface is part of the psychic (and phantasmatic) elaboration,
centering, and containment of one's own bodily contours. This process of
psychic projection or elaboration implies as well that the sense of one's own
body is not (only) achieved through differentiating from another (the maternal body), but that any sense of bodily contour, as projected, is articulated
through a necessary self-division and self-estrangement. In this sense,
Lacan's mirror stage can be read as a rewriting of Freud's introduction of
the bodily ego in *The Ego and the Id*, as well as the theory of narcissism. Here
it is not a question of whether the mother or the imago comes first or

whether they are fully distinct from one another, but, rather, how to account for individuation through the unstable dynamics of sexual differentiation and identification that take place through the elaboration of imaginary bodily contours.

For Lacan, the body or, rather, morphology is an imaginary formation,[16] but we learn in the second seminar that this percipi or visual production, the body, can be sustained in its phantasmatic integrity only through submitting to language and to a marking by sexual difference: "the percipi of man (sic) can only be sustained within a zone of nomination (*C'est par la nomination que l'homme fait subsister les objets dans une certaine consistance*)" (Lacan, *II*, 177/202). Bodies only become whole, i.e., totalities, by the idealizing and totalizing specular image which is sustained through time by the sexually marked name. To have a name is to be positioned within the Symbolic, the idealized domain of kinship, a set of relationships structured through sanction and taboo which is governed by the law of the father and the prohibition against incest. For Lacan, names, which emblematize and institute this paternal law, *sustain* the integrity of the body. What constitutes the integral body is not a natural boundary or organic telos, but the law of kinship that works through the name. In this sense, the paternal law produces versions of bodily integrity; the name, which installs gender and kinship, works as a politically invested and investing performative. To be named is thus to be inculcated into that law and to be formed, bodily, in accordance with that law.[17]

REWRITING THE MORPHOLOGICAL IMAGINARY

Consciousness occurs each time there is a surface such that it can produce what is called an image. That is a materialist definition. (Lacan, *II*, 49/65)

There is something originally, inaugurally, profoundly wounded in the human relation to the world...that is what comes out of the theory of narcissism Freud gave us, insofar as this framework introduces an indefinable, a *no exit*, marking all relations, and especially the libidinal relations of the subject. (Lacan, *II*, 167/199)

The following selective reading of Lacan will explore the consequences of the theory of narcissism for the formation of the bodily ego and its marking by sex. Insofar as the ego is formed from the psyche through projecting the body, and the ego *is* that projection, the condition of reflexive (mis)knowing, it is invariably a bodily ego. This projection of the body, which Lacan narrates as the mirror stage, rewrites Freud's theory of narcissism through the dynamics of projection and misrecognition (*méconnaissance*). In the course of that rewriting, Lacan establishes the morphology of the body as a psychically invested projection, an idealization or "fiction" of the body as a totality and locus of control. Moreover, he suggests that this narcissistic and idealizing projection that establishes morphology constitutes the condition for the generation of objects and the cognition of other bodies. The morphological scheme established through the mirror stage constitutes precisely that reserve of morphe from which the contours of objects are produced; both objects and others come to appear only through the mediating grid of this projected or imaginary morphology.

This Lacanian trajectory will be shown to become problematic on (at least) two counts: (1) the morphological scheme which becomes the epistemic condition for the world of objects and others to appear is marked as masculine, and, hence, becomes the basis for an anthropocentric and androcentric epistemological imperialism (this is one criticism of Lacan offered by Luce Irigaray and supplies the compelling reason for her project to articulate a feminine imaginary[18]); and (2) the idealization of the body as a center of control sketched in "The Mirror Stage" is rearticulated in Lacan's notion of the phallus as that which controls significations in discourse, in "The Signification of the Phallus" (1958). Although Lacan explicitly denounces the possibility that the phallus is a body part or an imaginary effect, that repudiation will be read as constitutive of the very symbolic status he confers on the phallus in the course of the later essay. As an idealization of a body part, the phantasmatic figure of the phallus within Lacan's essay undergoes a set of contradictions similar to those which unsettled Freud's analysis of erotogenic body parts. The lesbian phallus may be said to intervene as an unexpected consequence of the Lacanian scheme, an apparently contradictory signifier which, through a critical mimesis,[19] calls into question the ostensibly originating and controlling power of the Lacanian phallus, indeed, its installation as the privileged signifier of the symbolic order. The move emblematized by the lesbian phallus contests the relationship between the logic of non-contradiction and the legislation of compulsory heterosexuality at the level of the symbolic and bodily morphogenesis. Consequently, it seeks to open up a discursive site for reconsidering the tacitly political relations that constitute and persist in the divisions between body parts and wholes, anatomy and the imaginary, corporeality and the psyche.

In his seminar of 1953, Lacan argued that "the mirror stage is not simply a moment in development. It also has an exemplary function, because it reveals some of the subject's relations to his image, in so far as it is the *Urbild* of the ego" (Lacan, *I*, 74/88). In "The Mirror Stage," published four years earlier, Lacan argues that "we have…to understand the mirror stage *as an identification*…," and then slightly later in the essay suggests that the ego is the cumulative effect of its formative identifications.[20] Within the American reception of Freud, especially in ego psychology and certain versions of object relations, it is perhaps customary to suggest that the ego preexists its identifications, a notion confirmed by the grammar that insists that "an ego identifies with an object outside itself." The Lacanian position suggests not only that identifications *precede* the ego, but that the identificatory relation to the image establishes the ego. Moreover, the ego established through this identificatory relation is itself a relation, indeed, the cumulative history of such relations. As a result, the ego is not a self-identical substance, but a sedimented history of imaginary relations which locate the center of the ego outside itself, in the externalized *imago* which confers and produces bodily contours. In this sense, Lacan's mirror does not reflect or represent a preexisting ego, but, rather, provides the frame, the boundary, the spatial delineation for the projective elaboration of the ego itself. Hence, Lacan claims, "the image of the body gives the subject the first form which allows him to locate what pertains to the ego ["ce qui est du moi"] and what does not" (Lacan, *I*, 79/94).

Strictly speaking, then, the ego cannot be said to identify with an object outside itself; rather, it is through an identification with an imago, which is itself a relation, that the "outside" of the ego is first ambiguously demarcated, indeed, that a spatial boundary that negotiates "outside" and "inside" is established in and as the imaginary: "the function of the mirror stage [is] a particular case of the function of the *imago*, which is to establish a relation between the organism and its reality—or, as they say, between the *Innenwelt* and the *Umwelt*."[21] The specular image that the child sees, that is, the imagining that the child produces, confers a visual integrity and coherence on his own body (appearing as other) which compensates for his limited and pre-specular sense of motility and undeveloped motor control. Lacan goes on to identify this specular image with the ego-ideal (*je-ideal*) and with the subject, although these terms will in his later lectures be distinguished from one another on other grounds.[22]

Significantly, this idealized totality that the child sees is a mirror image. One might say that it confers an ideality and integrity on his body, but it is perhaps more accurate to claim that the very sense of the body is generated through this projection of ideality and integrity. Indeed, this mirroring transforms a lived sense of disunity and loss of control into an ideal of integrity and control ("la puissance") through that event of specularization. Shortly, we will argue that this idealization of the body articulated in "The Mirror Stage" reemerges unwittingly in the context of Lacan's discussion of the phallus as the idealization and symbolization of anatomy. At this point, it is perhaps enough to note that the *imago* of the body is purchased through a certain loss; libidinal dependency and powerlessness is phantasmatically overcome by the installation of a boundary and, hence, a hypostacized center which produces an idealized bodily ego; that integrity and unity is achieved through the ordering of a wayward motility or disaggregated sexuality not yet restrained by the boundaries of individuation: "the human object [*l'objet humain*] always constitutes itself through the intermediary of a first loss—nothing fruitful takes place in man [*rien de fécond n'a lieu pour l'homme*] save through the intermediary of a loss of an object" (Lacan, *II*, 136/F165).[23]

Lacan remarks in the second seminar that "the body in pieces [*le corps morcelé*] finds its unity in the image of the Other, which is its own anticipated image—a dual situation in which a polar, but non-symmetrical relation, is sketched out" (Lacan, *II*, 54/72). The ego is formed around the specular image of the body itself, but this specular image is itself an *anticipation*, a subjunctive delineation. The ego is first and foremost an object which cannot coincide temporally with the subject, a temporal *ek-stasis*; the ego's temporal futurity, and its exteriority as a *percipi*, establish its alterity to the subject. But this alterity is ambiguously located: first, within the circuit of a psyche which constitutes/finds the ego as a mistaken and decentering token of itself (hence, an interior alterity); second, as an object of perception, like other objects, and so at a radical epistemic distance from the subject: "The ego...is a particular object within the experience of the subject. Literally, the ego is an object—an object which fills a certain function which we here call the imaginary function" (Lacan, *II*, 44/60).[24] As imaginary, the ego as object is neither interior nor exterior to the subject, but the permanently unstable site where that spatialized distinction is perpetually negotiated; it is this ambiguity that marks the ego as *imago*, that is, as an identificatory relation. Hence, identifications are never simply or definitively *made* or *achieved*; they are insistently constituted, contested, and negotiated.

The specular image of the body itself is in some sense the image of the Other. But it is only on the condition that the anticipated, ambiguously located body furnishes an *imago* and a boundary for the ego that objects come into perception. "The object is always more or less structured as the image of the body of the subject. The reflection of the subject, its mirror stage [*image spéculaire*], is always found somewhere in every perceptual picture [*tableau perceptif*], and that is what gives it a quality, a special inertia" (Lacan, *II*, 167/199). Here we not only have an account of the social constitution of the ego, but the modes by which the ego is differentiated from its Other, and how that *imago* that sustains and troubles that differentiation *at the same time* generates objects of perception. "On the libidinal level, the object is only even apprehended through the grid of the narcissistic relation" (Lacan, *II*, 167). And this is made all the more complex when we see that the reflexive relation to/of the ego is always ambiguously related to a relation to the "Other." Far from being a merely narcissistic precondition of object genesis, this claim offers instead an irreducible equivocation of narcissism and sociality which becomes the condition of the epistemological generation of and access to objects.

The idealization of the body as a spatially bounded totality, characterized by a control exercized by the gaze, is lent out to the body as its own self-control. This will become crucial to the understanding of the phallus as a privileged signifier that appears to control the significations that it produces. Lacan suggests as much in the second seminar: "The issue is knowing which organs come into play in [*entrent en jeu dans*] the narcissistic imaginary relation to the other whereby the ego is formed, *bildet*. The imaginary structuration of the ego forms around the specular image of the body itself, of the image of the Other" (Lacan, *II*, 94-95/119).

But some parts of the body become the tokens for the centering and controlling function of the bodily *imago*: "certain organs are caught up in [*sont intéressés dans*] the narcissistic relation, insofar as it structures both the relation of the ego to the other and the constitution of the world of objects" (Lacan, *II*, 95/119). Although these organs are not named, it seems that they are, first of all, organs [*les organes*] and that they enter into play in the narcissistic relation; they are that which act as the token or conjectured basis for narcissism. If these organs are the male genitals, they function as both the site and token of a specifically masculine narcissism. Moreover, insofar as these organs are set into play by a narcissism which is said to provide the structure of relations to the Other and to the world of objects, then these organs become part of the imaginary elaboration of the ego's bodily boundary, token and "proof" of its integrity and control, and the imaginary epistemic condition of its access to the world. By entering into that narcissistic relation, the organs cease to be organs and become imaginary effects. One might be tempted to argue that in the course of being set into play by the narcissistic imaginary, the penis becomes the phallus. And yet, curiously and significantly, in Lacan's essay on "The Signification of the Phallus," he will deny that the phallus is either an organ or an imaginary effect; it is instead a "privileged signifier."[25] We will turn to the textual knots that those series of denials produce in Lacan's essay, but here it is perhaps important to note that these narcissistically engaged organs become part of the condition and structure of every object and Other that can be perceived.

"What did I try get across with the mirror stage?...The image of [man's] body is the principle of every unity he perceives in objects...all the objects of his world are always structured around the wandering shadow of his own ego [*c'est toujours autour de l'ombre errante de son propre moi que se structureront tous les objets de son monde*]" (Lacan, *II*, 166/198). This extrapolating function of narcissism becomes phallogocentrism at the moment in which the aforementioned organs, engaged by the narcissistic relation, become the model or principle by which any other object or Other is known. At this point, the organs are installed as a "privileged signifier." Within the orbit of this emerging phallogocentrism, "*Verliebtheit* [being in love] is fundamentally narcissistic. On the libidinal level, the object is only even apprehended through the grid of the narcissistic relation [*la grille du rapport narcissique*]" (Lacan, *II*, 167/199).

Lacan claims that the organs are "taken up" by a narcissistic relation, and that this narcissistically invested anatomy becomes the structure, the principle, the grid of all epistemic relations. In other words, it is the narcissistically imbued organ which is then elevated to a structuring principle which forms and gives access to all knowable objects. In the first place, this account of the genesis of epistemological relations implies that all knowable objects will have an anthropomorphic and androcentric character.[26] Secondly, this androcentric character will be phallic.

At this juncture it makes sense to consider the relation between the account of specular relations in "The Mirror Stage," the argument that morphology preconditions epistemological relations, and the later move in "The Signification of the Phallus" which asserts that the phallus is a privileged signifier. The differences between the language and aims of the two essays are marked: the earlier essay concerns epistemological relations which are not yet theorized in terms of signification; the latter appears to have emerged after a shift from epistemological to significatory models (or, rather, an embedding of the epistemological within the symbolic domain of signification). And yet, there is another difference here, one which might be understood as a reversal. In the earlier essay, the "organs" are taken up by the narcissistic relation and become the phantasmatic morphology which generates, through a specular extrapolation, the structure of knowable objects. In the later essay, Lacan introduces the phallus which functions as a privileged signifier and delimits the domain of the signifiable.

In a limited sense, the narcissistically invested organs in "The Mirror Stage" serve a function parallel to that of the phallus in "The Signification of the Phallus": the former establish the conditions for knowability; the latter establish the conditions for signifiability. Further, the theoretical context in which "The Signification of the Phallus" occurs is one in which signification is the condition of all knowability, and the image can be sustained only by the sign (the imaginary within the terms of the symbolic); it appears to follow that the narcissistically invested organs in the former essay are in some way maintained in and by the notion of the phallus. Even if we were to argue that "The Mirror Stage" documents an imaginary relation, whereas "The Signification of the Phallus" is concerned with signification at the level of the symbolic, it is unclear whether the former can be sustained without the latter and, perhaps more significantly, the latter (i.e., the Symbolic), without the former. And yet this logical conclusion is thwarted by Lacan himself in his insistence that the phallus is neither an anatomical part nor an imaginary relation. Is this repudiation of the anatomical and imaginary origins of the phallus to be read as a refusal to account for the very genealogical process of idealizing the body that Lacan himself provided in "The Mirror Stage"? Are we to accept the priority of the phallus without questioning the narcissistic investment by which an organ, a body part, has been elevated/erected to the structuring and centering principle of the world? If "The Mirror Stage" reveals how, through the synecdochal function of the imaginary, parts come to stand for wholes and a decentered body is transfigured into a totality with a center, then we might be led to ask which organs perform this centering and synecdochal function. "The Signification of the Phallus" effectively refuses the question that the former essay implicitly raised. For if the phallus in its symbolic function is neither an organ nor an imaginary effect, then it is not constructed through the imaginary, and maintains a status and integrity independent of it. This corresponds, of course, to the distinction that Lacan makes throughout his work between the imaginary and the symbolic. But if the phallus can be shown to be a synecdochal effect, if it both stands for the part, the organ, and is the imaginary trans-figuration of that part into the centering and totalizing function of the body, then the phallus appears *as symbolic only to the extent that its construction through the transfigurative and specular mechanisms of the imaginary is denied.* Indeed, if the phallus is an imaginary effect, a wishful transfigura-tion, then it is not merely the *symbolic* status of the phallus that is called into question, but the very distinction between the symbolic and the imaginary. If the phallus is the privileged signifier of the symbolic, the delimiting and ordering principle of what can be signified, then this signifier gains its privilege through becoming an imaginary effect that pervasively denies its own status as both imaginary and an effect. If this is true of the signifier that delimits the domain of the signifiable within the symbolic, then it is true of all that is signified as the symbolic. In other words, what operates under the sign of the symbolic may be nothing other than precisely that set of imaginary effects which have become natural-ized and reified as the law of signification.

"The Mirror Stage" and "The Signification of the Phallus" follow (at least) two very different narrative trajectories: the first follows the prema-ture and imaginary transformation of a decentered body—a body in pieces [*le corps morcelé*]—into the specular body, a morphological totality

invested with a center of motor control; the second follows the differential "accession" of bodies to sexed positions within the symbolic. In the
one instance, there is narrative recourse to a body before the mirror; in
the other, a body before the law. Such a discursive reference is one which,
within Lacan's own terms, is to be construed less as a developmental
explanation than as a necessary heuristic fiction.

In "The Mirror Stage," that body is figured "in pieces" [*une image
morcelée du corps*];[27] in Lacan's discussion of the phallus, the body and
anatomy are described only through negation: anatomy and, in particular,
anatomical parts, are *not the phallus, but only that which the phallus symbolizes*
(*Il est encore bien moins l'organe, pénis ou clitoris, qu'il symbolise* [690]). In the
former essay, then (shall we call it a "piece"?), Lacan narrates the overcoming of the partitioned body through the specular and phantasmatic
production of a morphological whole. In the latter essay, that drama is
enacted—or symptomatized—by the narrative movement of the theoretical performance itself, what we will consider briefly as the performativity
of the phallus. But if it is possible to read "The Signification of the Phallus" as symptomatizing the specular phantasm described in "The Mirror
Stage," it is also possible, and useful, to reread "The Mirror Stage" as
offering an implicit theory of "mirroring" as a signifying practice.

If the body is "in pieces" before the mirror, it follows that the mirroring
works as a kind of synecdochal extrapolation by which those pieces or parts
come to stand (in and by the mirror) for the whole; or, put differently, the
part substitutes for the whole and thereby becomes a token for the whole.
If this is right, then perhaps "The Mirror Stage" proceeds through a synecdochal logic that institutes and maintains a phantasm of control. It makes
sense to ask, then, whether the theoretical construction of the phallus
is such a synecdochal extrapolation. By changing the name of the penis
to "the phallus," is the part status of the former phantasmatically and
synecdochally overcome through the inauguration of the latter as "the
privileged signifier"? And does this name, like proper names, secure and
sustain the morphological distinctness of the masculine body, sustaining
the *percipi* through nomination?

In Lacan's discussion of what the phallus is, to be distinguished from
his discussion of who "is" the phallus, he quarrels with various psychoanalytic practitioners about who is entitled to name the phallus, who knows
where and how the name applies, who is in the position to name the

name. He objects to the relegation of the phallus to a "phallic stage" or to the conflation and diminution of the phallus to a "partial object." Lacan faults Karl Abraham in particular for introducing the notion of the partial object, but it is clear that he is most strongly opposed to Melanie Klein's theory of introjected body parts and with Ernest Jones's influential acceptance of these positions. Lacan associates the normalization of the phallus as partial object with the degradation of psychoanalysis on American soil, "*la dégradation de la psychanalyse, consécutive à sa transplantation américaine*" (Lacan, *Écrits*, 77/687). Other theoretical tendencies associated with this degradation are termed "culturalist" and "feminist." In particular, he is opposed to those psychoanalytic positions which consider the phallic phase to be an effect of repression, and the phallic object as a symptom. Here the phallus is negatively defined through a string of attributes: not partial, not an object, not a symptom. Moreover, the "not" which precedes each of these attributes is "not" to be read as a "*refoulement*" (repression); in other words, negation *in these textual instances* is not to be read psychoanalytically (Lacan, *Écrits*, 79/687).

How, then, can we read the symptomatic dimension of Lacan's text here? Does the rejection of the phallic phase and, in particular, of the figuration of the phallus as a partial or approximative object, seek to overcome a degradation in favor of an idealization, a specular one? Do these psychoanalytic texts fail to mirror the phallus as specular center, and do they threaten to expose the synecdochal logic by which the phallus is installed as privileged signifier? If the position for the phallus erected by Lacan symptomatizes the specular and idealizing mirroring of a decentered body in pieces before the mirror, then we can read here the phantasmatic rewriting of an organ or body part, the penis, as the phallus, a move effected by a transvaluative denial of its substitutability, dependency, diminuitive size, limited control, partiality. The phallus would then emerge as a symptom, and its authority could be established only through a metaleptic reversal of cause and effect. Rather than the postulated origin of signification or the signifiable, the phallus would be the effect of a signifying chain summarily suppressed.

But this analysis still needs to take into account why it is that the body is in pieces before the mirror and before the law. Why should the body be given in parts before it is specularized as a totality and center of control? How did this body come to be in pieces and parts? To have a sense of a piece or a part is to have in advance a sense for the whole to which they belong. Although "The Mirror Stage" attempts to narrate how a body comes to have a sense of its own totality for the first time, the very description of a body before the mirror as being in parts or pieces takes as its own precondition an *already* established sense of a whole or integral morphology. If to be in pieces is to be without control, then the body before the mirror is without the phallus, symbolically castrated; and by gaining specularized control through the ego constituted in the mirror, that body "assumes" or "comes to have" the phallus. But the phallus is, as it were, already in play in the very description of the body in pieces before the mirror; as a result, the phallus governs the description of its own genesis and, accordingly, wards off a genealogy that might confer on it a derivative or projected character.

Although Lacan claims quite explicitly that the phallus "is not an imaginary effect,"[28] that denial might be read as constitutive of the very formation of the phallus as privileged signifier; that denial appears to facilitate that privileging. As an imaginary effect, the phallus would be as decentered and tenuous as the ego. In an effort to recenter and ground the phallus, the phallus is elevated to the status of the privileged signifier, and it is offered at the end of a long list of improper usages for the term, ways in which the term has gotten out of hand, signified where it ought not to have and in ways that are wrong:

> ...the phallus is not a fantasy, if what is understood by that is an imaginary effect. Nor is it an object (part, internal, good, bad, etc....) in so far as this term tends to accentuate the reality involved in a relationship. It is even less the organ, penis or clitoris, which it symbolizes. And it is not by accident that Freud took his reference for it from the simulacrum which it represented for the Ancients.
>
> For the phallus is a signifier...[Rose, 79][29]

In this last pronouncement, Lacan seeks to relieve the term of its catachrestic wanderings, to reestablish the phallus as a site of control (as that which is "to designate as a whole the effect of there being a signified") and hence to position Lacan himself as the one to control the meaning of the phallus. As Jane Gallop has argued (to cite her is perhaps to transfer the phallus from him to her, but also then affirms my point that the phallus is fundamentally transferable): "And their inability to control the meaning of the word *phallus* is evidence of what Lacan calls symbolic castration"(126).

If not being able to control the significations that follow from the signifier phallus is evidence of symbolic castration, then the body "in pieces" and out of control before the mirror may be understood as symbolically castrated, and the specular and synecdochal idealization of the (phallic) body may be read as a compensatory mechanism by which this phantasmatic castration is overcome. Not unlike Freud's efforts to put a stop to the proliferation of erotogenic body parts in his text, parts which were also sites of pain, Lacan stalls the sliding of the signifier into a proliferative catachresis through a preemptive assertion of the phallus as privileged signifier. To claim for the phallus the status of a privileged signifier performatively produces and effects this privilege. The announcement of that privileged signifier is its performance. That performative assertion produces and enacts the very process of privileged signification, one whose privilege is potentially contested by the very list of alternatives it discounts, and the negation of which constitutes and precipitates that phallus. Indeed, the phallus is *not* a body part (but the whole), is *not* an imaginary effect (but the origin of all imaginary effects). These negations are constitutive; they function as disavowals that precipitate—and are then erased by-the idealization of the phallus.

The paradoxical status of the negation that introduces and institutes the phallus becomes clear in the grammar itself: "*Il est encore moins l'organe, pénis ou clitoris, qu'il symbolise.*" Here the sentence suggests that the phallus, "even less" than an imaginary effect, is not an organ. Here Lacan thus suggests gradations of negation: the phallus is more likely to be an imaginary effect than an organ; if it is either one, it is more of an imaginary effect than an organ. This is not to say that it is not at all an organ, but that the "copula"—that which asserts a linguistic and ontological identity—is the least adequate way of expressing the relation between them. In the very sentence in which the minimization of any possible identity between penis and phallus is asserted, an alternative relation between them is offered, namely, the relation of *symbolization*. The phallus *symbolizes* the penis; and insofar as it symbolizes the penis, retains the penis as that which it symbolizes; it *is* not the penis. To be the object of symbolization is precisely not to be that which symbolizes. To the extent that the phallus symbolizes the penis, it is not that which it symbolizes. The more symbolization occurs, the less ontological connection there is between symbol and symbolized. Symbolization presumes and produces the ontological difference between that which symbolizes—or signifies—and that which is symbolized—or signified. Symbolization depletes that which is symbolized of its ontological connection with the symbol itself.

But what is the status of this particular assertion of ontological difference if it turns out that this symbol, the phallus, always takes the penis as that which it symbolizes?[30] What is the character of this bind whereby the phallus symbolizes the penis to the extent that it differentiates itself from the penis, where the penis becomes the privileged referent to be negated? If the phallus *must* negate the penis in order to symbolize and signify in its privileged way, then the phallus is bound to the penis, not through simple identity, but through determinate negation. If the phallus only signifies to the extent that it is *not* the penis, and the penis is qualified as that body part that it must *not be*, then the phallus is fundamentally dependent upon the penis in order to symbolize at all. Indeed, the phallus would be nothing without the penis. And in that sense in which the phallus requires the penis for its own constitution, the identity of the phallus includes the penis, that is, a relation of identity holds between them. And this is, of course, not only a logical point, for we have seen that the phallus not only opposes the penis in a logical sense, but is itself instituted through the repudiation of its partial, decentered, and substitutable character.

The question, of course, is why it is assumed that the phallus requires that particular body part to symbolize, and why it could not operate through symbolizing other body parts. The viability of the lesbian phallus depends on this displacement. Or, to put it more accurately, the displace-ability of the phallus, its capacity to symbolize in relation to other body parts or other body-like things, opens the way for the lesbian phallus, an otherwise contradictory formulation. And here it should be clear that the lesbian phallus crosses the orders of *having* and *being*, it both wields the threat of castration (which is in that sense a mode of "being" the phallus, as women "are") and suffers from castration anxiety (and so is said "to have" the phallus, and to fear its loss).

To suggest that the phallus might symbolize body parts other than the penis is compatible with the Lacanian scheme. But to argue that certain body parts or body-like things other than the penis are symbolized as "having" the phallus is to call into question the mutually exclusive trajectories of castration anxiety and penis envy.[31] Indeed, if men are said to "have" the phallus symbolically, their anatomy is also a site marked by having lost it; the anatomical part is never commensurable with the phallus itself. In this sense, men might be understood to be both castrated (already) and driven by penis envy (more properly understood as phallus envy).[32] Conversely, insofar as women might be said to "have" the phallus and fear its loss (and there is no reason why that could not be true in both lesbian and heterosexual exchange, raising the question of an implicit heterosexuality in the former, and homosexuality in the latter), they may be driven by castration anxiety.[33]

Although a number of theorists have suggested that lesbian sexuality is outside the economy of phallogocentrism, that position has been critically countered by the notion that lesbian sexuality is *as* constructed as any other form of sexuality within contemporary sexual regimes. Of interest here is not whether the phallus persists in lesbian sexuality as a structuring principle, but *how* it persists, how it is constructed, and what happens to the "privileged" status of that signifier within this form of constructed exchange. I am not arguing that lesbian sexuality is only or even primarily structured by the phallus, or even that such an impossible monolith as "lesbian sexuality" exists. But I do want to suggest that the phallus constitutes an ambivalent site of identification and desire that is significantly different from the scene of normative heterosexuality to which it is related. If Lacan claimed that the phallus only operates as "veiled," we might ask in return what kind of "veiling" the phallus invariably performs. And what is the logic of "veiling" and, hence, of "exposure" that emerges within lesbian sexual exchange in relation to the question of the phallus?

Clearly, there is no single answer, and the kind of culturally textured work that might approximate an answer to this question will doubtless need to take place elsewhere; indeed, "the" lesbian phallus is a fiction, but perhaps a theoretically useful one, for there are questions of imitation, subversion, and the recirculation of phantasmatic privilege that a psychoanalytically informed reading might attend.

If the phallus is that which is excommunicated from the feminist orthodoxy on lesbian sexuality as well as the "missing part," the sign of an inevitable dissatisfaction that is lesbianism in homophobic and misogynist constructions, then the admission of the phallus into that exchange faces two convergent prohibitions: first, the phallus signifies the persistence of the "straight mind," a masculine or heterosexist identification and, hence, the defilement or betrayal of lesbian specificity; secondly, the phallus signifies the insuperability of heterosexuality and constitutes lesbianism as a vain and/or pathetic effort to mime the real thing. Thus, the phallus enters lesbian sexual discourse in the mode of a transgressive "confession" conditioned and confronted by both the feminist and misogynist forms of repudiation: it's not the real thing (the lesbian thing) or it's not the real thing (the straight thing). What is "unveiled" is precisely the repudiated desire, that which is abjected by heterosexist logic and that which is defensively foreclosed through the effort to circumscribe a specifically feminine morphology for lesbianism. In a sense, what is unveiled or exposed is a desire that is produced through a prohibition.

And yet, the phantasmatic structure of this desire will operate as a "veil" precisely at the moment in which it is "revealed." That phantasmatic transfiguration of bodily boundaries will not only expose its own tenuousness, but will turn out to *depend on* that tenuousness and transience in order to signify at all. The phallus as signifier within lesbian sexuality will engage the spectre of shame and repudiation delivered by that feminist theory which would secure a feminine morphology in its radical distinctness from the masculine (a binarism that is secured through heterosexual presumption), a spectre delivered in a more pervasive way by the masculinist theory which would insist on the male morphology as the only possible figure for the human body. Traversing those divisions, the lesbian phallus signifies a desire that is produced historically at the crossroads of these prohibitions, and is never fully free of the normative demands that condition its possibility and that it nevertheless seeks to subvert. Insofar as the phallus is an idealization of morphology, it produces a necessary effect of inadequation, one which, in the cultural context of lesbian relations, can be quickly assimilated to the sense of an inadequate derivation from the supposedly real thing, and, hence, a source of shame.

But precisely *because* it is an idealization, one which no body can adequately approximate, the phallus is a transferable phantasm, and its naturalized link to masculine morphology can be called into question through an aggressive reterritorialization. That complex identificatory fantasies inform morphogenesis, and that they cannot be fully predicted, suggests that morphological idealization is both a necessary and unpredictable ingredient in the constitution of both the bodily ego and the dispositions of desire.

It also means that there is not necessarily one imaginary schema for the bodily ego, and that cultural conflicts over the idealization and degradation of specific masculine and feminine morphologies will be played out at the site of the morphological imaginary in complex and conflicted ways. It may well be through a degradation of a feminine morphology, an imaginary and cathected degrading of the feminine, that the lesbian phallus comes into play, or it may be through a castrating occupation of that central masculine trope, fueled by the kind of defiance which seeks to overturn that very degradation of the feminine.

It is important to underscore, however, the way in which the stability of both "masculine" and "feminine" morphologies is called into question by a lesbian resignification of the phallus which depends on the crossings of phantasmatic identification. If the morphological distinctness of "the feminine" depends on its purification of all masculinity, and if this bodily boundary and distinctness is instituted in the service of the laws of a heterosexual symbolic, then that repudiated masculinity is *presumed* by the feminized morphology, and will emerge either as an impossible ideal that shadows and thwarts the feminine or as a disparaged signifier of a patriarchal order against which a specific lesbian-feminism defines itself. In either case, the relation to the phallus is constitutive; an identification is made which is at once disavowed.

Indeed, it is this disavowed identification that enables and informs the production of a "distinct" feminine morphology from the start. It is doubtless possible to take account of the structuring presence of cross-identifications in the elaboration of the bodily ego, and to frame these identifications in a direction beyond a logic of repudiation by which one identification is always and only worked at the expense of another. For the "shame" of the lesbian phallus presumes that it will come to represent the "truth" of lesbian desire, a truth which will be figured as a falsehood, a vain imitation or derivation from the heterosexual norm. And the counterstrategy of confessional defiance presumes as well that what has been excluded from dominant sexual discourses on lesbianism thereby constitutes its "truth." But if the "truth" is, as Nietzsche suggests, only a series of mistakes configured in relation to one another or, in Lacanian terms, a set of constituting *méconnaissances*, then the phallus is but one signifier among others in the course of lesbian exchange, neither the originating signifier nor the unspeakable outside. The phallus will thus always operate as both veil and confession, a deflection from an erotogenicity that includes and exceeds the phallus, an exposure of a desire which attests to a morphological transgression and, hence, to the instability of the imaginary boundaries of sex.

CONCLUSION

If the phallus is an imaginary effect (which is reified as the privileged signifier of the symbolic order), then its structural place is no longer determined by the logical relation of mutual exclusion entailed by a heterosexist version of sexual difference in which men are said to "have" and women to "be" the phallus. This logical and structural place is secured through the move that claims that by virtue of the penis, one is symbolized as "having"; that structural bond (or bind) secures a relation of identity between the phallus and the penis that is explicitly denied (it also performs a synecdochal collapse of the penis and the one who has it). If the phallus only symbolizes to the extent that there is a penis there to be symbolized, then the phallus is not only fundamentally dependent upon the penis, but cannot exist without it. But is this true?

If the phallus operates as a signifier whose privilege is under contest, if its privilege is shown to be secured precisely through the reification of logical and structural relations within the symbolic, then the structures within which it is put into play are more various and revisable than the Lacanian scheme can affirm. Consider that "having" the phallus can be symbolized by an arm, a tongue, a hand (or two), a knee, a thigh, a pelvic bone, an array of purposefully instrumentalized body-like things. And that this "having" exists in relation to a "being the phallus" which is both part of its own signifying effect (the phallic lesbian as potentially castrating) and that which it encounters in the woman who is desired (as the one who, offering or withdrawing the specular guarantee, wields the power to castrate). That this scene can reverse, that being and having can be confounded, upsets the logic of non-contradiction that serves the either-or of normative heterosexual exchange. In a sense, the simultaneous acts of depriveging the phallus and removing it from the normative heterosexual form of exchange, and recirculating and reprivileging it between women deploys the phallus to break the signifying chain in which it conventionally operates. If a lesbian "has" it, it is also clear that she does not "have" it in the traditional sense; her activity furthers a crisis in the sense of what it means to "have" one at all. The phantasmatic status of "having" is redelineated, rendered transferable, substitutable, plastic; and the eroticism produced within such an exchange depends on the displacement from traditional masculinist contexts as well as the critical redeployment of its central figures of power.

Clearly, the phallus operates in a privileged way in contemporary sexual cultures, but that operation is secured by a linguistic structure or position that is not independent of its perpetual reconstitution. Inasmuch as the phallus signifies, it is also always in the process of being signified and resignified. In this sense, it is not the incipient moment or origin of a signifying chain, as Lacan would insist, but part of a reiterable signifying practice and, hence, open to resignification: signifying in ways and in places that exceed its proper structural place within the Lacanian symbolic and contest the necessity of that place. If the phallus is a privileged signifier, it gains that privilege through being reiterated. And if the cultural construction of sexuality compels a repetition of that signifier, there is nevertheless in the very force of repetition, understood as resignification or recirculation, the possibility of deprivileging that signifier.

If what comes to signify under the sign of the phallus are a number of body parts, discursive performatives, alternative fetishes, to name a few, then the symbolic position of "having" has been dislodged from the penis as its privileged anatomical (or non-anatomical) occasion. The phantasmatic moment in which a part suddenly stands for and produces a sense of the whole or is figured as the center of control, in which a certain kind of "phallic" determination is made by virtue of which meaning appears radically generated, underscores the very plasticity of the phallus, the way in which it exceeds the structural place to which it has been consigned by the Lacanian scheme, the way in which that structure, to remain a structure, has to be *reiterated* and, as reiterable, becomes open to variation and plasticity.[34] When the phallus is lesbian, then it is and is not a masculinist figure of power; the signifier is significantly split, for it both recalls and displaces the masculinism by which it is impelled. And insofar as it operates at the site of anatomy, the phallus (re)produces the spectre of the penis only to enact its vanishing, to reiterate and exploit its perpetual vanishing as the very occasion of the phallus. This opens up anatomy—and sexual difference itself—as a site of proliferative resignifications.

In a sense, the phallus as I offer it here is both occasioned by Lacan and exceeds the purview of that form of heterosexist structuralism. It is not enough to claim that the signifier is not the same as the signified (phallus/penis), if both terms are nevertheless bound to each other by an essential relation in which that difference is contained. The offering of the lesbian phallus suggests that the signifier can come to signify *in excess* of its structurally mandated position; indeed, the signifier can be repeated in contexts and relations that come to *displace* the privileged status of that signifier. The "structure" by which the phallus signifies the penis as its privileged occasion exists only through being instituted and reiterated, and, by virtue of that temporalization, is unstable and open to subversive repetition. Moreover, if the phallus symbolizes only through taking anatomy as its occasion, then the more various and unanticipated the anatomical (and non-anatomical) occasions for its symbolization, the more unstable that signifier becomes. In other words, the phallus has no existence separable from the occasions of its symbolization; it cannot symbolize without its occasion. Hence, the lesbian phallus offers the occasion (a set of occasions) for the phallus to signify differently, and in so signifying, to resignify, unwittingly, its own masculinist and heterosexist privilege.

The notion of the bodily ego in Freud and that of the projective idealization of the body in Lacan suggest that the very contours of the body, the delimitations of anatomy, are in part the consequence of an externalized identification. That identificatory process is itself motivated by a transfigurative wish. And that wishfulness proper to all morphogenesis is itself prepared and structured by a culturally complex signifying chain that not only constitutes sexuality, but establishes sexuality as a site where bodies and anatomies are perpetually reconstituted. If these central identifications cannot be strictly regulated, then the domain of the imaginary in which the body is partially constituted is marked by a constitutive vacillation. The anatomical is only "given" through its signification, and yet it appears to exceed that signification, to provide the elusive referent in relation to which the variability of signification performs. Always already caught up in the signifying chain by which sexual difference is negotiated, the anatomical is never given outside its terms, and yet it is also that which exceeds and compels that signifying chain, that reiteration of difference, an insistent and inexhaustible demand.

If the heterosexualization of identification and morphogenesis is historically contingent, however hegemonic, then identifications, which are always already imaginary, as they cross gender boundaries, reinstitute sexed bodies in variable ways. In crossing these boundaries, such morphogenetic identifications reconfigure the mapping of sexual difference itself. The bodily ego produced through identification is not *mimetically* related to a preexisting biological or anatomical body (that former body could only become available through the imaginary schema I am proposing here, so that we would be immediately caught up in an infinite regress or vicious circle). The body in the mirror does not represent a body that is, as it were, before the mirror: the mirror, even as it is instigated by that unrepresentable body "before" the mirror, produces that body as its delirious effect—a delirium, by the way, which we are compelled to live.

In this sense, to speak of the lesbian phallus as a possible site of desire is not to refer to an *imaginary* identification and/or desire that can be measured against a *real* one; on the contrary, it is simply to promote an alternative *imaginary* to a hegemonic imaginary and to show, through that assertion, the ways in which the hegemonic imaginary constitutes itself through the naturalization of an exclusionary heterosexual morphology. In this sense, it is important to note that it is the lesbian *phallus* and not the *penis* that is considered here. For what is needed is not a new body part, as it were, but a displacement of the hegemonic symbolic of (heterosexist) sexual difference and the critical release of alternative imaginary schemas for constituting sites of erotogenic pleasure.

3

PHANTASMATIC IDENTIFICATION AND
THE ASSUMPTION OF SEX

> How does it happen that the human subject makes himself [sic] into
> an object of possible knowledge, through what forms of rationality,
> through what historical necessities, and at what price? My question
> is this: How much does it cost the subject to be able to tell the truth
> about itself?
> —Michel Foucault, "How Much Does It Cost to Tell the Truth?"

When one asks whether or not sexual identities are constructed, a
more or less tacit set of questions is implicitly raised: Is sexuality so
highly constrained from the start that it ought to be conceived as fixed?
If sexuality is so constrained from the start, does it not constitute a kind
of essentialism at the level of identity? At stake is a way to describe this
deeper and perhaps irrecoverable sense of *constitutedness and constraint* in
the face of which the notions of "choice" or "free play" appear not only
foreign, but unthinkable and sometimes even cruel. The constructed
character of sexuality has been invoked to counter the claim that sexuality
has a natural and normative shape and movement, that is, one which
approximates the normative phantasm of a compulsory heterosexuality.
The efforts to denaturalize sexuality and gender have taken as their main
enemy those normative frameworks of compulsory heterosexuality that
operate through the naturalization and reification of heterosexist norms.
But is there a risk in the affirmation of *denaturalization* as a strategy? The
turn to phylogenetic essentialism among some gay theorists marks a
desire to take account of a domain of constitutive constraints, a domain
that the discourse on denaturalization has appeared in part to overlook.

In this chapter, I will try to locate the sense of constraint in sexuality in
terms of the logic of repudiation by which the normalization of
(hetero)sexuality is instituted. In the next chapter, "Gender Is Burning," I
will consider the limits of denaturalization as a critical strategy.

It may be useful to shift the terms of the debate from constructivism versus essentialism to the more complex question of how "deep-seated" or constitutive constraints can be posed in terms of symbolic limits in their intractability and contestability. What has been understood as the performativity of gender—far from the exercise of an unconstrained voluntarism—will prove to be impossible apart from notions of such political constraints registered psychically. It may well be useful to separate the notion of constraints or limits from the metaphysical endeavor to ground those constraints in a biological or psychological essentialism. This latter effort seeks to establish a certain "proof" of constraint over and against a constructivism which is illogically identified with voluntarism and free play. Those essentialist positions which seek recourse to a sexual nature or to a precultural structuring of sexuality in order to secure a metaphysical site or cause for this sense of constraint become highly contestable even on their own terms.[1]

Such efforts to underscore the fixed and constrained character of sexuality, however, need to be read carefully, especially by those who have insisted on the constructed status of sexuality. For sexuality cannot be summarily made or unmade, and it would be a mistake to associate "constructivism" with "the freedom of a subject to form her/his sexuality as s/he pleases." A construction is, after all, not the same as an artifice. On the contrary, constructivism needs to take account of the domain of constraints without which a certain living and desiring being cannot make its way. And every such being is constrained by not only what is difficult to imagine, but what remains radically unthinkable: in the domain of sexuality these constraints include the radical unthinkability of desiring otherwise, the radical unendurability of desiring otherwise, the absence of certain desires, the repetitive compulsion of others, the abiding repudiation of some sexual possibilities, panic, obsessional pull, and the nexus of sexuality and pain.

There is a tendency to think that sexuality is either constructed or determined; to think that if it is constructed, it is in some sense free, and if it is determined, it is in some sense fixed. These oppositions do not describe the complexity of what is at stake in any effort to take account of the conditions under which sex and sexuality are assumed. The "performative" dimension of construction is precisely the forced reiteration of norms. In this sense, then, it is not only that there are constraints to performativity; rather, constraint calls to be rethought as the very condition of performativity. Performativity is neither free play nor theatrical self-presentation; nor can it be simply equated with performance. Moreover, constraint is not necessarily that which sets a limit to performativity; constraint is, rather, that which impels and sustains performativity.

Here, at the risk of repeating myself, I would suggest that performativity cannot be understood outside of a process of iterability, a regularized and constrained repetition of norms. And this repetition is not performed *by* a subject; this repetition is what enables a subject and constitutes the temporal condition for the subject. This iterability implies that "performance" is not a singular "act" or event, but a ritualized production, a ritual reiterated under and through constraint, under and through the force of prohibition and taboo, with the threat of ostracism and even death controlling and compelling the shape of the production, but not, I will insist, determining it fully in advance.

How are we to think through this notion of performativity as it relates to prohibitions that effectively generate sanctioned and unsanctioned sexual practices and arrangements? In particular, how do we pursue the question of sexuality and the law, where the law is not only that which represses sexuality, but a prohibition that *generates* sexuality or, at least, compels its directionality? Given that there is no sexuality outside of power, and that power in its productive mode is never fully free from regulation, how can regulation itself be construed as a productive or generative constraint on sexuality? Specifically, how does the capacity of the law to produce and constrain at once play itself out in the securing for every body a sex, a sexed position within language, a sexed position which is in some sense presumed by any body who comes to speak as a subject, an "I," one who is constituted through the act of taking its sexed place within a language that insistently forces the question of sex?

IDENTIFICATION, PROHIBITION, AND THE INSTABILITY OF "POSITIONS"

The introduction of a psychoanalytic discourse on sexual difference, and the turn to the work of Jacques Lacan by feminists, has been in part an effort to reassert the kinds of symbolic constraints under which becoming "sexed" occurs. Over and against those who argued that sex is a simple question of anatomy, Lacan maintained that sex is a symbolic position that one assumes under the threat of punishment, that is, a position one is constrained to assume, where those constraints are operative in the very structure of language and, hence, in the constitutive relations of cultural life. Some feminists have turned to Lacan in an effort to temper a certain kind of utopianism that held that the radical reorganization of kinship relations could imply the radical reorganization of the psyche, sexuality, and desire. The symbolic domain which compelled the assumption of a sexed position within language was held to be more fundamental than any specific organization of kinship. So that one might rearrange kinship relations outside of the family scene, but still discover one's sexuality to be constructed through more deep-seated constraining and constitutive symbolic demands. What are these demands? Are they prior to the social, to kinship, to politics? If they do operate as constraints, are they for that reason fixed?

I propose to consider the symbolic demand to assume a sexed position and what is implied by that demand. Although this chapter will not consider the full domain of constraints on sex and sexuality (a limitless task), it does propose in a general way to take account of constraints as the limits of what can and cannot be constructed. In the oedipal scenario, the symbolic demand that institutes "sex" is accompanied by the threat of punishment. Castration is the figure for punishment, the fear of castration motivating the assumption of the masculine sex, the fear of not being castrated motivating the assumption of the feminine. Implicit in the figure of castration, which operates differentially to constitute the constraining force of gendered punishment, are at least two inarticulate figures of abject homosexuality, the feminized fag and the phallicized dyke; the Lacanian scheme presumes that the terror over occupying either of these positions is what compels the assumption of a sexed position within language, a sexed position that is sexed by virtue of its heterosexual positioning, and that is assumed through a move that excludes and abjects gay and lesbian possibilities.

The point of this analysis is not to affirm the constraints under which sexed positions are assumed, but to ask how the fixity of such constraints is established, what sexual (im)possibilities have served as the constitutive constraints of sexed positionality, and what possibilities of reworking those constraints arise from within its own terms. If to assume a sexed position is to identify with a position marked out within the symbolic domain, and if to identify involves fantasizing the possibility of approximating that symbolic site, then the heterosexist constraint that compels the assumption of sex operates through the regulation of phantasmatic identification.[2] The oedipal scenario depends for its livelihood on the threatening power of its threat, on the resistance to identification with masculine feminization and feminine phallicization. But what happens if the law that deploys the spectral figure of abject homosexuality as a threat becomes itself an inadvertent site of eroticization? If the taboo becomes eroticized precisely for the transgressive sites that it produces, what happens to oedipus, to sexed positionality, to the fast distinction between an imaginary or fantasized identification and those social and linguistic positions of intelligible "sex" mandated by the symbolic law? Does the refusal to concur with the abjection of homosexuality necessitate a critical rethinking of the psychoanalytic economy of sex?

Three critical points must first be made about the category of sex and the notion of sexual difference in Lacan. First, the use of "sexual difference" to denote a relation simultaneously anatomical and linguistic implicates Lacan in a tautological bind. Second, another tautology appears when he claims that the subject emerges only as a consequence of sex and sexual difference, and yet insists that the subject must accomplish and assume its sexed position within language. Third, the Lacanian version of sex and sexual difference implicates his descriptions of anatomy and development in an unexamined framework of normative heterosexuality.

As for the claim that Lacan offers a tautological account of the category of "sex," one might well reply that *of course* that is true; indeed, that tautology constitutes the very scene of a necessary redoubling in which "sex" is assumed. On the one hand, the category of sex is assumed; there are sexed positions that persist within a symbolic domain which preexist their appropriation by individuals and cannot be reduced to the various moments in which the symbolic subjects and subjectivates individual bodies according to sex. On the other hand, the category of sex is presumed already to have marked that individual body which is, as it were, delivered up to the symbolic law to receive its mark. Hence, "sex" is that which marks the body prior to its mark, staging in advance which symbolic position will mark it, and it is this latter "mark" which appears to postdate the body, retroactively attributing a sexual position to a body. This mark and position constitute that symbolic condition through which the body becomes signifiable at all. But here there are at least two conceptual knots: first, the body is marked by sex, but the body is marked prior to that mark, for it is the first mark that prepares the body for the second one, and, second, the body is only signifiable, only occurs as that which can be signified within language, by being marked in this second sense. This means that any recourse to the body before the symbolic can take place only within the symbolic, which seems to imply that there is no body prior to its marking. If this last implication is accepted, we can never tell a story about how it is that a body comes to be marked by the category of sex, for the body before the mark is constituted as signifiable only *through* the mark. Or, rather, any story we might tell about such a body making its way toward the marker of sex will be a fictional one, even if, perhaps, a necessary fiction.

For Lacan, sexual desire is initiated through the force of prohibition. Indeed, desire is marked off from *jouissance* precisely through the mark of the law. Desire travels along metonymic routes, through a logic of displacement, impelled and thwarted by the impossible fantasy of recovering a full pleasure before the advent of the law. This return to that site of phantasmatic abundance cannot take place without risking psychosis. But what is this psychosis? And how is it figured? Psychosis appears not only as the prospect of losing the status of a subject and, hence, of life within language, but as the terrorizing spectre of coming under an unbearable censor, a death sentence of sorts.

The breaking of certain taboos brings on the spectre of psychosis, but to what extent can we understand "psychosis" as relative to the very prohibitions that guard against it? In other words, what precise cultural possibilities threaten the subject with a psychotic dissolution, marking the boundaries of livable being? To what extent is the fantasy of psychotic dissolution itself the effect of a certain prohibition against those sexual possibilities which abrogate the heterosexual contract? Under what conditions and under the sway of what regulatory schemes does homosexuality itself appear as the living prospect of death?[3] To what extent do deviations from oedipalized identifications call into question the structural stasis of sexual binarisms and their relation to psychosis?

What happens when the primary prohibitions against incest produce displacements and substitutions which do not conform to the models outlined above? Indeed, a woman may find the phantasmatic remainder of her father in another woman or substitute her desire for her mother in a man, at which point a certain crossing of heterosexual and homosexual desires operates at once. If we grant the psychoanalytic presumption that primary prohibitions not only produce deflections of sexual desire but consolidate a psychic sense of "sex" and sexual difference, then it appears to follow that the coherently heterosexualized deflections require that identifications be effected on the basis of similarly sexed bodies and that desire be deflected across the sexual divide to members of the opposite sex. But if a man can identify with his mother, and produce desire from that identification (a complicated process, no doubt, that I cannot justly delineate here), he has already confounded the psychic description of stable gender development. And if that same man desires another man, or a woman, is his desire homosexual, heterosexual, or even lesbian? And what is to restrict any given individual to a single identification? Identifications are multiple and contestatory, and it may be that we desire most strongly those individuals who reflect in a dense or saturated way the possibilities of multiple and simultaneous substitutions, where a substitution engages a fantasy of recovering a primary object of a love lost—and produced—through prohibition. Insofar as a number of such fantasies can come to constitute and saturate a site of desire, it follows that we are not in the position of *either* identifying with a given sex *or* desiring someone else of that sex; indeed, we are not, more generally, in a position of finding identification and desire to be mutually exclusive phenomena.

Of course, I use the grammar of an "I" or a "we" as if these subjects precede and activate their various identifications, but this is a grammatical fiction—one I am willing to use even though it runs the risk of enforcing an interpretation counter to the one that I want to make. For there is no "I" prior to its assumption of sex, and no assumption that is not at once an impossible yet necessary identification. And yet, I use the grammar that denies this temporality—as I am doubtless used by it—only because I cannot find in myself a desire to replicate too closely Lacan's sometimes tortured prose (my own is difficult enough).

To identify is not to oppose desire. Identification is a phantasmatic trajectory and resolution of desire; an assumption of place; a territorializing of an object which enables identity through the temporary resolution of desire, but which remains desire, if only in its repudiated form.

My reference to multiple identification does not mean to suggest that everyone is compelled by being or having such identificatory fluidity. Sexuality is as much motivated by the fantasy of retrieving prohibited objects as by the desire to remain protected from the threat of punishment that such a retrieval might bring on. In Lacan's work, this threat is usually designated as the Name of the Father, that is, the father's law as it determines appropriate kinship relations which include appropriate and mutually exclusive lines of identification and desire. When the threat of punishment wielded by that prohibition is too great, it may be that we desire someone who will keep us from ever seeing the desire for which we are punishable, and in attaching ourselves to that person, it may be that we effectively punish ourselves in advance and, indeed, generate desire in and through and for that self-punishment.

Or it may be that certain identifications and affiliations are made, certain sympathetic connections amplified, precisely in order to institute a *dis*identification with a position that seems too saturated with injury or aggression, one that might, as a consequence, be occupiable only through imagining the loss of viable identity altogether. Hence, the peculiar logic in the sympathetic gesture by which one objects to an injury done to another to deflect attention from an injury done to oneself, a gesture that then becomes the vehicle of displacement by which one feels for oneself *through and as the other*. Inhibited from petitioning the injury in one's own name (for fear of being further steeped in that very abjection and/or launched infelicitously into rage), one makes the petition in the name of another, perhaps going as far as denouncing those who would turn the tables and make the claim for oneself. If this "altruism" constitutes the displacement of narcissism or self-love, then the exterior site of identification inevitably becomes saturated with the resentment that accompanies the expropriation, the loss of narcissism. This accounts for the ambivalence at the heart of political forms of altruism.

Identifications, then, can ward off certain desires or act as vehicles for desire; in order to facilitate certain desires, it may be necessary to ward off others: identification is the site at which this ambivalent prohibition and production of desire occurs. If to assume a sex is in some sense an "identification," then it seems that identification is a site at which prohibition and deflection are insistently negotiated. To identify with a sex is to stand in some relation to an imaginary threat, imaginary and forceful, forceful precisely because it is imaginary.

In "The Signification of the Phallus," after an aside on castration, Lacan remarks that man (*Mensch*) is confronted with an antinomy internal to the assumption of his sex. And then he offers a question: "Why must he take up its [sex's] attributes only by means of a threat, or even in the guise of a privation?" (Rose, 75).[4] The symbolic marks the body by sex through threatening that body, through the deployment/production of an imaginary threat, a castration, a privation of some bodily part: this must be the masculine body that will lose the member it refuses to submit to the symbolic inscription; without symbolic inscription, that body will be negated. And so, to whom is this threat delivered? There must be a body trembling before the law, a body whose fear can be compelled by the law, a law that produces the trembling body prepared for its inscription, a law that marks the body *first* with fear only then to mark it again with the symbolic stamp of sex. To assume the law, to accede to the law is to produce an imaginary alignment with the sexual position marked out by the symbolic, but also always to fail to approximate that position, and to feel the distance between that imaginary identification and the symbolic as the threat of punishment, the failure to conform, the spectre of abjection.

It is said, of course, that women are always already punished, castrated, and that their relation to the phallic norm will be penis envy. And this must have happened first, since men are said to look over and see this figure of castration and fear any identification there. Becoming like her, becoming her, that is the fear of castration and, hence, the fear of falling into penis envy as well. The symbolic position that marks a sex as masculine is one through which the masculine sex is said to "have" the phallus; it is one that compels through the threat of punishment, that is, the threat of feminization, an imaginary and, hence, inadequate identification. Hence, there is then *presupposed* in the imaginary masculine effort to identify with this position of having the phallus, a certain inevitable failure, a failure to have and a yearning to have a penis envy which is not the *opposite* of the fear of castration, but *its very presupposition.* Castration could not be feared if the phallus were not already detachable, already elsewhere, already dispossessed; it is not simply the spectre that it will become lost that constitutes the obsessive preoccupation of castration anxiety. *It is the spectre of the recognition that it was always already lost, the vanquishing of the fantasy that it might ever have been possessed—the loss of nostalgia's referent.* If the phallus exceeds every effort to identify with it, then this failure to approximate the phallus constitutes the necessary relation of the imaginary to the phallus. In this sense, the phallus is always already lost, and the fear of castration is a fear that phantasmatic identification will collide with and dissolve against the symbolic, a fear of the recognition that there can be no final obedience to that symbolic power, and this must be a recognition that, in some already operative way, one already has made.

The symbolic marks a body as feminine through the mark of privation and castration, but can it compel that accession to castration through the threat of punishment? If castration is the very figure for the punishment with which the masculine subject is threatened, it seems that assuming the feminine position is not only compelled by the threat of punishment (her fate is apparently the alternative that follows the disjunctive "or," but the French "voire" is less oppositional than emphatic, better translated as "even" or "indeed"). The feminine position is constituted as the figural enactment of that punishment, the very figuration of that threat and, hence, is produced as a lack only in relation to the masculine subject. To assume the feminine position is to take up the figure of castration or, at least, to negotiate a relation to it, symbolizing at once the threat to the masculine position as well as the guarantee that the masculine "has" the phallus. Precisely because the guarantee can be relinquished for the threat of castration, the feminine position must be taken up in its reassuring mode. This "identification" is thus *repeatedly* produced, and in the demand that the identification be *reiterated* persists the possibility, the threat, that it will *fail* to repeat.

But how, then, is the assumption of feminine castration compelled? What serves as a punishment for the one who refuses to accede to punishment? We might expect that this refusal or resistance would be figured as a punishable phallicism. The failure to approximate the symbolic position of the feminine—a failure that would characterize any imaginary effort to identify with the symbolic—would be construed as a failure to submit to castration and to effect the necessary identification with the (castrated) mother and, through that identification, to produce a displaced version of the (imaginary) father to desire. The failure to submit to castration appears capable of producing only its opposite, the spectral figure of the castrator with Holophernes's head in hand. This figure of excessive phallicism, typified by the phallic mother, is devouring and destructive, the negative fate of the phallus when attached to the feminine position. Significant in its misogyny, this construction suggests that "having the phallus" is much more destructive as a feminine operation than as a masculine one, a claim that symptomatizes the displacement of phallic destructiveness and implies that there is no other way for women to assume the phallus except in its most killing modalities.

The "threat" that compels the assumption of masculine and feminine attributes is, for the former, a descent into feminine castration and abjection and, for the latter, the monstrous ascent into phallicism. Are both of these figures of hell, figures which constitute the state of punishment threatened by the law, in part figures of homosexual abjection, a gendered afterlife? The feminized "fag" and the phallicized "dyke"? And are these undelineated figures the structuring absences of symbolic demand? If a man refuses too radically the "having of the phallus," he will be punished with homosexuality, and if a woman refuses too radically her position as castration, she will be punished with homosexuality. Here the sexed positions that are said to inhere in language are stabilized through a hierarchized and differentiated specular relation (he "has"; she "reflects his having" and has the power to offer or withdraw that guarantee; therefore, she "is" the phallus, castrated, potentially threatening castration). This specular relation, however, is itself established through the exclusion and abjection of a domain of relations in which all the wrong identifications are pursued; men wishing to "be" the phallus for other men, women wishing to "have" the phallus for other women, women wishing to "be" the phallus for other women, men wishing both to have and to be the phallus for other men in a scene in which the phallus not only transfers between the modalities of being and having, but between partners within a volatile circuit of exchange, men wishing to "be" the phallus for a woman who "has" it, women wishing to "have it" for a man who "is" it.

And here it is important to note that it is not only that the phallus circulates out of line, but that it also can be an absent, indifferent, or otherwise diminished structuring principle of sexual exchange. Further, I do not mean to suggest that there are only two figures of abjection, the inverted versions of the heterosexualized masculinity and femininity; on the contrary, these figures of abjection, which are inarticulate yet organizing figures within the Lacanian symbolic, foreclose precisely the kind of complex crossings of identification and desire which might exceed and contest the binary frame itself. Indeed, it is this range of identificatory contestation that is foreclosed from the binary figuration of normalized heterosexuality and abjected homosexuality. The binarism of feminized male homosexuality, on the one hand, and masculinized female homosexuality, on the other, is itself produced as the restrictive spectre that constitutes the defining limits of symbolic exchange. Importantly, these are spectres produced *by* that symbolic as its threatening outside to safeguard its continuing hegemony.

Assuming the mark of castration, a mark which is after all a lack, a lack which designates absently the domain of the feminine, can precipitate a set of crises that cannot be predicted by the symbolic scheme that purports to circumscribe them. If identification with the symbolic position of castration is bound to fail, if it can only figure repeatedly and vainly a phantasmatic approximation of that position and never fully bind itself to that demand, then there is always some critical distance between what the law compels and the identification that the feminine body offers up as the token of her loyalty to the law. The body marked as feminine occupies or inhabits its mark at a critical distance, with radical unease or with a phantasmatic and tenuous pleasure or with some mixture of anxiety and desire. If she is marked as castrated, she must nevertheless *assume* that mark, where "assumption" contains both the wish for an identification as well as its impossibility.[5] For if she must assume, accomplish, accede to her castration, there is at the start some *failure* of socialization here, some excessive occurrence of that body outside and beyond its mark, in relation to that mark.[6] There is some body to which/to whom the threat or punishment encoded and enacted by the mark is addressed, in whom some fear of punishment is insistently compelled, who is not yet or not ever a figure of strict compliance. Indeed, there is a body which has failed to perform its castration in accord with the symbolic law, some locus of resistance, some way in which the desire to have the phallus has not been renounced and continues to persist.

If this analysis invites the charge of penis envy, it also forces a reconsideration of the unstable status of identification in any envious act: there is in the very structure of envy the possibility of an imaginary identification, a crossing over into a "having" of the phallus that is both acknowledged and blocked. And if there is a law that must compel a feminine identification with a position of castration, it appears that this law "knows" that identification could function differently, that a feminine effort to identify with "having" the phallus could resist its demand, and that this possibility must be renounced. Although the feminine position is figured as already castrated and, hence, subject to penis envy, it seems that penis envy marks not only the masculine relation to the symbolic, but marks every relation to the having of the phallus, that vain striving to approximate and possess what no one ever can have, but anyone sometimes can have in the transient domain of the imaginary.

But where or how does identification occur? When can we say with confidence that an identification has happened? Significantly, it never can be said to have taken place; identification does not belong to the world of events. Identification is constantly figured as a desired event or accomplishment, but one which finally is never achieved; identification is the phantasmatic staging of the event.[7] In this sense, identifications belong to the imaginary; they are phantasmatic efforts of alignment, loyalty, ambiguous and cross-corporeal cohabitation; they unsettle the "I"; they are the sedimentation of the "we" in the constitution of any "I," the structuring presence of alterity in the very formulation of the "I." Identifications are never fully and finally made; they are incessantly reconstituted and, as such, are subject to the volatile logic of iterability. They are that which is constantly marshaled, consolidated, retrenched, contested, and, on occasion, compelled to give way. That *resistance* is here linked only with the possibility of *failure* will be shown as the political inadequacy of this conception of the law, for the formulation suggests that the law, the injunction, that produces this failure cannot itself be reworked or recalled by virtue of the kind of resistances that it generates. What is the status of this law as a site of power?

Understood as a phantasmatic effort subject to the logic of iterability, an identification always takes place in relation to a law or, more specifically, a prohibition that works through delivering a threat of punishment. The law, understood here as the demand and threat issued by and through the symbolic, compels the shape and direction of sexuality through the instillation of fear. If identification seeks to produce an ego, which Freud insists is "first and foremost a bodily ego," in compliance with a symbolic position, then the *failure* of identificatory phantasms constitutes the site of resistance to the law. But the failure or refusal to reiterate the law does not in itself change the structure of the demand that the law makes. The law continues to make its demand, but the failure to comply with the law produces an instability in the ego at the level of the imaginary. Disobedience to the law becomes the promise of the imaginary and, in particular, of the incommensurability of the imaginary with the symbolic. But the law, the symbolic, is left intact, even as its authority to compel strict compliance with the "positions" it lays out is called into question.

This version of resistance has constituted the promise of psychoanalysis to contest strictly opposed and hierarchical sexual positions for some feminist readers of Lacan. But does this view of resistance fail to consider the status of the symbolic as immutable law?[8] And would the mutation of that law call into question not only the compulsory heterosexuality attributed to the symbolic, but also the stability and discreteness of the distinction between symbolic and imaginary registers within the Lacanian scheme? It seems crucial to question whether resistance to an immutable law is *sufficient* as a political contestation of compulsory heterosexuality, where this resistance is safely restricted to the imaginary and thereby restrained from entering into the structure of the symbolic itself.[9] To what extent is the symbolic unwittingly elevated to an incontestable position precisely through domesticating resistance within the imaginary? If the symbolic is structured by the Law of the Father, then the feminist resistance to the symbolic unwittingly *protects* the father's law by relegating feminine resistance to the less enduring and less efficacious domain of the imaginary. Through this move, then, feminine resistance is both valorized in its specificity and reassuringly disempowered. By accepting the radical divide between symbolic and imaginary, the terms of feminist resistance reconstitute sexually differentiated and hierarchized "separate spheres." Although resistance constitutes a temporary escape from the constituting power of the law, it cannot enter into the dynamic by which the symbolic reiterates its power and thereby alter the structural sexism and homophobia of its sexual demands.[10]

The symbolic is understood as the normative dimension of the constitution of the sexed subject within language. It consists in a series of demands, taboos, sanctions, injunctions, prohibitions, impossible idealizations, and threats—performative speech acts, as it were, that wield the power to produce the field of culturally viable sexual subjects: performative acts, in other words, with the power to produce or materialize subjectivating effects. But what cultural configuration of power organizes these normative and productive operations of subject-constitution?

"Sex" is always produced as a reiteration of hegemonic norms. This productive reiteration can be read as a kind of performativity. Discursive performativity appears to produce that which it names, to enact its own referent, to name and to do, to name and to make. Paradoxically, however, this productive capacity of discourse is derivative, a form of cultural iterability or rearticulation, a practice of *re*signification, not creation ex nihilo. Generally speaking, a performative functions to produce that which it declares. As a discursive practice (performative "acts" must be *repeated* to become efficacious), performatives constitute a locus of *discursive production*. No "act" apart from a regularized and sanctioned practice can wield the power to produce that which it declares. Indeed, a performative act apart from a reiterated and, hence, sanctioned set of conventions can appear only as a vain effort to produce effects that it cannot possibly produce.

Consider the relevance of the deconstructive reading of juridical imperatives to the domain of the Lacanian symbolic. The authority/the judge (let us call him "he") who effects the law through naming does not harbor that authority in his person. As one who efficaciously speaks in the name of the law, the judge does not originate the law or its authority; rather, he "cites" the law, consults and reinvokes the law, and, in that reinvocation, reconstitutes the law. The judge is thus installed in the midst of a signifying chain, receiving and reciting the law and, in the reciting, echoing forth the authority of the law. When the law functions as ordinance or sanction, it operates as an imperative that brings into being that which it legally enjoins and protects. The performative speaking of the law, an "utterance" that is most often within legal discourse inscribed in a book of laws, works only by reworking a set of already operative conventions. And these conventions are grounded in no other legitimating authority than the echo-chain of their own reinvocation.

Paradoxically, what is *invoked* by the one who speaks or inscribes the law is *the fiction* of a speaker who wields the authority to make his words binding, the legal incarnation of the divine utterance. And yet, if the judge is citing the law, he is not himself the authority who invests the law with its power to bind; on the contrary, he seeks recourse to an authoritative legal convention that precedes him. His discourse becomes a site for the reconstitution and resignification of the law. And yet the already existing law that he cites, from where does that law draw its authority? Is there an original authority, a primary source, or is it, rather, *in* the very practice of citation, potentially infinite in its regression, that the ground of authority is constituted as perpetual *deferral*? In other words, it is precisely through the infinite deferral of authority to an irrecoverable past that authority itself is constituted. That deferral is the repeated act by which legitimation occurs. The pointing to a ground which is never recovered becomes authority's groundless ground.[11]

Is "assuming" a sex like a speech act? Or is it, or is it like, a citational strategy or resignifying practice?

To the extent that the "I" is secured by its sexed position, this "I" and its "position" can be secured only by being *repeatedly* assumed, whereby "assumption" is not a singular act or event, but, rather, an iterable practice. If to "assume" a sexed position is to seek recourse to a legislative norm, as Lacan would claim, then "assumption" is a question of *repeating* that norm, citing or miming that norm. And a citation will be at once an interpretation of the norm and an occasion to expose the norm itself as a privileged interpretation.

This suggests that "sexed positions" are not localities but, rather, citational practices instituted within a juridical domain—a domain of constitutive constraints. The embodying of sex would be a kind of "citing" of the law, but neither sex nor the law can be said to preexist their various embodyings and citings. Where the law appears to predate its citation, that is where a given citation has become established as "the law." Further, the failure to "cite" or instantiate it correctly or completely would be at once the mobilizing condition of such a citation and its punishable consequence. Since the law must be repeated to remain an authoritative law, the law perpetually reinstitutes the possibility of its own failure.

The excessive power of the symbolic is itself *produced* by the citational instance by which the law is embodied. It is not that the symbolic law, the norms that govern sexed positions (through threats of punishment) are in themselves larger and more powerful than any of the imaginary efforts to identify with them. For how do we account for how the symbolic becomes invested with power? The imaginary practice of identification must itself be understood as a double movement: in citing the symbolic, an identification (re)invokes and (re)invests the symbolic law, seeks recourse to it as a constituting authority that precedes its imaginary instancing. The priority and the authority of the symbolic is, however, constituted *through* that recursive turn, such that citation, here as above, effectively brings into being the very prior authority to which it then defers. The subordination of the citation to its (infinitely deferred) origin is thus a ruse, a dissimulation whereby the prior authority proves to be *derived from* the contemporary instance of its citation. There is then no prior position which legislates, initiates, or motivates the various efforts to embody or instantiate that position; rather, that position is the fiction produced in the course of its instancings. In this sense, then, the instance produces the fiction of the priority of sexed positions.

The question suggested, then, by the above discussion of performativity is whether the symbolic is not precisely the kind of law to which the citational practice of sex refers, the kind of "prior" authority that is, in fact, produced as the effect of citation itself. And further, whether citation in this instance requires repudiation, takes place through a set of repudiations, invokes the heterosexual norm through the exclusion of contestatory possibilities.

If the figures of homosexualized abjection *must* be repudiated for sexed positions to be assumed, then the return of those figures as sites of erotic cathexis will refigure the domain of contested positionalities within the symbolic. Insofar as any *position* is secured through differentiation, none of these positions would exist in simple opposition to normative heterosexuality. On the contrary, they would refigure, redistribute, and resignify the constituents of that symbolic and, in this sense, constitute a subversive rearticulation of that symbolic.

Foucault's point in *The History of Sexuality, Volume One*, however, was even stronger: the juridical law, the regulative law, seeks to confine, limit, or prohibit some set of acts, practices, subjects, but in the process of articulating and elaborating that prohibition, the law provides *the discursive occasion* for a resistance, a resignification, and potential self-subversion of that law. Generally, Foucault understands the process of signification that governs juridical laws to exceed their putative ends; hence, a prohibitive law, by underscoring a given practice in discourse, produces the occasion for a public contest that may inadvertently enable, refigure, and proliferate the very social phenomenon it seeks to restrict. In his words, "In general, I would say that the interdiction, the refusal, the prohibition, far from being essential forms of power, are only its limits: the frustrated or extreme forms of power. The relations of power are, above all, productive."[12] In the case of sexuality, which is no ordinary instance, the prohibitive law runs the risk of eroticizing the very practices that come under the scrutiny of the law. The enumeration of prohibited practices not only brings such practices into a public, discursive domain, but it thereby produces them as potential erotic enterprises and so invests erotically in those practices, even if in a negative mode.[13] Further, prohibitions can themselves become objects of eroticization, such that coming under the censure of the law becomes what Freud called a necessary condition for love.[14]

In the above analysis of the symbolic, we considered that certain wayward identifications functioned within that economy as figures for the very punishments by which the assumption of sexed positions were compelled. The phallicized dyke and the feminized fag were two figures for this state of gender punishment, but there are clearly more: the lesbian femme who refuses men, the masculine gay man who challenges the presumptions of heterosexuality, and a variety of other figures whose characterizations by conventional notions of femininity and masculinity are confounded by their manifest complexity. In any case, the heterosexual presumption of the symbolic domain is that apparently inverted identifications will effectively and exclusively signal abjection *rather than* pleasure, or signal abjection without at once signaling the possibility of a pleasurable insurrection against the law or an erotic turning of the law against itself. The presumption is that the law will constitute sexed subjects along the heterosexual divide to the extent that its threat of punishment effectively instills fear, where the object of fear is figured by homosexualized abjection.

Importantly, the erotic redeployment of prohibitions and the production of new cultural forms for sexuality is not a transient affair within an imaginary domain that will inevitably evaporate under the prohibitive force of the symbolic. The resignification of gay and lesbian sexuality through and against abjection is itself an unanticipated reformulation and proliferation of the symbolic itself.

That this vision of a differently legitimated sexual future is construed by some as a merely vain imagining attests to the prevalence of a heterosexual psyche that wishes to restrict its homosexual fantasies to the domain of culturally impossible or transient dreams and fancies. Lacan provides that guarantee, preserving the heterosexism of culture through relegating homosexuality to the unrealizable life of passing fantasy. To affirm the unrealizability of homosexuality as a sign of weakness in that symbolic domain is, thus, to mistake the most insidious effect of the symbolic as the sign of its subversion. On the other hand, the entrance of homosexuality into the symbolic will alter very little if the symbolic itself is not radically altered in the course of that admission. Indeed, the legitimation of homosexuality will have to resist the force of normalization for a queer resignification of the symbolic to expand and alter the normativity of its terms.

POLITICAL AFFILIATION BEYOND THE LOGIC OF REPUDIATION

In this reformulation of psychoanalytic theory, sexed positions are themselves secured through the repudiation and abjection of homosexuality and the assumption of a normative heterosexuality. What in Lacan would be called "sexed positions," and what some of us might more easily call "gender," appears then to be secured through the depositing of non-heterosexual identifications in the domain of the culturally impossible, the domain of the imaginary, which on occasion contests the symbolic, but which is finally rendered illegitimate through the force of the law. What is then outside the law, before the law, has been relegated there by and through a heterosexist economy that disempowers contestatory possibilities by rendering them culturally unthinkable and unviable from the start. I have been referring to "normative" heterosexuality in the above because it is not always or necessarily the case that heterosexuality be rooted in such a full-scale repudiation and rejection of homosexuality.

The very logic of repudiation which governs and destabilizes the assumption of sex in this scheme presupposes a heterosexual relationality that relegates homosexual possibility to the transient domain of the imaginary. Homosexuality is not fully repudiated, because it is entertained, but it will always remain "entertainment," cast as the figure of the symbolic's "failure" to constitute its sexed subjects fully or finally, but also and always a subordinate rebellion with no power to rearticulate the terms of the governing law.

But what does it mean to argue that sexed positions are assumed at the price of homosexuality or, rather, through the abjection of homosexuality? This formulation implies that there is a linkage between homosexuality and abjection, indeed, a possible identification *with* an abject homosexuality at the heart of heterosexual identification. This economy of repudiation suggests that heterosexuality and homosexuality are mutually exclusive phenomena, that they can only be made to coincide through rendering the one culturally viable and the other a transient and imaginary affair. The abjection of homosexuality can take place only through an identification with that abjection, an identification that must be disavowed, an identification that one fears to make only because one has already made it, an identification that institutes that abjection and sustains it.

The response to this schema is not simply to proliferate "positions" within the symbolic, but, rather, to interrogate the exclusionary moves through which "positions" are themselves invariably assumed; that is, the acts of repudiation that enable and sustain the kind of normative "citing" of sexed positions suggested before. The logic of repudiation that governs this normativizing heterosexuality, however, is one that can govern a number of other "sexed positions" as well. Heterosexuality does not have a monopoly on exclusionary logics. Indeed, they can characterize and sustain gay and lesbian identity positions which constitute themselves through the production and repudiation of a heterosexual Other; this logic is reiterated in the failure to recognize bisexuality as well as in the normativizing interpretation of bisexuality as a kind of failure of loyalty or lack of commitment—two cruel strategies of erasure.

What is the economic premise operating in the assumption that one identification is purchased at the expense of another? If heterosexual identification takes place *not* through the refusal to identify as homosexual but *through* an identification with an abject homosexuality that must, as it were, never show, then can we extrapolate that normative subject-positions more generally depend on and are articulated through a region of abjected identifications? How does this work when we consider, on the one hand, hegemonic subject-positions like whiteness and heterosexuality and, on the other hand, subject-positions that either have been erased or have been caught in a constant struggle to achieve an articulatory status? Clearly, the power differentials by which such subjects are instituted and sustained are quite different. And yet, there is some risk that in making the articulation of a subject-position into *the* political task, some of the strategies of abjection wielded through and by hegemonic subject-positions have come to structure and contain the articulatory struggles of those in subordinate or erased positionalities.

Although gay and lesbian subjects do not wield the social power, the signifying power, to abject heterosexuality in an efficacious way (that reiteration cannot compare with the one which has regularized the abjection of homosexuality), there is nevertheless sometimes within the formation of gay and lesbian identity an effort to disavow a constitutive relationship to heterosexuality. This disavowal is enacted as a political necessity to *specify* gay and lesbian identity over and against its ostensible opposite, heterosexuality. This very disavowal, however, culminates paradoxically in a weakening of the very constituency it is meant to unite. Not only does such a strategy attribute a false unity to heterosexuality, but it misses the political opportunity to work the weakness in heterosexual subjectivation, and to refute the logic of mutual exclusion by which heterosexism proceeds. Moreover, a full-scale denial of that interrelationship can constitute a rejection of heterosexuality that is to some degree an identification *with* a rejected heterosexuality. Important to this economy, however, is the refusal to recognize this identification that is, as it were, already made, a refusal which absently designates the domain of a specifically gay melancholia, a loss which cannot be recognized and, hence, cannot be mourned. For a gay or lesbian identity-position to sustain its appearance as coherent, heterosexuality must remain in that rejected and repudiated place. Paradoxically, its heterosexual *remains* must be *sustained* precisely through the insistence on the seamless coherence of a specifically gay identity. Here it should become clear that a radical refusal to identify with a given position suggests that on some level an identification has already taken place, an identification that is made and disavowed, a disavowed identification whose symptomatic appearance is the insistence on, the overdetermination of, the identification by which gay and lesbian subjects come to signify in public discourse.

This raises the political question of the cost of articulating a coherent identity-position if that coherence is produced through the production, exclusion and repudiation of abjected spectres that threaten those very subject-positions? Indeed, it may be only by risking the *incoherence* of identity that connection is possible, a political point that correlates with Leo Bersani's insight that only the decentered subject is available to desire.[15] For what cannot be avowed as a constitutive identification of any given subject-position runs the risk of becoming not only externalized in a degraded form, but repeatedly repudiated and subjected to a policy of disavowal. To a certain extent constitutive identifications are precisely those which are always disavowed, for, contrary to Hegel, the subject cannot reflect on the entire process of its formation. But certain forms of disavowal do reappear as external and externalized figures of abjection who receive the repudiation of the subject time and again. It is this repeated repudiation by which the subject installs its boundary and constructs the claim to its "integrity" that concerns us here. This is not a buried identification that is left behind in a forgotten past, but an identification that must be leveled and buried again and again, the compulsive repudiation by which the subject incessantly sustains his/her boundary (this will guide our understanding of the operation by which both whiteness and heterosexuality are anxiously secured in Nella Larsen's *Passing* in chapter six).

The task is not, as a consequence, to multiply numerically subject-positions *within* the existing symbolic, the current domain of cultural viability, even as such positions are necessary in order to occupy available sites of empowerment within the liberal state—to become recipients of health care, to have partnerships honored legally, to mobilize and redirect the enormous power of public recognition. Occupying such positions, however, is not a matter of ascending to preexisting structural locales within a contemporary symbolic order; on the contrary, certain "occupations" constitute fundamental ways of rearticulating, in the Gramscian sense, possibilities of enunciation. In other words, it is not the case that a "subject-position" preexists the enunciation that it occasions, for certain kinds of enunciations dismantle the very "subject-positions" by which they are ostensibly enabled. There is no relation of radical exteriority between "position" and "enunciation"; certain claims extend the boundaries of the symbolic itself, produce a displacement within and of the symbolic, temporalizing the entire vocabulary of "position" and "structural place." For what do we make of the enunciation that *establishes* a position where there was none, or that marks the zones of exclusion and displacement by which available subject-positions are themselves established and stabilized?

To the extent that subject-positions are produced in and through a logic of repudiation and abjection, the specificity of identity is purchased through the loss and degradation of connection, and the map of power which produces and divides identities differentially can no longer be read. The multiplication of subject-positions along a pluralist axis would entail the multiplication of exclusionary and degrading moves that could only produce a greater factionalization, a proliferation of differences without any means of negotiating among them. The contemporary political demand on thinking is to map out the interrelationships that connect, without simplistically uniting, a variety of dynamic and relational posi-tionalities within the political field. Further, it will be crucial to find a way both to occupy such sites *and* to subject them to a democratizing contestation in which the exclusionary conditions of their production are perpetually reworked (even though they can never be fully overcome) in the direction of a more complex coalitional frame. It seems important, then, to question whether a political insistence on coherent identities can ever be the basis on which a crossing over into political alliance with other subordinated groups can take place, especially when such a conception of alliance fails to understand that the very subject-positions in question are themselves a kind of "crossing," are themselves the lived scene of coalition's difficulty. The insistence on coherent identity as a point of departure presumes that what a "subject" is is already known, already fixed, and that that ready-made subject might enter the world to renegotiate its place. But if that very subject produces its coherence at the cost of its own complexity, the crossings of identifications of which it is itself composed, then that subject forecloses the kinds of contestatory connections that might democratize the field of its own operation.

Something more is at stake in such a reformulation of the subject than the promise of a kinder, gentler psychoanalytic theory. The question here concerns the tacit cruelties that sustain coherent identity, cruelties that include self-cruelty as well, the abasement through which coherence is fictively produced and sustained. Something on this order is at work most obviously in the production of coherent heterosexuality, but also in the production of coherent lesbian identity, coherent gay identity, and within those worlds, the coherent butch, the coherent femme. In each of these cases, if identity is constructed through opposition, it is also constructed through rejection. It may be that if a lesbian opposes heterosexuality absolutely, she may find herself more in its power than a straight or bisex-ual woman who knows or lives its constitutive instability. And if butchness requires a strict opposition to femmeness, is this a refusal of an identifica-tion or is this an identification with femmeness that has already been made, made and disavowed, a disavowed identification that sustains the butch, without which the butch qua butch cannot exist?

The point here is not to prescribe the taking on of new and different identifications. I invest no ultimate political hope in the possibility of avowing identifications that have conventionally been disavowed. It is doubtless true that certain disavowals are fundamentally enabling, and that no subject can proceed, can act, without disavowing certain possibilities and avowing others. Indeed, certain kinds of disavowals function as constitutive constraints, and they cannot be willed away. But here a reformulation is in order, for it is not, strictly speaking, that a subject disavows its identifications, but, rather, that certain exclusions and foreclosures institute the subject and persist as the permanent or constitutive spectre of its own destabilization. The ideal of transforming all excluded identifications into inclusive features—of appropriating all difference into unity—would mark the return to a Hegelian synthesis which has no exterior and that, in appropriating all difference as exemplary features of itself, becomes a figure for imperialism, a figure that installs itself by way of a romantic, insidious, and all-consuming humanism.

But there remains the task of thinking through the potential cruelties that follow from an intensification of identification that cannot afford to acknowledge the exclusions on which it is dependent, exclusions that must be refused, identifications that must remain as refuse, as abjected, in order for that intensified identification to exist. This is an order of refusal which not only culminates in the rigid occupation of exclusionary identities, but which tends to enforce that exclusionary principle on whomever is seen to deviate from those positions as well.

To prescribe an exclusive identification for a multiply constituted subject, as every subject is, is to enforce a reduction and a paralysis, and some feminist positions, including my own, have problematically prioritized gender as the identificatory site of political mobilization at the expense of race or sexuality or class or geopolitical positioning/displacement.[16] And here it is not simply a matter of honoring the subject as a plurality of identifications, for these identifications are invariably imbricated in one another, the vehicle for one another: a gender identification can be made in order to repudiate or participate in a race identification; what counts as "ethnicity" frames and eroticizes sexuality, or can itself be a sexual marking. This implies that it is not a matter of relating race and sexuality and gender, as if they were fully separable axes of power; the pluralist theoretical separation of these terms as "categories" or indeed as "positions" is itself based on exclusionary operations that attribute a false uniformity to them and that serve the regulatory aims of the liberal state. And when they are considered analytically as discrete, the practical consequence is a continual enumeration, a multiplication that produces an ever-expanding list that effectively separates that which it purports to connect, or that seeks to connect through an enumeration which cannot consider the crossroads, in Gloria Anzaldúa's sense, where these categories converge, a crossroads that is not a subject, but, rather, the unfulfillable demand to rework convergent signifiers in and through each other.[17]

What appear within such an enumerative framework as separable categories are, rather, the conditions of articulation *for* each other: How is race lived in the modality of sexuality? How is gender lived in the modality of race? How do colonial and neo-colonial nation-states rehearse gender relations in the consolidation of state power? How have the humiliations of colonial rule been figured as emasculation (in Fanon), or racist violence as sodomization (JanMohammed); and where and how is "homosexuality" at once the imputed sexuality of the colonized, and the incipient sign of Western imperialism (Walter Williams)? How has the "Orient" been figured as the veiled feminine (Lowe, Chow); and to what extent has feminism pillaged the "Third World" in search of examples of female victimization that would support the thesis of a universal patriarchal subordination of women (Mohanty)?[18]

And how is it that available discursive possibilities meet their limit in a "subaltern feminine," understood as a catachresis, whose exclusion from representation has become the condition of representation itself (Spivak)? To ask such questions is still to continue to pose the question of "identity," but no longer as a preestablished position or a uniform entity; rather, as part of a dynamic map of power in which identities are constituted and/or erased, deployed and/or paralyzed.

The despair evident in some forms of identity politics is marked by the elevation and regulation of identity-positions *as* a primary political policy. When the articulation of coherent identity becomes its own policy, then the policing of identity takes the place of a politics in which identity works dynamically in the service of a broader cultural struggle toward the rearticulation and empowerment of groups that seeks to overcome the dynamic of repudiation and exclusion by which "coherent subjects" are constituted.[19]

None of the above is meant to suggest that identity is to be denied, overcome, erased. None of us can fully answer to the demand to "get over yourself!" The demand to overcome radically the constitutive constraints by which cultural viability is achieved would be its own form of violence. But when that very viability is itself the consequence of a repudiation, a subordination, or an exploitative relation, the negotiation becomes increasingly complex. What this analysis does suggest is that an economy of difference is in order in which the matrices, the crossroads at which various identifications are formed and displaced, force a reworking of that logic of non-contradiction by which one identification is always and only purchased at the expense of another. Given the complex vectors of power that constitute the constituency of any identity-based political group, a coalitional politics that requires one identification at the expense of another thereby inevitably produces a violent rift, a dissension that will come to tear apart the identity wrought through the violence of exclusion.

Doubtlessly crucial is the ability to wield the signs of subordinated identity in a public domain that constitutes its own homophobic and racist hegemonies through the erasure or domestication of culturally and politically constituted identities. And insofar as it is imperative that we insist upon those specificities in order to expose the fictions of an imperialist humanism that works through unmarked privilege, there remains the risk that we will make the articulation of ever more specified identities into the aim of political activism. Thus every insistence on identity must at some point lead to a taking stock of the constitutive exclusions that reconsolidate hegemonic power differentials, exclusions that each articulation was forced to make in order to proceed. This critical reflection will be important in order not to replicate at the level of identity politics the very exclusionary moves that initiated the turn to specific identities in the first place.

If through its own violences, the conceits of liberal humanism have compelled the multiplication of culturally specific identities, then it is all the more important not to repeat that violence without a significant difference, reflexively and prescriptively, within the articulatory struggles of those specific identities forged from and through a state of siege. That identifications shift does not necessarily mean that one identification is repudiated for another; that shifting may well be one sign of hope for the possibility of avowing an expansive set of connections. This will not be a simple matter of "sympathy" with another's position, since sympathy involves a substitution of oneself for another that may well be a colonization of the other's position *as* one's own. And it will not be the abstract

inference of an equivalence based on an insight into the partially constituted character of all social identity. It will be a matter of tracing the ways in
which identification is implicated in what it excludes, and to follow the lines
of that implication for the map of future community that it might yield.

4

GENDER IS BURNING: QUESTIONS
OF APPROPRIATION AND SUBVERSION

> We all have friends who, when they knock on the door and we ask, through the door, the question, "Who's there?," answer (since "it's obvious") "It's me." And we recognize that *"it is him," or "her"* [my emphasis].
> —Louis Althusser, "Ideology and Ideological State Apparatuses"

> The purpose of "law" is absolutely the last thing to employ in the history of the origin of law: on the contrary,...the cause of the origin of a thing and its eventual utility, its actual employment and place in a system of purposes, lie worlds apart; whatever exists, having somehow come into being, is again and again reinterpreted to new ends, taken over, transformed, and redirected.
> —Friedrich Nietzsche, *On the Genealogy of Morals*

In Althusser's notion of interpellation, it is the police who initiate the call or address by which a subject becomes socially constituted. There is the policeman, the one who not only represents the law but whose address "Hey you!" has the effect of binding the law to the one who is hailed. This "one" who appears not to be in a condition of trespass prior to the call (for whom the call establishes a given practice as a trespass) is not fully a social subject, is not fully subjectivated, for he or she is not yet reprimanded. The reprimand does not merely repress or control the subject, but forms a crucial part of the juridical and social *formation* of the subject. The call is formative, if not *per*formative, precisely because it initiates the individual into the subjected status of the subject.

Althusser conjectures this "hailing" or "interpellation" as a unilateral act, as the power and force of the law to compel fear at the same time that it offers recognition at an expense. In the reprimand the subject not only receives recognition, but attains as well a certain order of social existence, in being transferred from an outer region of indifferent, questionable, or impossible being to the discursive or social domain of the subject. But does this subjectivation take place as a direct effect of the reprimanding utterance or must the utterance wield the power to compel the fear of punishment and, from that compulsion, to produce a compliance and obedience to the law? Are there are other ways of being addressed and constituted by the law, ways of being occupied and occupying the law, that disarticulate the power of punishment from the power of recognition?

Althusser underscores the Lacanian contribution to a structural analysis of this kind, and argues that a relation of misrecognition persists between the law and the subject it compels.[1] Although he refers to the possibility of "bad subjects," he does not consider the range of *disobedience* that such an interpellating law might produce. The law might not only be refused, but it might also be ruptured, forced into a rearticulation that calls into question the monotheistic force of its own unilateral operation. Where the uniformity of the subject is expected, where the behavioral conformity of the subject is commanded, there might be produced the refusal of the law in the form of the parodic inhabiting of conformity that subtly calls into question the legitimacy of the command, a repetition of the law into hyperbole, a rearticulation of the law against the authority of the one who delivers it. Here the performative, the call by the law which seeks to produce a lawful subject, produces a set of consequences that exceed and confound what appears to be the disciplining intention motivating the law. Interpellation thus loses its status as a simple performative, an act of discourse with the power to create that to which it refers, and creates more than it ever meant to, signifying in excess of any intended referent.

It is this constitutive failure of the performative, this slippage between discursive command and its appropriated effect, which provides the linguistic occasion and index for a consequential disobedience.

Consider that the use of language is itself enabled by first having been *called a name*, the occupation of the name is that by which one is, quite without choice, situated within discourse. This "I," which is produced through the accumulation and convergence of such "calls," cannot extract itself from the historicity of that chain or raise itself up and confront that chain as if it were an object opposed to me, which is not me, but only what others have made of me; for that estrangement or division produced by the mesh of interpellating calls and the "I" who is its site is not only violating, but enabling as well, what Gayatri Spivak refers to as "an enabling violation." The "I" who would oppose its construction is always in some sense drawing from that construction to articulate its opposition;

further, the "I" draws what is called its "agency" in part through being implicated in the very relations of power that it seeks to oppose. To be *implicated* in the relations of power, indeed, enabled by the relations of power that the "I" opposes is not, as a consequence, to be reducible to their existing forms.

You will note that in the making of this formulation, I bracket this "I" in quotation marks, but I am still here. And I should add that this is an "I" that I produce here for you in response to a certain suspicion that this theoretical project has lost the person, the author, the life; over and against this claim, or rather, in response to having been called the site of such an evacuation, I write that this kind of bracketing of the "I" may well be crucial to the thinking through of the constitutive ambivalence of being socially constituted, where "constitution" carries both the enabling and violating sense of "subjection." If one comes into discursive life through being called or hailed in injurious terms, how might one occupy the interpellation by which one is already occupied to direct the possibilities of resignification against the aims of violation?

This is not the same as censoring or prohibiting the use of the "I" or of the autobiographical as such; on the contrary, it is the inquiry into the ambivalent relations of power that make that use possible. What does it mean to have such uses repeated in one's very being, "messages implied in one's being," as Patricia Williams claims, only to repeat those uses such that subversion might be derived from the very conditions of violation. In this sense, the argument that the category of "sex" is the instrument or effect of "sexism" or its interpellating moment, that "race" is the instrument and effect of "racism" or its interpellating moment, that "gender" only exists in the service of heterosexism, does *not* entail that we ought never to make use of such terms, as if such terms could only and always reconsolidate the oppressive regimes of power by which they are spawned. On the contrary, precisely because such terms have been produced and constrained within such regimes, they ought to be repeated in directions that reverse and displace their originating aims. One does not stand at an instrumental distance from the terms by which one experiences violation. Occupied by such terms and yet occupying them oneself risks a complicity, a repetition, a relapse into injury, but it is also the occasion to work the mobilizing power of injury, of an interpellation one never chose. Where one might understand violation as a trauma which can only induce a

destructive repetition compulsion (and surely this is a powerful consequence of violation), it seems equally possible to acknowledge the force
of repetition as the very condition of an affir-mative response to violation.
The compulsion to repeat an injury is not necessarily the compulsion to
repeat the injury in the same way or to stay fully within the traumatic orbit
of that injury. The force of repetition in language may be the paradoxical
condition by which a certain agency—not linked to a fiction of the ego as
master of circumstance—is derived from the *impossibility* of choice.

It is in this sense that Irigaray's critical mime of Plato, the fiction of the
lesbian phallus, and the rearticulation of kinship in *Paris Is Burning* might
be understood as repetitions of hegemonic forms of power which fail to
repeat loyally and, in that failure, open possibilities for resignifying the
terms of violation against their violating aims. Cather's occupation of the
paternal name, Larsen's inquiry into the painful and fatal mime that is
passing for white, and the reworking of "queer" from abjection to politicized affiliation will interrogate similar sites of ambivalence produced at
the limits of discursive legitimacy.

The temporal structure of such a subject is chiasmic in this sense: in
the place of a substantial or self-determining "subject," this juncture of
discursive demands is something like a "crossroads," to use Gloria
Anzaldúa's phrase, a crossroads of cultural and political discursive forces,
which she herself claims cannot be understood through the notion of the
"subject."[2] There is no subject prior to its constructions, and neither is the
subject determined by those constructions; it is always the nexus, the non-
space of cultural collision, in which the demand to resignify or repeat the
very terms which constitute the "we" cannot be summarily refused, but
neither can they be followed in strict obedience. It is the space of this
ambivalence which opens up the possibility of a reworking of the very
terms by which subjectivation proceeds—and fails to proceed.

AMBIVALENT DRAG

From this formulation, then, I would like to move to a consideration of the
film *Paris Is Burning*, to what it suggests about the simultaneous production and subjugation of subjects in a culture which appears to arrange
always and in every way for the annihilation of queers, but which nevertheless produces occasional spaces in which those annihilating norms, those

killing ideals of gender and race, are mimed, reworked, resignified. As much as there is defiance and affirmation, the creation of kinship and of glory in that film, there is also the kind of reiteration of norms which cannot be called subversive, but which lead to the death of Venus Xtravaganza, a Latina/preoperative transsexual, cross-dresser, prostitute, and member of the "House of Xtravanganza." To what set of interpellating calls does Venus respond, and how is the reiteration of the law to be read in the manner of her response?

Venus, and *Paris Is Burning* more generally, calls into question whether parodying the dominant norms is enough to displace them; indeed, whether the denaturalization of gender cannot be the very vehicle for a reconsolidation of hegemonic norms. Although many readers understood *Gender Trouble* to be arguing for the proliferation of drag performances as a way of subverting dominant gender norms, I want to underscore that there is no necessary relation between drag and subversion, and that drag may well be used in the service of both the denaturalization and reidealization of hyperbolic heterosexual gender norms. At best, it seems, drag is a site of a certain ambivalence, one which reflects the more general situation of being implicated in the regimes of power by which one is constituted and, hence, of being implicated in the very regimes of power that one opposes.

To claim that all gender is like drag, or is drag, is to suggest that "imitation" is at the heart of the *heterosexual* project and its gender binarisms, that drag is not a secondary imitation that presupposes a prior and original gender, but that hegemonic heterosexuality is itself a constant and repeated effort to imitate its own idealizations. That it must repeat this imitation, that it sets up pathologizing practices and normalizing sciences in order to produce and consecrate its own claim on originality and propriety, suggests that heterosexual performativity is beset by an anxiety that it can never fully overcome, that its effort to become its own idealizations can never be finally or fully achieved, and that it is consistently haunted by that domain of sexual possibility that must be excluded for heterosexualized gender to produce itself. In this sense, then, drag is subversive to the extent that it reflects on the imitative structure by which hegemonic gender is itself produced and disputes heterosexuality's claim on naturalness and originality.

But here it seems that I am obliged to add an important qualification: heterosexual privilege operates in many ways, and two ways in which it operates include naturalizing itself and rendering itself as the original and the norm. But these are not the only ways in which it works, for it is clear that there are domains in which heterosexuality can concede its lack of originality and naturalness but still hold on to its power. Thus, there are forms of drag that heterosexual culture produces for itself—we might think of Julie Andrews in *Victor, Victoria* or Dustin Hoffmann in *Tootsie* or Jack Lemmon in *Some Like It Hot* where the anxiety over a possible homosexual consequence is both produced and deflected within the narrative trajectory of the films. These are films which produce and contain the homosexual excess of any given drag performance, the fear that an apparently heterosexual contact might be made before the discovery of a nonapparent homosexuality. This is drag as high het entertainment, and though these films are surely important to read as cultural texts in which homophobia and homosexual panic are negotiated,[3] I would be reticent to call them subversive. Indeed, one might argue that such films are functional in providing a ritualistic release for a heterosexual economy that must constantly police its own boundaries against the invasion of queerness, and that this displaced production and resolution of homosexual panic actually fortifies the heterosexual regime in its self-perpetuating task.

In her provocative review of *Paris Is Burning,* bell hooks criticized some productions of gay male drag as misogynist, and here she allied herself in part with feminist theorists such as Marilyn Frye and Janice Raymond.[4] This tradition within feminist thought has argued that drag is offensive to women and that it is an imitation based in ridicule and degradation. Raymond, in particular, places drag on a continuum with cross-dressing and transsexualism, ignoring the important differences between them, maintaining that in each practice women are the object of hatred and appropriation, and that there is nothing in the identification that is respectful or elevating. As a rejoinder, one might consider that identification is always an ambivalent process. Identifying with a gender under contemporary regimes of power involves identifying with a set of norms that are and are not realizable, and whose power and status precede the identifications by which they are insistently approximated. This "being a man" and this "being a woman" are internally unstable affairs. They are always beset by ambivalence precisely because there is a cost in every identification, the loss of some other set of identifications, the forcible approximation of a norm one never chooses, a norm that chooses us, but which we occupy, reverse, resignify to the extent that the norm fails to determine us completely.

The problem with the analysis of drag as only misogyny is, of course, that it figures male-to-female transsexuality, cross-dressing, and drag as male homosexual activities—which they are not always—and it further diagnoses male homosexuality as rooted in misogyny. The feminist analysis thus makes male homosexuality *about* women, and one might argue that at its extreme, this kind of analysis is in fact a colonization in reverse, a way for feminist women to make themselves into the center of male homosexual activity (and thus to reinscribe the heterosexual matrix, paradoxically, at the heart of the radical feminist position). Such an accusation follows the same kind of logic as those homophobic remarks that often follow upon the discovery that one is a lesbian: a lesbian is one who must have had a bad experience with men, or who has not yet found the right one. These diagnoses presume that lesbianism is acquired by virtue of some failure in the heterosexual machinery, thereby continuing to install heterosexuality as the "cause" of lesbian desire; lesbian desire is figured as the fatal effect of a derailed heterosexual causality. In this framework, heterosexual desire is always true, and lesbian desire is always and only a mask and forever false. In the radical feminist argument against drag, the displacement of women is figured as the aim and effect of male-to-female drag; in the homophobic dismissal of lesbian desire, the disappointment with and displacement of men is understood as the cause and final truth of lesbian desire. According to these views, drag is nothing but the displacement and appropriation of "women," and hence fundamentally based in a misogyny, a hatred of women; and lesbianism is nothing but the displacement and appropriation of men, and so fundamentally a matter of hating men—misandry.

These explanations of displacement can only proceed by accomplishing yet another set of displacements: of desire, of phantasmatic pleasures, and of forms of love that are not reducible to a heterosexual matrix and the logic of repudiation. Indeed, the only place love is to be found is *for* the ostensibly repudiated object, where love is understood to be strictly produced through a logic of repudiation; hence, drag is nothing but the effect of a love embittered by disappointment or rejection, the incorporation of the Other whom one originally desired, but now hates. And lesbianism is nothing other than the effect of a love embittered by disappointment or rejection, and of a recoil from that love, a defense against it or, in the case of butchness, the appropriation of the masculine position that one originally loved.

This logic of repudiation installs heterosexual love as the origin and truth of both drag and lesbianism, and it interprets both practices as symptoms of thwarted love. But what is displaced in this explanation of displacement is the notion that there might be pleasure, desire, and love that is not solely determined by what it repudiates.[5] Now it may seem at first that the way to oppose these reductions and degradations of queer practices is to assert their radical specificity, to claim that there is a lesbian desire radically different from a heterosexual one, with *no* relation to it, that is neither the repudiation nor the appropriation of heterosexuality, and that has radically other origins than those which sustain heterosexuality. Or one might be tempted to argue that drag is not related to the ridicule or degradation or appropriation of women: when it is men in drag as women, what we have is the destabilization of gender itself, a destabilization that is denaturalizing and that calls into question the claims of normativity and originality by which gender and sexual oppression sometimes operate. But what if the situation is neither exclusively one nor the other; certainly, some lesbians have wanted to retain the notion that their sexual practice is rooted in part in a repudiation of heterosexuality, but also to claim that this repudiation does not account for lesbian desire, and cannot therefore be identified as the hidden or original "truth" of lesbian desire. And the case of drag is difficult in yet another way, for it seems clear to me that there is both a sense of defeat and a sense of insurrection to be had from the drag pageantry in *Paris Is Burning,* that the drag we see, the drag which is after all framed for us, filmed for us, is one which both appropriates and subverts racist, misogynist, and homophobic norms of oppression. How are we to account for this ambivalence? This is not first an appropriation and then a subversion. Sometimes it is both at once; sometimes it remains caught in an irresolvable tension, and sometimes a fatally unsubversive appropriation takes place.

Paris Is Burning (1991) is a film produced and directed by Jennie Livingston about drag balls in New York City, in Harlem, attended by, performed by "men" who are either African-American or Latino. The balls are contests in which the contestants compete under a variety of categories. The categories include a variety of social norms, many of which are established in white culture as signs of class, like that of the "executive" and the Ivy League student; some of which are marked as feminine, ranging from high drag to butch queen; and some of them, like that of the "bangie," are taken from straight black masculine street culture. Not all of the categories, then, are taken from white culture; some of them are replications of a straightness which is not white, and some of them are focused on class, especially those which almost require that expensive women's clothing be "mopped" or stolen for the occasion. The competition in military garb shifts to yet another register of legitimacy, which enacts the performative and gestural conformity to a masculinity which parallels the performative or reiterative production of femininity in other categories. "Realness" is not exactly a category in which one competes; it is a standard that is used to judge any given performance within the established categories. And yet what determines the effect of realness is the ability to compel belief, to produce the naturalized effect. This effect is itself the result of an embodiment of norms, a reiteration of norms, an impersonation of a racial and class norm, a norm which is at once a figure, a figure of a body, which is no particular body, but a morphological ideal that remains the standard which regulates the performance, but which no performance fully approximates.

Significantly, this is a performance that works, that effects realness, to the extent that it *cannot* be read. For "reading" means taking someone down, exposing what fails to work at the level of appearance, insulting or deriding someone. For a performance to work, then, means that a reading is no longer possible, or that a reading, an interpretation, appears to be a kind of transparent seeing, where what appears and what it means coincide. On the contrary, when what appears and how it is "read" diverge, the artifice of the performance can be read as artifice; the ideal splits off from its appropriation. But the impossibility of reading means that the artifice works, the approximation of realness appears to be achieved, the body performing and the ideal performed appear indistinguishable.

But what is the status of this ideal? Of what is it composed? What reading does the film encourage, and what does the film conceal? Does the denaturalization of the norm succeed in subverting the norm, or is this a denaturalization in the service of a perpetual reidealization, one that can only oppress, even as, or precisely when, it is embodied most effectively? Consider the different fates of Venus Xtravaganza. She "passes" as a light-skinned woman, but is—by virtue of a certain failure to pass completely—

clearly vulnerable to homophobic violence; ultimately, her life is taken presumably by a client who, upon the discovery of what she calls her "little secret," mutilates her for having seduced him. On the other hand, Willi Ninja can pass as straight; his voguing becomes foregrounded in het video productions with Madonna et al., and he achieves post-legendary status on an international scale. There is passing and then there is passing, and it is—as we used to say—"no accident" that Willi Ninja ascends and Venus Xtravaganza dies.

Now Venus, Venus Xtravaganza, she seeks a certain transubstantiation of gender in order to find an imaginary man who will designate a class and race privilege that promises a permanent shelter from racism, homophobia, and poverty. And it would not be enough to claim that for Venus gender is *marked by* race and class, for gender is not the substance or primary substrate and race and class the qualifying attributes. In this instance, gender is the vehicle for the phantasmatic transformation of that nexus of race and class, the site of its articulation. Indeed, in *Paris Is Burning*, becoming real, becoming a real woman, although not everyone's desire (some children want merely to "do" realness, and that, only within the confines of the ball), constitutes the site of the phantasmatic promise of a rescue from poverty, homophobia, and racist delegitimation.

The contest (which we might read as a "contesting of realness") involves the phantasmatic attempt to approximate realness, but it also exposes the norms that regulate realness as *themselves* phantasmatically instituted and sustained. The rules that regulate and legitimate realness (shall we call them symbolic?) constitute the mechanism by which certain sanctioned fantasies, sanctioned imaginaries, are insidiously elevated as the parameters of realness. We could, within conventional Lacanian parlance, call this the ruling of the symbolic, except that the symbolic assumes the primacy of sexual difference in the constitution of the subject. What *Paris Is Burning* suggests, however, is that the order of sexual difference is not prior to that of race or class in the constitution of the subject; indeed, that the symbolic is also and at once a racializing set of norms, and that norms of realness by which the subject is produced are racially informed conceptions of "sex" (this underscores the importance of subjecting the entire psychoanalytic paradigm to this insight).[6]

This double movement of approximating and exposing the phantasmatic status of the realness norm, the symbolic norm, is reinforced by the diagetic movement of the film in which clips of so-called "real" people moving in and out of expensive stores are juxtaposed against the ballroom drag scenes.

In the drag ball productions of realness, we witness and produce the phantasmatic constitution of a subject, a subject who repeats and mimes the legitimating norms by which it itself has been degraded, a subject founded in the project of mastery that compels and disrupts its own repetitions. This is not a subject who stands back from its identifications and decides instrumentally how or whether to work each of them today; on the contrary, the subject is the incoherent and mobilized imbrication of identifications; it is constituted in and through the iterability of its performance, a repetition which works at once to legitimate and delegitimate the realness norms by which it is produced.

In the pursuit of realness this subject is produced, a phantasmatic pursuit that mobilizes identifications, underscoring the phantasmatic promise that constitutes any identificatory move—a promise which, taken too seriously, can culminate only in disappointment and disidentification. A fantasy that for Venus, because she dies—killed apparently by one of her clients, perhaps after the discovery of those remaining organs—cannot be translated into the symbolic. This is a killing that is performed by a symbolic that would eradicate those phenomena that require an opening up of the possibilities for the resignification of sex. If Venus wants to become a woman, and cannot overcome being a Latina, then Venus is treated by the symbolic in precisely the ways in which women of color are treated. Her death thus testifies to a tragic misreading of the social map of power, a misreading orchestrated by that very map according to which the sites for a phantasmatic self-overcoming are constantly resolved into disappointment. If the signifiers of whiteness and femaleness—as well as some forms of hegemonic maleness constructed through class privilege—are sites of phantasmatic promise, then it is clear that women of color and lesbians are not only everywhere excluded from this scene, but constitute a site of identification that is consistently refused and abjected in the collective phantasmatic pursuit of a transubstantiation into various forms of drag, transsexualism, and uncritical miming of the hegemonic. That this fantasy involves becoming in part like women and, for some of the children, becoming like black women, falsely constitutes black women as a site of privilege; they can catch a man and be protected by him, an impossible

idealization which of course works to deny the situation of the great numbers of poor black women who are single mothers without the support of
men. In this sense, the "identification" is composed of a denial, an envy,
which is the envy of a phantasm of black women, an idealization that
produces a denial. On the other hand, insofar as black men who are queer
can become feminized by hegemonic straight culture, there is in the performative dimension of the ball a significant *reworking* of that feminization,
an occupation of the identification that is, as it were, *already* made between
faggots and women, the feminization of the faggot, the feminization of the
black faggot, which is the black feminization of the faggot.

The performance is thus a kind of talking back, one that remains
largely constrained by the terms of the original assailment: If a white
homophobic hegemony considers the black drag ball queen to be a
woman, that woman, constituted already by that hegemony, will become
the occasion for the rearticulation of its terms; embodying the excess of
that production, the queen will out-woman women, and in the process
confuse and seduce an audience whose gaze must to some degree be
structured through those hegemonies, an audience who, through the
hyperbolic staging of the scene, will be drawn into the abjection it wants
both to resist and to overcome. The phantasmatic excess of this production constitutes the site of women not only as marketable goods within
an erotic economy of exchange,[7] but as goods which, as it were, are also
privileged consumers with access to wealth and social privilege and
protection. This is a full-scale phantasmatic transfiguration not only of
the plight of poor black and Latino gay men, but of poor black women
and Latinas, who are the figures for the abjection that the drag ball scene
elevates as a site of idealized identification. It would, I think, be too simple to reduce this identificatory move to black male misogyny, as if that
were a discrete typology, for the feminization of the poor black man
and, most trenchantly, of the poor, black, gay man, is a strategy of abjection that is already underway, originating in the complex of racist,
homophobic, misogynist, and classist constructions that belong to larger
hegemonies of oppression.

These hegemonies operate, as Gramsci insisted, through *rearticulation*,
but here is where the accumulated force of a historically entrenched and
entrenching rearticulation overwhelms the more fragile effort to build an
alternative cultural configuration from or against that more powerful

regime. Importantly, however, that prior hegemony also works through and as its "resistance" so that the relation between the marginalized community and the dominative is not, strictly speaking, oppositional. The citing of the dominant norm does not, in this instance, displace that norm; rather, it becomes the means by which that dominant norm is most painfully reiterated as the very desire and the performance of those it subjects.

Clearly, the denaturalization of sex, in its multiple senses, does not imply a liberation from hegemonic constraint: when Venus speaks her desire to become a whole woman, to find a man and have a house in the suburbs with a washing machine, we may well question whether the denaturalization of gender and sexuality that she performs, and performs well, culminates in a reworking of the normative framework of heterosexuality. The painfulness of her death at the end of the film suggests as well that there are cruel and fatal social constraints on denaturalization. As much as she crosses gender, sexuality, and race performatively, the hegemony that reinscribes the privileges of normative femininity and whiteness wields the final power to *re*naturalize Venus's body and cross out that prior crossing, an erasure that is her death. Of course, the film brings Venus back, as it were, into visibility, although not to life, and thus constitutes a kind of cinematic performativity. Paradoxically, the film brings fame and recognition not only to Venus but also to the other drag ball children who are depicted in the film as able only to attain local legendary status while longing for wider recognition.

The camera, of course, plays precisely to this desire, and so is implicitly installed in the film as the promise of legendary status. And yet, is there a filmic effort to take stock of the place of the camera in the trajectory of desire that it not only records, but also incites? In her critical review of the film, bell hooks raises the question not only of the place of the camera, but also that of the filmmaker, Jennie Livingston, a white lesbian (in other contexts called "a white Jewish lesbian from Yale," an interpellation which also implicates this author in its sweep), in relation to the drag ball community that she entered and filmed. hooks remarks that,

> Jennie Livingston approaches her subject matter as an outsider looking in. Since her presence as white woman/lesbian filmmaker is "absent" from *Paris Is Burning,* it is easy for viewers to imagine that they are watching an ethnographic film documenting the life of

black gay "natives" and not recognize that they are watching a work shaped and formed from a perspective and standpoint specific to Livingston. By cinematically masking this reality (we hear her ask questions but never see her) Livingston does not oppose the way hegemonic whiteness "represents" blackness, but rather assumes an imperial overseeing position that is in no way progressive or counterhegemonic.

Later in the same essay, hooks raises the question of not merely whether or not the cultural location of the filmmaker is absent from the film, but whether this absence operates to form tacitly the focus and effect of the film, exploiting the colonialist trope of an "innocent" ethnographic gaze: "Too many critics and interviewers," hooks argues, "...act as though she somehow did this marginalized black gay subculture a favor by bringing their experience to a wider public. Such a stance obscures the substantial rewards she has received for this work. Since so many of the black gay men in the film express the desire to be big stars, it is easy to place Livingston in the role of benefactor, offering these 'poor black souls' a way to realize their dreams" (63).

Although hooks restricts her remarks to black men in the film, most of the members of the House of Xtravaganza, are Latino, some of whom are light-skinned, some of whom engage in crossing and passing, some of who only do the ball, some who are engaged in life projects to effect a full transubstantiation into femininity and/or into whiteness. The "houses" are organized in part along ethnic lines. This seems crucial to underscore precisely because neither Livingston nor hooks considers the place and force of ethnicity in the articulation of kinship relations.

To the extent that a transubstantiation into legendary status, into an idealized domain of gender and race, structures the phantasmatic trajectory of the drag ball culture, Livingston's camera enters this world as the promise of phantasmatic fulfillment: a wider audience, national and international fame. If Livingston is the white girl with the camera, she is both the object and vehicle of desire; and yet, as a lesbian, she apparently maintains some kind of identificatory bond with the gay men in the film and also, it seems, with the kinship system, replete with "houses," "mothers," and "children," that sustains the drag ball scene and is itself organized by it. The one instance where Livingston's body might be said to appear allegorically on camera is when Octavia St. Laurent is posing for the camera, as a moving model would for a photographer. We hear a voice tell her that she's terrific, and it is unclear whether it is a man shooting the film as a proxy for Livingston, or Livingston herself. What is suggested by this sudden intrusion of the camera into the film is something of the camera's desire, the desire that motivates the camera, in which a white lesbian phallically organized by the use of the camera (elevated to the status of disembodied gaze, holding out the promise of erotic recognition) eroticizes a black male-to-female transsexual—presumably preoperative—who "works" perceptually as a woman.

What would it mean to say that Octavia is Jennie Livingston's kind of girl? Is the category or, indeed, "the position" of white lesbian disrupted by such a claim? If this is the production of the black transsexual for an exoticizing white gaze, is it not also the transsexualization of lesbian desire? Livingston incites Octavia to become a woman for Livingston's own camera, and Livingston thereby assumes the power of "having the phallus," i.e., the ability to confer that femininity, to anoint Octavia as model woman. But to the extent that Octavia receives and is produced by that recognition, the camera itself is empowered as phallic instrument. Moreover, the camera acts as surgical instrument and operation, the vehicle through which the transubstantiation occurs. Livingston thus becomes the one with the power to turn men into women who, then, depend on the power of her gaze to become and remain women. Having asked about the transsexualization of lesbian desire, then, it follows that we might ask more particularly: what is the status of the desire to feminize black and Latino men that the film enacts? Does this not serve the purpose, among others, of a visual pacification of subjects by whom white women are imagined to be socially endangered?

Does the camera promise a transubstantiation of sorts? Is it the token of that promise to deliver economic privilege and the transcendence of social abjection? What does it mean to eroticize the holding out of that promise, as hooks asks, when the film will do well, but the lives that they record will remain substantially unaltered? And if the camera is the vehicle for that transubstantiation, what is the power assumed by the one who wields the camera, drawing on that desire and exploiting it? Is this not its own fantasy, one in which the filmmaker wields the power to transform what she records? And is this fantasy of the camera's power not directly counter to the ethnographic conceit that structures the film?

hooks is right to argue that within this culture the ethnographic conceit of a neutral gaze will always be a white gaze, an unmarked white gaze, one which passes its own perspective off as the omniscient, one which presumes upon and enacts its own perspective as if it were no perspective at all. But what does it mean to think about this camera as an instrument and effect of lesbian desire? I would have liked to have seen the question of Livingston's cinematic desire reflexively thematized in the film itself, her intrusions into the frame as "intrusions," the camera *implicated* in the trajectory of desire that it seems compelled to incite. To the extent that the camera figures tacitly as the instrument of transubstantiation, it assumes the place of the phallus, as that which controls the field of signification. The camera thus trades on the masculine privilege of the disembodied gaze, the gaze that has the power to produce bodies, but which is itself no body.

But is this cinematic gaze only white and phallic, or is there in this film a decentered place for the camera as well? hooks points to two competing narrative trajectories in the film, one that focuses on the pageantry of the balls and another that focuses on the lives of the participants. She argues that the spectacle of the pageantry arrives to quell the portraits of suffering that these men relate about their lives outside the ball. And in her rendition, the pageantry represents a life of pleasurable fantasy, and the lives outside the drag ball are the painful "reality" that the pageantry seeks phantasmatically to overcome. hooks claims that "at no point in Livingston's film are the men asked to speak about their connections to a world of family and community beyond the drag ball. The cinematic narrative makes the ball the center of their lives. And yet who determines this? Is this the way the black men view their reality or is this the reality that Livingston constructs?"

Clearly, this *is* the way that Livingston constructs their "reality," and the insights into their lives that we do get are still tied in to the ball. We hear about the ways in which the various houses prepare for the ball, we see "mopping," and we see the differences among those who walk in the ball as men, those who do drag inside the parameters of the ball, those who cross-dress all the time in the ball and on the street and, among the cross-dressers, those who resist transsexuality, and those who are transsexual in varying degrees. What becomes clear in the enumeration of the kinship system that surrounds the ball is not only that the "houses" and the "mothers" and the "children" sustain the ball, but that the ball is itself an occasion for the building of a set of kinship relations that manage and sustain those who belong to the houses in the face of dislocation, poverty, homelessness. These men "mother" one another, "house" one another, "rear" one another, and the resignification of the family through these terms is not a vain or useless imitation, but the social and discursive building of community, a community that binds, cares, and teaches, that shelters and enables. This is doubtless a cultural reelaboration of kinship that anyone outside of the privilege of heterosexual family (and those within those "privileges" who suffer there) needs to see, to know, and to learn from, a task that makes none of us who are outside of heterosexual "family" into absolute outsiders to this film. Significantly, it is in the elaboration of kinship forged through a resignification of the very terms which effect our exclusion and abjection that such a resignification creates the discursive and social space for community, that we see an appropriation of the terms of domination that turns them toward a more enabling future.

In these senses, then, *Paris Is Burning* documents neither an efficacious insurrection nor a painful resubordination, but an unstable coexistence of both. The film attests to the painful pleasures of eroticizing and miming the very norms that wield their power by foreclosing the very reverse-occupations that the children nevertheless perform.

This is not an appropriation of dominant culture in order to remain subordinated by its terms, but an appropriation that seeks to make over the terms of domination, a making over which is itself a kind of agency, a power in and as discourse, in and as performance, which repeats in order to remake—and sometimes succeeds. But this is a film that cannot achieve this effect without implicating its spectators in the act; to watch this film means to enter into a logic of fetishization which installs the ambivalence of that "performance" as related to our own. If the ethnographic conceit allows the performance to become an exotic fetish, one from which the audience absents itself, the commodification of heterosexual gender ideals will be, in that instance, complete. But if the film establishes the ambivalence of embodying—and failing to embody—that which one sees, then a distance will be opened up *between* that hegemonic call to normativizing gender and its critical appropriation.

SYMBOLIC REITERATIONS

The resignification of the symbolic terms of kinship in *Paris Is Burning* and in the cultures of sexual minorities represented and occluded by the film raises the question of how precisely the apparently static workings of the symbolic order become vulnerable to subversive repetition and resignification. To understand how this resignification works in the fiction of Willa Cather, a recapitulation of the psychoanalytic account of the formation of sexed bodies is needed. The turn to Cather's fiction involves bringing the question of the bodily ego in Freud and the status of sexual differentiation in Lacan to bear on the question of naming and, particularly, the force of the name in fiction. Freud's contention that the ego is always a bodily ego is elaborated with the further insight that this bodily ego is projected in a field of visual alterity. Lacan insists that the body as a visual projection or imaginary formation cannot be sustained except through submitting to the name, where the "name" stands for the Name of the Father, the law of sexual differentiation. In "The Mirror Stage," Lacan remarks that the ego is produced "in a fictional direction," that its contouring and projection are psychic works of fiction; this fictional directionality is arrested and immobilized through the emergence of a symbolic order that legitimates sexually differentiated fictions as "positions." As a visual fiction, the ego is inevitably a site of *méconnaissance*; the sexing of the ego by the symbolic seeks to subdue this instability of the ego, understood as an imaginary formation.

Here it seems crucial to ask where and how language emerges to effect this stabilizing function, particularly for the fixing of sexed positions. The capacity of language to fix such positions, that is, to enact its symbolic effects, depends upon the permanence and fixity of the symbolic domain itself, the domain of signifiability or intelligibility.[8] If, for Lacan, the name secures the bodily ego in time, renders it identical through time, and this "conferring" power of the name is derived from the conferring power of the symbolic more generally, then it follows that a crisis in the symbolic will entail a crisis in this identity-conferring function of the name, and in the stabilizing of bodily contours according to sex allegedly performed by the symbolic. *The crisis in the symbolic, understood as a crisis over what constitutes the limits of intelligibility, will register as a crisis in the name and in the morphological stability that the name is said to confer.*

The phallus functions as a synecdoche, for insofar as it is a figure of the penis, it constitutes an idealization and isolation of a body part and, further, the investment of that part with the force of symbolic law. If bodies are differentiated according to the symbolic positions that they occupy, and those symbolic positions consist in either having or being the phallus, bodies are thus differentiated and sustained in their differentiation by being subjected to the Law of the Father which dictates the "being" and "having" positions; men become men by approximating the "having of the phallus," which is to say they are compelled to approximate a "position" which is itself the result of a synecdochal collapse of masculinity into its "part" and a corollary idealization of that synecdoche as the governing symbol of the symbolic order. According to the symbolic, then, the assumption of sex takes place through an approximation of this synecdochal reduction. This is the means by which a body assumes sexed integrity as masculine or feminine: the sexed integrity of the body is paradoxically achieved through an identification with its reduction into idealized synecdoche ("having" or "being" the phallus). The body which fails to submit to the law or occupies that law in a mode contrary to its dictate, thus loses its sure footing—its cultural gravity—in the symbolic and reappears in its imaginary tenuousness, its fictional direction. Such bodies contest the norms that govern the intelligibility of sex.

Is the distinction between the symbolic and the imaginary a stable distinction? And what of the distinction between the name and the bodily ego? Does the name, understood as the linguistic token which designates sex, only work to *cover over* its fictiveness, or are there occasions in which *the fictive and unstable status of that bodily ego trouble the name, expose the name as a crisis in referentiality?* Further, if body parts do not reduce to their phallic idealizations, that is, if they become vectors for other sorts of phantasmatic investments, then to what extent does the synecdochal logic through which the phallus operates lose its differentiating capacity? In other words, the phallus itself presupposes the regulation and reduction of phantasmatic investment such that the penis is either idealized as the phallus or mourned as the scene of castration, and desired in the mode of an impossible compensation. If these investments are deregulated or, indeed, diminished, to what extent can having/being the phallus still function as that which secures the differentiation of the sexes?

In Cather's fiction, the name not only designates a gender uncertainty, but produces a crisis in the figuration of sexed morphology as well. In this sense, Cather's fiction can be read as the foundering and unraveling of the symbolic on its own impossible demands. What happens when the name and the part produce divergent and conflicting sets of sexual expectations? To what extent do the unstable descriptions of gendered bodies and body parts produce a crisis in the referentiality of the name, the name itself as the very fiction it seeks to cover? If the heterosexism of the Lacanian symbolic depends on a set of rigid and prescribed identifications, and if those identifications are precisely what Cather's fiction works through and against the symbolically invested name, then the contingency of the symbolic—and the heterosexist parameters of what qualifies as "sex"—undergo a rearticulation that works the fictive grounding of what only appears as the fixed limits of intelligibility.

Cather cites the paternal law, but in places and ways that mobilize a subversion under the guise of loyalty. Names fail fully to gender the characters whose femininity and masculinity they are expected to secure. The name fails to sustain the identity of the body within the terms of cultural intelligibility; body parts disengage from any common center, pull away from each other, lead separate lives, become sites of phantasmatic investments that refuse to reduce to singular sexualities. And though it appears that the normativizing law prevails by forcing suicide, the sacrifice of homosexual eroticism, or closeting homosexuality, the text exceeds the text, the life of the law exceeds the teleology of the law, enabling an erotic contestation and disruptive repetition of its own terms.

PART *two*

5

"DANGEROUS CROSSING":
WILLA CATHER'S MASCULINE NAMES

"Dangerous Crossing"; it's painted on signboards all over the world!
— Willa Cather, "Tom Outland's Story"

It is not easy to know how to read gender or sexuality in Willa Cather's fiction. Cather has appeared not to place herself in a legible relation to women or to lesbianism. For her reader, then, to place or affirm her with a name engages a certain violence against her texts, texts which have as one of their persistent features the destabilization of gender and sexuality through the name. At issue is how to read the name as a site of identification, a site where the dynamic of identification is at play, and to read the name as an occasion for the retheorization of cross-identification or, rather, the crossing that is, it seems, at work in every identificatory practice.

This question of how to read identification in relation to the fictional name is for the most part unproblematized in the reception of Cather. Some feminists have argued that she is a male-identified writer, one whose stories presume a masculine narrator or foreground a masculine protagonist. Feminist biographer Sharon O'Brien argues that Cather moves from an early male identification (when she calls herself "Will") to a female identification through the course of her literary production, and that the early Cather's loyalty to her father and uncle is replaced in time with a loyalty to and identification with her maternal forebears.[1] The intensification of this putative identificatory bond with her mother accounts for O'Brien's assertion that the trajectory of Cather's career can be read as a growing affirmation of herself not only as a woman, but as a woman writer. O'Brien traces this psychological shift by mobilizing the presumption that psychic identifications become legible through the characters that the author produces, that characters are the mimetic reflections of these identifications, and that identification is a sign of loyalty and affiliation rather than, say, unresolved aggression or, minimally,

ambivalence. Although O'Brien affirms the importance of Cather's lesbianism to her authorship, she does not consider the place of cross-identification in the articulation of that sexuality; indeed, she presumes that
lesbianism is not only the love of women, but the intensification of a
maternal identificatory bond. In the recent biography written by
Hermione Lee, however, cross-identification and cross-dressing become
part of the spectacle of the literary Cather, but cross-gendered identification is forcefully disengaged from the question of Cather's sexuality.[2]
Here it seems that cross-dressing and cross-writing are not to be read as
sexual enactments, but almost exclusively as a voluntarist production of a
spectacular self.

Eve Sedgwick offers a more complex reading of cross-identification in
Cather's novel *The Professor's House* (1925), in which a homoerotic relationship between two men is quite literally contained within the narrative frame
of a heterosexual family arrangement, arid almost to the point of death.[3]
According to Sedgwick, Cather makes two "cross-translations," one across
gender and another across sexuality" (68); Cather assumes the position of
men and that of male homosexuality. How are we to understand this
assumption; at what cost is it performed? Sedgwick writes: "what becomes
visible in this double refraction are the shadows of the brutal suppressions
by which a lesbian love did not in Willa Cather's time and culture freely
become visible as itself" (69). Here Sedgwick offers us the choice between a
refracted love, one which is articulated through a double-translation, and
one which has the possibility of a direct and transparent visibility, what she
refers to as "lesbian truths" which appear to exist prior to the possibility of
their constitution in a legitimating historical discourse (69).

And yet it is Sedgwick who also argues in *The Epistemology of the Closet*
that such absences, constituting the apparatus of the closet, are not only
the site of brutal suppressions, but persist in consequence of their prohibition as an array of indirections, substitutions, and textual vacillations that
call for a specific kind of reading.[4] In interpreting Cather to be performing
a translation into the masculine gender through the character of Tom
Outland in *The Professor's House*, Sedgwick overlooks another Tommy, the
one in 1896 who appears as a young woman, a tomboy to be precise, in
Cather's "Tommy the Unsentimental"; in that text the name does not reflect
a gender, but becomes the site of a certain crossing, a transfer of gender,
which raises the question of whether for Cather the name stages an

exchange of gender identifications that the substantializing of gender and sexuality conceal. The postulation of an original "truth" of lesbian sexuality which awaits its adequate historical representation presumes an ahistorical sexuality constituted and intact prior to the discourses by which it is represented. This speculation rests on a missed opportunity to read lesbian sexuality *as* a specific practice of dissimulation produced through the very historical vocabularies that seek to effect its erasure. The prohibition that is said to work effectively to quell the articulation of lesbian sexuality in Cather's fiction is, I would argue, precisely the occasion of its constitution and exchange. It is perhaps less that the legibility of lesbianism is perpetually endangered in Cather's text than that lesbian sexuality within the text is produced as a perpetual challenge to legibility. Adrienne Rich remarks on this challenge when she writes, "…for Willa Cather, lesbian—the marker is mute."[5] In this sense, the "refraction" that Sedgwick isolates in Cather is a sign of not only a violation of lesbianism, but the very condition and possibility of lesbianism as a refracted sexuality, constituted in translation and displacement. Within Cather's text, this sexuality never qualifies as a truth, radically distinct from heterosexuality. It is almost nowhere figured mimetically, but is to be read as an exchange in which sacrifice and appropriation converge, and where the name becomes the ambivalent site of this prohibited taking, this anguished giving away.

BURDENSOME NAMES

In 1918, Cather began her novel *My Ántonia* with a prologue in which an "I" emerges, a narrating figure, who is never introduced, indeed, never named.[6] This prologue is in fact called an "introduction," as if written by someone other than the author, perhaps as an introduction to the author himself, Jim Burden. This installation of Jim Burden as author takes place through the production and gradual effacement the anonymous "I" (1-2). Indeed, what Cather couples for us at the outset of her text is an anonymous narrator and a named one, two figures who coincide, indeed, who "are old friends," and who, within a single sentence, appear to traverse the conventions of past and present tense. "Last summer, in a season of intense heat, Jim Burden and I happened to be crossing Iowa on the same train." There is circumstance and already a question of crossing, and then the uncertainty repeats itself in the next sentence, which slides almost eerily from the certain present of the relationship to the question of whether it is only memory: "He and I are old friends, we grew up together in the same Nebraska town, and we had a great deal to say to one another."

The relationship, we learn, does not survive into the present tense where each lives in New York, and where Jim Burden appears to have a wife whom the anonymous narrator dislikes. This wife, we learn, is handsome but "unimpressionable," energetic, but "incapable of enthusiasm." But this figure who separates them is replaced in the course of the page by another who binds them: Ántonia, who Jim at the window appears to conjure from the burning landscape. The burning horizon resolves into a burning figure, a figure of desire who not only joins the "I" and "Jim," but becomes the occasion for the displacement of the "I" by Jim: "More than any other person we remembered, this girl seemed to mean to us the country, the conditions, the whole adventure of our childhood" (2). And it is, then, through the phantasmatic retrieval of Ántonia that Jim is said to renew a friendship with our nameless narrator, a friendship that the narrator, right before vanishing altogether, claims was invaluable. And this narrating "I," receding in accelerated fashion into an almost illegible anonymity, thus parallels the state of Nebraska, a receding perspective from the point of view of the train burning its way toward New York. The "I" dissimulated as fading horizon becomes the story's nonthematic condition; this condition is installed through the transferring of narrative authority from the shifting pronoun to the figure of Jim. And this transfer is thus the temporary resolution of the ambiguously referring "I" in and by a masculine figure supported by a masculine name, but a name, "Jim Burden," that announces the burdensome quality of carrying the weight of that resolution and whose capacity to refer will be intermittently disrupted by the trajectory of the narrative that it appears to ground. How are we to read this transfer of authority and desire in the name?

We might read the precipitating "I" of *My Ántonia* as a site in which the conventions of anonymity are negotiated with the conventions of traditional masculine authorship. This "I" is a receding mark, one which enacts the withdrawal into anonymity, a pronominal mark which comes to erase itself, thereby becoming the unspoken condition that reappears as a nonthematic textual disruption within the very matrix of heterosexual convention.

In giving over narrative authority, the "I" figures the ideal reader as one whose enjoyment is achieved through a displaced identification. Jim's passion for the figure of Ántonia is thus relayed to the "I" whose passion for her is reawakened through his: "I had lost sight of her altogether, but Jim had found her again after long years, and had renewed a friendship that meant a great deal to him. His mind was full of her that day. He made me see her again, feel her presence, revived all my old affection for her" (2). Here it is Jim's figuration of Ántonia that appears to be the occasion for the "I"'s desire, an enabling displacement that ostensibly transfers desire from him to the anonymous reader.

The passion of this nameless "I" thus appears to follow Jim's, and yet at the moment after this "I" narrates the "I"'s own affection, Jim speaks for the first time, assuming the authorial function that will become exclusively his in the course of the next two paragraphs and throughout the text that follows. Hence, the marking of the "I"'s desire, which is attributed to the power of Jim's phantasm, is thus directly eclipsed through the installation of Jim as the source and origin of the desirous revery that will constitute the text. Does Jim eclipse this desire, or is this an eclipse of the "I" which then carries, as it were, the burden of that "I"'s desire? When Jim speaks, it is a discourse without address, a revery indifferent to its listener, casting the once narrating "I" into the position of an impressionable reader within the text, but inadvertently strengthening the narrative authority of the text: "'From time to time I've been writing down what I remember about Ántonia,' he told me..." The "I" now functions as the vehicle of dictation, but here the "I," fully dissimulated as a citational strategy, records his speech, and thus confers an unmarked authority on that speech. As Jim appears to eclipse the "I" as the narrator, the "I" becomes the illegible condition of Jim's narration. His narration, on the other hand, is now a citation which thus acquires its origin and its ground retrospectively in the one who cites, the nameless one who, in the citing, or, rather, *as* the citing, is displaced in the act. Indeed, the anonymous narrator figures an ideal reader for this future text, and Jim advises this "I," in what may be the only occasion of direct address, that she/he "should certainly see it," referring to the text, a joke worthy of Kafka, casting the author as a wanting reader, denying the crossing of Jim with that self-sacrificial author and thereby producing Jim, the name, as the effect and token of that sacrifice. And yet, it is unclear whether Jim has taken the place of this narrator or whether the narrator now more fully possesses Jim, a possession which is enacted through the very logic of sacrifice.

We learn in the course of this introduction that another reason for the emotional distance between the anonymous narrator and Jim Burden is that Jim became legal counsel for one of the Western railways, and this seems to suggest that the anonymous narrator takes some distance from the law or is herself under a kind of censor. Jim, on the other hand, represents the law: his legal status returns at the end of the introduction when he arrives at the narrator's apartment with the manuscript encased in legal cover, wearing the stamp of the law, with Jim as the signatory, carrying the weight of legitimation. "Here is the thing about Ántonia." "I simply wrote down pretty much all that her name recalls to me": "I suppose it hasn't any form" he remarks, and then, "It hasn't any title either." And then in the presence of the narrator, Jim writes the title "Ántonia," erases it with a frown and, then, with "satisfaction," lays claim to the proper name: "My Ántonia," he writes (2).

Jim's title thus converges with Cather's, and the repetition displaces the act by which Jim appeared to have supplanted the narrator in the text. We know that this is, after all, Cather's text, which implies that she is perhaps the anonymous one who dictates what Jim narrates. Figured as an "impressionable" reader, an impressionability which recalls an idealized feminine reader, the one who receives and dictates the text written by a man, Cather first dissimulates through this feminine convention, then disappears in order finally to "possess" the text that she appears to give away. In other words, she stages the laying of the claim to authorial rights by transferring them to the one who represents the law, a transfer that, in its redoubling, is a kind of fraud, one which facilitates the claim to the text that she only appears to give away.

The false transfer is, I think, a recurring movement within her texts, a figure for the crossing of identification which both enables and conceals the workings of desire. This is a crossing that I will consider soon in the context of her short story "Tommy the Unsentimental" where identification is always an ambivalent process, a taking on of a position that is at once a taking over, a dispossession, and a sacrifice.[7] Indeed, this is a fraudulent gift, an apparent sacrifice, in which a feminine authorship appears to yield in favor of a masculine one, a signing-over that, I will try to show, resolves into an exacting exchange, and, in "Tommy the Unsentimental," becomes the production of a masculine debt. If Cather's texts often appear to idealize masculine authorship through a displaced identification, it may be that the displacement of identification is the very condition for the possibility of her fiction.

Jim's authorship is assumed only through a literal repetition of Cather's own title, which suggests that Cather in some sense retains the title in both its literary and legal terms and, therefore, retains the title to the authorship that is Jim's burden to carry. As a repetition and citation, Jim's authorship is thus understood to be derived, and the impressionable feminine listener retains full control. But what about the derived status of the fictional author is a burden? What is the weight or curse of this authorship? And what can we make of Jim as both Cather's designated representative and as emblem of the law, the force of prohibition which necessitates that very substitution?

Ántonia is Bohemian, and like other Bohemian girls in Cather's fiction, she belongs to the German-speaking communities derived from a land called "Bohemia" in the Austrian Empire who settled in Nebraska after the wars of 1848. The English term "bohemian" is traced to a French usage that began in the fifteenth century when gypsies, reputedly from Bohemia, started to arrive in western regions of Europe. In 1848, Thackeray began to transfer the sense of the term to anyone who is in exile within a given community; writing in *Vanity Fair*, he applied the term to young women who were considered "wild" and "roving." He applied the term again in the 1860s to refer to "literary gypseys," who, in a novel transposition of Civil War rhetoric, he described as "seceding" from conventionality. The term was subsequently extended to apply to anyone who holds contempt for social convention or, as the *OED* explains, "one who leads a free, vagabond, or irregular life."[8]

Ántonia is first introduced in Cather's text in a situation of linguistic exile and disorientation, full of hunger to learn English and, in particular, how names refer. When Ántonia meets Jim she touches his *shoulder* and asks, "Name? What Name?" (19) in order to know Jim's name, but also to signal the synecdochal collapse of Jim into his shoulder, the site on which burdens are carried. Ántonia then turns to trees and to the landscape, reiterating the question, "Name. What Name?" But no name appears to satisfy. How are we to read Ántonia's incessant pursuit of names which proliferate sites of linguistic dissatisfaction, as if what cannot be named or named with satisfaction exceeds every apparently satisfying act of nomination, as if Ántonia, rather than a name produced and possessed by Jim Burden, becomes herself a figure for an unmasterable excess produced by the conceits of nomination, one which proliferates into an infinite hunger for names that never quite satisfy.[9]

Jim tries to assuage this linguistic need by feeding Ántonia with English words. But this appropriation does not quite work, producing a situation that leads to greater confusion rather than the acquisition of conceptual mastery. Exploring what might be read as a figure for this misconnection, Jim and Ántonia encounter a "gravel bed" riddled with holes (31). Jim then reports what emerges from these gaps in the visible landscape: "I was walking backward, in a crouching position, when I heard Ántonia scream. She was standing opposite me, pointing behind me and shouting something in Bohemian. I whirled around, and there, on one of those dry gravel beds, was the biggest snake I had ever seen. He was sunning himself, after the cold night, and he must have been asleep when Ántonia screamed. When I turned, he was lying in loose waves, like a letter 'W.' He twitched and began to coil slowly. He was not merely a big snake, I thought—he was a circus monstrosity" (31). The truncated "W" introduces an abbreviated Willa into the text, and connects her with the loose waves of the letter, linking the question of grammatical morphology with the morphological figure of the snake that bears the movements of desire.[10] But this partial emergence from the hole, this breaking through of the supporting fiction of this narrative, can be only a "circus monstrosity," a spectacle, entertaining and terrifying.

Moreover, the emergence of the snake occasions a restaging of the splitting of the "I" from the "he," this time between the "I" of Jim and the "he" of the snake. Jim narrates the movements of the snake with a fascination and horror that puts into question the difference between them: "His abominable muscularity, his loathsome, fluid motion, somehow made me sick. He was as thick as my leg, and looked as if millstones couldn't crush the disgusting vitality out of him." In the figuring of Jim's leg as an instrument of disgusting vitality, the loathing of the snake is thus transferred to the narrative "I," presumably still Jim, who thereby figures his own body as an object of self-loathing and self-destruction. But because this "circus monstrosity" assumed the form of a "W," implicating yet cutting short, if not castrating, the monstrosity of Willa, who remains not quite named, exceeding and conditioning nomination in the text, it appears that the snake, not unlike Ántonia in the prologue, facilitates a transfer of egregious phallicism from Willa to that disgustingly vital leg that appears to belong to Jim, but that might equally well be construed as a free-floating limb of phantasmatic phallic transfer.

The terms of the analogy become increasingly unstable. The differentiating distance between Jim and the snake begins to close as Jim anticipates the snake: "now he would spring, spring his length." Yet it is not the snake who springs, but Jim, who then performs a veritable decapitation of the snake, preempting by enacting the very phallicism he fears: "I drove at his head with my spade, struck him fairly across the neck, and in a minute he was all about my feet in wavy loops" (32). Jim continues to beat the snake's "ugly head flat," but "his body kept on coiling and winding, doubling and falling back on itself." The snake thus resists Jim's murderous attempts, and this resistance can be read as the act by which the snake continues to signify in that doubling and winding way, like the letter "W," like the morphological movement of writing itself, another significant "W," which is, after all, that which sustains and produces Jim as its effect and which Jim is finally powerless to destroy. In this sense, Jim becomes the "circus monstrosity," and Willa and her potential monstrosity recede into the unobtrusive "W," the undulating movements of writing and, in particular, the winding, doubling, and falling back on itself that constitutes that abbreviated token of her signature. And "W" might also signify "woman," the term most fully dissimulated by Cather's narrator.[11]

The "W" is capitalized, suggesting a proper name. This "W" not only is a foreshortened Willa (one which she, earlier in her life, conventionally performed through taking on the name of "Will"), but enacts in advance the scene of castration/decapitation that Jim performs. As an abbreviation, it is clearly cut back, but this cutting back is also the condition of its dissimulating strategy or, rather, a specific kind of narrative that works with and against the prohibitions that would figure its own enabling sexuality as a masculinized monstrosity. Just as the "I" in the prologue recedes into the Nebraska landscape as Jim is installed in the first-person position, this cutting back of the proper name is the condition of the phantasmatic redistribution of the author-subject in and through the narrative. And it is not as if the narrative thus inversely represents the "I" who is dissimulated in its terms. On the contrary, the opacity of the "I" is the permanent condition of this redistribution. This is an "I" constituted in its opacity by the prohibition set against its desire, a prohibition that produces a set of narrative displacements that not only persistently raise the question of which name *could* satisfy, but which also effect the prohibition on the speaking of the name that could. Ántonia, the name that might be expected to satisfy, can be only the occasion to reiterate that displacement: "Name? What Name?"

Of course, it was in the prosecution of Oscar Wilde that homosexuality became associated with the unspoken and unspeakable name. The love that dare not speak its name becomes for Cather a love that proliferates names at the site of that nonspeaking, establishing a possibility for fiction as this displacement, reiterating that prohibition and at the same time *working, indeed, exploiting that prohibition for the possibilities of its repetition and subversion.*

The name thus functions as a kind of prohibition, but also as an enabling occasion. Consider that the name is a token of a symbolic order, an order of social law, that which legislates viable subjects through the institution of sexual difference and compulsory heterosexuality. In what ways can these institutions be worked against themselves to spawn possibilities that begin to question their hegemony?

In Lacan's *Seminar II*, he remarks that "naming constitutes a pact by which two subjects simultaneously come to an agreement to recognize the same object." This social function of the name is always to some extent an effort to stabilize a set of multiple and transient imaginary identifications, those that compose for Lacan the circuit of the ego, but not yet the subject within the symbolic. He writes, "If objects had only a narcissistic relationship with the subject," that is, if they were only sites for an imaginary and ecstatic identification, "they would only ever be perceived in a momentary fashion. The word, the word which names, is the identical" (169). The imaginary relation, the one constituted through narcissistic identification, is always tenuous precisely because it is an external object that is determined to be oneself; this failure to close the distance between the ego who identifies elsewhere and the elsewhere which is the defining site of that ego haunts that identification as its constitutive discord and failure. The name, as part of a social pact and, indeed, a social system of signs, overrides the tenuousness of imaginary identification and confers on it a social durability and legitimacy. The instability of the ego is thus subsumed or stabilized by a symbolic function, designated through the name: the "permanent appearance over time" of the human subject is, Lacan claims, "strictly only recognizable through the intermediary of the name. The name is the time of the object" (169).

It is this function of the name to secure the identity of the subject over time that Slavoj Žižek underscores in *The Sublime Object of Ideology* as the ideological dimension of the name. Žižek argues that what the philosopher Saul Kripke understands as the proper name's status as a rigid designator is parallel to this identity-conferring function of the name in Lacan.[12] For Žižek, the proper name elaborates no content; it is a function of speech that designates an identity without providing implicitly or explicitly any description of that identity. Like Lacan, Kripke understands the proper name to secure the identity of the object over time; the proper name is referential, and the identity to which it refers cannot be substituted for by any set of descriptions. Lacan's phrase might hold for Kripke as well: "The word, the word which names, is the identical."

Significantly, both Kripke and Lacan agree to hypostatize a *pact*, a social agreement that invests the name with its power to confer durability and recognizability on that which it names. And in both cases, it is always a social pact based on the Law of the Father, a patrilineal organization that implies that it is *patronymic* names that endure over time, as nominal zones of phallic control. Enduring and viable identity is thus purchased through subjection to and subjectivation by the patronym. But because this patronymic line can only be secured through the ritual exchange of women, there is required for women a certain shifting of patronymic alliance and, hence, a change in name. For women, then, propriety is achieved through having a changeable name, through the exchange of names, which means that the name is never permanent, and that the identity secured through the name is always dependent on the social exigencies of paternity and marriage. Expropriation is thus the condition of identity for women. Identity is secured precisely in and through the transfer of the name, the name as a site of transfer or substitution, the name, then, as precisely what is always impermanent, different from itself, more than itself, the non-self-identical.

Clearly, neither Žižek nor Kripke have this problematic in mind when the name is said to secure the permanence of that which it names. The changeableness of the feminine name is essential to the permanent appearance of the patronym, indeed, to the securing of an illusory permanence through a continuing patrilineality. Moreover, the proper name can be conceived as referential and *not* descriptive only to the extent that the social pact which confers legitimacy on the name remains uninterrogated for its masculinism and heterosexual privilege. Once the proper name is elaborated as a patronym, then it can be read as an abbreviation for a social pact or symbolic order that structures the subjects named through their position in a patrilineal social structure. The durability of the subject named is not, then, a function of the proper name, but a function of a patronym, the abbreviated instance of a hierarchical kinship regime.

The name as patronym does not only bear the law, but institutes the law. Insofar as the name secures and structures the subject named, it appears to wield the power of subjectivation: producing a subject on the basis of a prohibition, a set of laws that differentiates subjects through the compulsory legislation of sexed social positionalities. When Jim Burden writes on his legal portfolio the title of his writings, "My Ántonia," he couples the name with the possessive, rendering explicit what is usually implied by the missing patronym. His own patronym is itself the burden of the name, the burdensome investment that the patronym carries. This is not unlike Tom Outland of *The Professor's House*, whose patrilineage is unknown and whose last name substitutes a trope of exile and excess at the site where a patronymic token of social cohesion might be expected. The appropriation and displacement of the patronym in Cather displaces the social basis of its identity-conferring function and leaves the question of the referent open as a site of contested gendered and sexual meanings.

The title of Cather's short story "Tommy the Unsentimental," published in 1896, is itself an inversion of the title of J.M. Barrie's novel, *Sentimental Tommy*, signaling a certain inversion of Barrie's inversion, working a tradition of "inversion" against that of the sentimental novel and its associations with femininity.[13] Cather wrote her story about Tommy Shirley, a young woman whose very name inverts the patronymic expectation not only by placing the boy's name first, but by taking Charlotte Brontë's coinage of "Shirley" as a girl's name and coining it again as a patronym.[14] The terms "Tom" and "Tommy" had accrued a number of meanings by the time Cather used the name in her story.[15] Since the sixteenth century, "Tom" had functioned as a quasi-proper name for what is masculine, as in "Tom All-Thumbs" or "Tom True-Tongue." In the nineteenth century, "Tom" was also the name for a clown, for one who dissimulates or flatters (as in the racial marking of a "Tom" as in "Uncle Tom"), and also for a prostitute or for a girl who resists convention. These last two senses are related to the notion of the tomboy, a term reserved for boys in the sixteenth century, but which came to characterize girls in the seventeenth century, especially romping ones. Then, in the early nineteenth century, the physical wildness of the tomboy was associated with "women who trespass against the delicacy of their sex" (*OED*), and, by 1888, the tomboy became linked to those who show other girls "uncouth signs of affection." There were also Tommy shops in the 1860s in which wages for labor were paid in goods rather than money, "Tommy" being the name for such an exchange. And in 1895, it appears that the defiance of convention associated with female Toms—that is, tomboys and prostitutes—led the *Chicago Advance* to declaim, "A whole school of what has been humorously called erotic and tommyrotic realists [are]...asserting that progress in art requires the elimination of moral ideas."[16]

The history of these shifts resonates in the name, and Cather begins her story with a conversation in which two voices muse over the relative inabilities of a certain man. Names emerge in the course of the paragraph, but Tommy's gender is left unmarked, that is, she is assumed to be a man speaking within a heterosexual set of conventions. The conversation concerns Jessica's desire, whether she finds the man under consideration, Jay, reprehensible, and in the course of saying that she does, she suggests that she doesn't at all. At the end of the paragraph, Tommy turns away from her, "baffled" by the contradiction which appears to be her desire, but also by the toiletries that engage Jessica, toiletries that appear to constitute something like the epistemic limit to Tommy's comprehension of feminine conventions.

It is only at the outset of the next paragraph that what is not at all obvious is made disingenuously to appear as if it is: "Needless to say, Tommy was not a boy, although her keen gray eyes and wide forehead were scarcely girlish, and she had the lank figure of an active half-grown lad. Her real name is Theodosia, but during Thomas Shirley's frequent absences from the bank she had attended to his business and correspondence signing herself "T. Shirley," until everyone in Southdown called her 'Tommy'" (63).

The father is only present in this story as a name; in assuming his name, Tommy assumes and covers over his absent place. The name becomes not only a site of a (dissimulated) phantasmatic transfer of patrilineal authority, but this name, Thomas Shirley, performs the very inversion and appropriation that it masks. For this is not a simple identificatory loyalty of daughter to father, but an aggressive appropriation as well: the repetition of the name feminizes the patronym, positioning the masculine as subordinate, contingent, and subject to exchange. This is not a name that secures the singularity of identity over time, but, rather, it functions as a shifting vector of prohibition, propriety, and cross-gender appropriations.

The name takes the place of an absence, covers that absence, and reterritorializes that vacated position. Inasmuch as the name emerges as a site of loss, substitution, and phantasmatic identification, it fails to stabilize identity. The absence of Tommy's father necessitates that she sign in his place, appropriate his signature, which produces Tommy's fiscal authorship through the course of that displacement.[17] Inversions, however, do not stop there, for Tommy's identification is not without its costs. She is herself described as enormously fond of Jay Ellington Harper, but also as knowing that she is foolish for this fondness: "As she expressed it, she was not of his sort, and never would be." The seven Old Boys of the town, elders who are described as having "taken the place of Tommy's mother," appear to have this unspoken knowledge as well. And while they appear to trust her not to override her good sense and fall in with Jay, they are nevertheless distraught with what appears to be the other alternative, the one that makes itself apparent when Tommy returns from school in the East with Jessica in tow:

> The only unsatisfactory thing about Tommy's return was that she
> brought with her a girl she had grown fond of at school, a dainty,
> white, languid bit of a thing, who used violet perfumes and carried a
> sunshade. The Old Boys said it was a bad sign when a rebellious girl
> like Tommy took to being sweet and gentle to one of her own sex,
> the worst sign in the world [66].

Here the third person narrative voice and that of the Old Boys begin to merge, leaving imprecise who regards Jessica as a "languid bit of a thing." From the start, however, Tommy holds Jessica in contempt, and it appears that whatever the fondness between them, there is from the start a persistent repudiation—the working of prohibition in desire, the working of a prohibition in desire that necessitates the sacrifice of desire. Earlier

Tommy herself claims that it is difficult to find women with whom she could speak in Southdown, for they seem only to be concerned with "babies and salads"; and Miss Jessica's toiletries are an occasion for bafflement and a certain turning away. Jessica is devalued not only by the narrator and the Old Boys, but by Tommy herself; indeed, there is no textual evidence for this sweetness and kindness. Throughout the course of the story, Jessica becomes increasingly degraded by Tommy. The judgment of the Old Boys is reiterated as Tommy's own judgment; indeed, her degradation appears to be both the condition of Tommy's desire, the guarantor of that desire's transience, and the narrative grounds for the sacrifice of her that Tommy eventually enacts.

Jay Ellington appears to constitute his desire for Jessica on the occasion of Tommy's bringing her into town. Displaced at the bank by Tommy, who seems able to amass capital more effectively, Jay develops his interest in Jessica at the same time that he loses control over his bank's assets. His investors, the Bohemians again, arrive at the door one morning, and Jay wires Tommy to save the day. Significantly, Tommy has saved enough in her own bank to make the loan which will vouch for Jay's bank; she arrives with the cash and avoids a closing; she acts as his guarantor and his signatory. Indeed, Tommy now signs for both her father and Jay.

Jay is under siege by the Bohemians, and Tommy, sustaining some unspoken affiliation with them, has the peculiar power to turn back the demands that would deplete him of his resources. Tommy "saves" him, not only from losing the bank, but from losing Jessica as well. Tommy directs him to the place in the road where he left the girl, and advises him to leave quickly to retrieve her. In Cather's story, the success of capital appears to require the sacrifice of homosexuality or, rather, an exchange that Tommy enacts *of* homosexuality for capital, a self-absenting of Tommy's desire which acts as the guarantor for both the solvency of the bank and the future of normative heterosexuality. Tommy "saves" and fails to spend, holds back both money and desire, but enhances her credit, strengthening the power of her signature. What will be owed this name? And if Tommy sacrifices Jessica, what does she receive in return?

But before we consider this curious exchange, let us return to the triangular scene in which Jessica's desire becomes the site of a consequential speculation. In fact, her desire is figured as inscrutable, and although the story proceeds as if the reader will discover which one Jessica prefers, in an important way her desire is constituted as the effect of the exchange. One of the Old Boys describes the problem this way: "The heart of the cad [Jay] is gone out to the little muff, as is right and proper and in accordance with the eternal fitness of things. But there's the other girl who has the blindness that may not be cured, and she gets all the rub of it. It's no use, I can't help her…" (66) A year after the trial of Oscar Wilde in which the prosecution asks him whether he is guilty of "the love that dare not speak its name," Cather restages the grammatical cadence of that accusation in "the blindness that may not be cured." But Cather's restaging introduces an indeterminacy that the prosecutorial phrase clearly lacks. This is a blindness that may or may not be cured.[18] Tommy's desire is figured less as a fatality than as a wager, the outcome of which is uncertain. And that uncertainty is underscored by the phrase that is supposed to forecast Tommy's inevitable injury, but that also concedes the benefits of tribadic pleasure: after all, she "gets all the rub of it."

Jay sends a telegram asking Tommy to represent Jay to Tommy's father, but the father is, as if by definition, permanently absent, so Tommy ascends to his place. Tommy amasses the cash and mounts her bicycle, the only way to get to Jay's forsaken abode on time. Jessica begs to ride on the bike as well, and Tommy allows it, but then proceeds to ignore her and finally drives Jessica to the point of unendurable pain: "Jessica soon found that with the pedaling that had to be done there was little time left for emotion of any sort, or little sensibility for anything but the throbbing, dazzling heat that had to be endured…Jessica began to feel that unless she could stop and get some water she was not much longer for this vale of tears. She suggested this possibility to Tommy, but Tommy only shook her head, 'take too much time,' and bent over her handle bars, never lifting her eyes from the road in front of her" (68). If Jessica's desire were not already decided, Tommy's cycling becomes the argument by which Jessica's desire, if it was ever for Tommy, becomes successfully deflected:

> It flashed upon Miss Jessica that Tommy was not only very unkind, but that she sat very badly on her wheel and looked aggressively masculine and professional when she bent her shoulders and pumped like that. But just then Miss Jessica found it harder than ever to breathe, and the bluffs across the river began doing serpentines and skirt dances, and more important and personal considerations occupied the young lady.

Precisely at the moment when Miss Jessica, in what is described in terms nearly orgasmic, finds it harder than ever to breathe, she is propelled by that strength in Tommy that she does not like seeing, but one which she rides nevertheless to make the deflection away from her. Indeed, it is the strength of Tommy's movements which sustain and fuel that transport into visions of serpentine and skirt dances, a figure that embraces the masculine and feminine, reintroducing that roving phallus, in the service of a fantasy, not of Tommy, but presumably of Jay. Tommy's pedaling verges on a disclosure of a sexuality that is too graphic for Jessica to bear, an unseemly aggression that recalls the circus monstrosity of that W-shaped snake, a violence that is the verging on an explicitness that threatens to reverse the blindness that may not be cured. If this appearance of sexuality is figured as a kind of incurable blindness, is this a fatality vainly denied, or is it, rather, that which defines the margins of the visible, as that which is seen and denied at once? Does Cather bring us close enough to that visibility to disclose not the truth of that sexuality, but the cultural vacillations of vision through which that sexuality is constituted, the denial in which it thrives? And if Jessica cannot bear to see Tommy in that pumping posture, does Miss Jessica not typify a refusal to see that is attributed to lesbianism as the blindness to the eternal fitness of things that may not be cured, but that more properly characterizes the homophobic failure of vision which refuses to see what it sees, and then attributes that blindness to precisely what it itself refuses to see?[19]

Paradoxically, Jessica dismounts from physical duress, sending Tommy on to "save" Jay, constituting herself as a stranded commodity, which then conditions the exchange between Tommy and Jay over who will savor the phallic identification and who will get the girl. For it is here, in this story, a disjunctive relation in which having the phallus designates the sacrifice of desire, an equation that only works within the context of a homophobic economy of the law. Tommy's butch demeanor fails to install her in the heterosexual matrix that might legitimate and sustain her desire. The more efficacious Tommy becomes, the more she "approximates" the masculine position, the more her social castration is guaranteed. Thus, Tommy saves the bank; tells Jay that Jessica is waiting for him; takes up a position behind Jay's desk at the bank, the place of another always absent father, that is, the place of a paternal ideal for which no instance exists; and then does what fathers do and gives the girl away. Tommy thus presides over an exchange in which her sentimentality is sacrificed so that Jay may have his.

As if mocking Cather's efforts to construct the credible fiction of a man, Jay remarks to Tommy before leaving that "You almost made a man of even me." And as if warning against a reading that would reduce Jay to this masculine position, Tommy answers, "Well, I certainly didn't succeed" (70). After he is gone, Tommy picks up a white flower that Jay dropped and the text gestures toward a possible confession of sentiment. But which sentiment? This is an expectation of a confession that the text both produces and withdraws. The stray flower in Cather's stories becomes a motif that engages the conventions of the dandy. In 1905, Cather wrote "Paul's Case" in which gender-troubled Paul is said to wear a red carnation in his buttonhole: "This latter adornment the faculty [at his school] somehow felt was not properly significant of the contrite spirit befitting a boy under the ban of suspension."[20] In the appendix to Wilde's trial it is ascertained that in France homosexuals wear green carnations to signal their availability, and Wilde flagrantly allies himself with this practice in the wearing of such flowers himself. What does it mean that Jay both wears and drops a white flower? Is this a veiled allusion that not everyone can read? Or is it, in fact, the return of Jessica herself, described by the Old Boys as "a dainty white languid bit of a thing"? If so, how do we read the following: "[Tommy] picked it up and stood holding it a moment, biting her lip. Then she dropped it into the grate and turned away, shrugging her thin shoulders" (71). Jay might be read as a homonym for "J," which is also the foreshortened version of Jessica. It may be that Cather here abbreviates the grief over the loss of Jessica through the initial "J," the grammatical closet that both deflects and enables the moment of sentiment.

The final line appears then within quotation marks, restaging the degendered voice that opens the story: there is some question over who speaks it; whether it is a citation; whether it is credible, ironic, parodic; and to whom it is addressed: "They are awful idiots, half of them, and never think of anything beyond their own dinner. But O, how we do like 'em!" (71).

The "they" appears to be half of "them," and so it could be men or women; it could be men like Harper who don't think beyond the satisfactions of the moment and can't run banks, or it could be women who seem to think only about babies and salads. And who is the "we" who appears to like them? Is this women who like men, as the Old Boys claim is right according to the eternal fitness of things, or is this the moment of an identification with men in which women are constructed as those awful idiots who Tommys everywhere are condemned to love?

This is, after all, an unattributed citation with Tommy only implied as the speaker, implied—but at a distance: suspended graphically as its own paragraph, these words are the reassuring recirculation of locally iterable truths, what we might understand as the mutterings of the symbolic, mutterings in search of a subject to speak them.

The story begins with the citation of an ungendered set of voices, a conversation among voices in which the masculine object remains unanchored from any proper name, sliding it seems between Tommy and the unnamed "he." And it concludes, it seems, by rendering even that pronoun indefinite, a move that one might read as a retraction of lesbian truth or, to prefer Sedgwick's other terms, a refraction, a deferral of vision, not quite the blindness that may not be cured, but a deflection from figuration that enables precisely the sexuality it thematically forecloses.

Tommy is not left utterly bereft. She finances the bank and heterosexuality at once, providing the loan that puts both institutions in her debt. Banking on heterosexual desire as immediate consumption, Tommy excludes herself from the circuit of exchange and profits from the exchange that her exclusion enables. She is thus installed at the desk of the father, the director, but this position of idealized control is also at the same time a sacrifice of desire, achieved at the expense of desire, constituting Tommy as the expendable third in this triangle, the expenditure without which the heterosexual scene cannot take place, the site of its absenting mediation.[21]

The narrative trajectory of this story can be read as a kind of sacrifice, one that takes place for Tommy through the appropriation of the father's place; and if there is, to recall Sedgwick's phrase, a brutal suppression here, it is the reflexive sacrifice of desire, a double-directioned misogyny that culminates in the degradation of lesbian love. This may be the price of cross-identification when it becomes the strategy for the obliteration of desire, but perhaps most painfully, the price of identifying with the *place* of the father, when that name installs a prohibition, when that prohibition orchestrates both identification and the foreclosure of desire. Here "Tommy" becomes a name that refers to no thing, no identity, but to the incitement to appropriation and expropriation produced by the prohibition on homosexuality—the name, then, as a site in which what is taken is also given away, in which the impermanence of lesbian desire is institutionalized. And yet in making the loan to Jay, Tommy continues to save, becomes herself an offering of a future, awaiting a return, a future satisfaction, with no guarantee, but perhaps an expectation.

BODIES UNDER THE BAN OF SUSPENSION

To read Cather's text as a lesbian text is to initiate a set of complications that cannot be easily summarized, for the challenge takes place, often painfully, within the very norms of heterosexuality that the text also mocks. If what we might now be tempted to call "lesbian" is itself constituted in and through the discursive sites at which a certain transfer of sexuality takes place, a transfer which does not leave intact the sexuality that it transfers, then it is not some primary truth awaiting its moment of true and adequate historical representation and which in the meantime appears only in substitute forms. Rather, substitutability is a condition for this sexuality. It is doubtless with any, but here, it is the historically specific consequence of a prohibition on a certain naming, a prohibition against speaking the name of this love that nevertheless and insistently speaks through the very displacements that that prohibition produces, the very refractions of vision that the prohibition on the name engenders.

That the unspoken name produces, as it were, a refraction of vision in Cather suggests one way to read the relation between prohibition and the contouring and partitioning of bodies. Bodies appear as collections of parts, and parts appear invested with an almost autonomous significance, thus figurally thwarting the ideal integrity of the body, which appears to be a male body, but which also vacillates between genders at key moments. The introduction to schoolboy Paul in "Paul's Case" makes clear that he is a figure "under the ban of suspension." Suspended, then, but not quite expelled, Paul inhabits a temporary exteriority to the law; he is set into that exteriority by the law. But what is also "suspended" here is some decision about his status, an allegory of this fiction in which what Sedgwick calls Paul's liminal sexual and gender status remains in question. As he is called in front of the local school authorities, his clothes are described as not quite or, rather, no longer, fitting the body within, and this incommensurability between the body and its clothes is recapitulated in the unexpectedly "suave and smiling" demeanor of the body that suggests "something of the dandy about him," and in the "adornments," including the Wilde-reminiscent "carnation" which "the faculty somehow felt was not properly significant of the contrite spirit befitting a body under the ban of suspension" (149).

But what would "befit" this body and signify properly? If the unbefittingness of donning the red carnation under the ban of suspension suggests an improper kind of signifying, then perhaps that figure can be read as an allegory for the ensuing narrative. If the story is as much about the dandy as it is about the liminal zone in which the figure of the dandy also carries for Cather the liminal predicament of the lesbian, then we might read "Paul" less as a mimetic reflection of "boys at the time" than as a figure with the capacity to convey and confound what Sedgwick has described as the passages *across* gender and sexuality. But I would add that this "across" ought not to be read as a "beyond," that is, as a fictional transcendence of "women" or "lesbian" in order to animate a vicarious figure of the "male homosexual." For the figures of boys and men in Cather retain the residue of that crossing, and their often brilliant resistance to gender and sexual coherence results from the impossibility of making that "dangerous crossing"—to borrow a phrase from "Tom Outland's Story"—fully or finally.[22]

Considering the historical importance of "crossing" and "passing" for lesbians at the turn of the century—and Cather's own early penchant for pseudonymous writing—it may be that what we find in Cather is a narrative specification of that social practice, an authorial "passing" that succeeds only by producing the final indecipherability or irreducibility of the fictional directions that it mobilizes and sustains.[23] The "ban of suspension" under which Paul appears, then, puts into doubt to which gender and sexuality "Paul" refers, confounding a reading that claims to "settle" the question of which vectors of sexuality Paul embodies. As a figure, "Paul" becomes the site of that transference as well as the impossibility of its resolution into any of the gendered or sexual elements that it transfers.

Paul's body refuses to cohere in an ordinary sense, and the body parts which nevertheless hang together appear discordant precisely because of a certain happy and anxious refusal to assume the regulatory norm. Just as his coat in the first paragraph no longer fits, suggesting an appearance outgrown, even "frayed," Paul's body in the second paragraph is given only in parts, inhabited, separated from itself, and deprived by the "ban" under which he appears. He is "tall" and "thin," "with high cramped shoulders and a narrow chest" (149). A strain of feminizing "hysteria" is noted, but this highly symptomatic state does not, as one might expect, signify a somaticized consciousness seized by movements beyond its control. On the contrary, hysteria in this text is a kind of hyper-consciousness: "His eyes were remarkable for a certain hysterical brilliancy, and he used them in a conscious, theatrical sort of way, peculiarly offensive in a boy" (150). Here the offense is further elaborated as a kind of trickery or lying, in which the normative expectation of a heterosexual reading of Paul is thwarted by his own departure from that norm. The hysterical brilliancy is presumably inoffensive in women or, at least, expected, but that hysteria is theatricalized suggests a certain rehearsing of the feminine that is at once a distance from its place as a signifier of the unconscious. For this is a hysteria endowed with "will," and though those same eyes, "abnormally large," recall as well "an addiction to belladonna," they are somehow too theatrical, too full of "glassy glitter" for that to be true. If the drug, literally "beautiful woman," is the addiction that the large eyes recall, it may be that Paul both could not possibly be addicted to beautiful women and that the urgency of his desire recalls and refracts precisely the urgency of that desire for women which, also under the ban of suspension, might well be lesbian.

The "eyes" are, as it were, watched with such close scrutiny, appearing increasingly detached and detachable from a body that is otherwise composed of cramped shoulders, narrow chest, and a precocious tallness. The anonymous and watchful narrator of this story records for us the eyes which are "abnormally large" and thus participates in the very watchfulness it describes. The narration is a kind of hyper-consciousness, a magnified searching that scours every corner of these eyes, heightening the expectation of a final deciphering of "Paul" only to refuse that satisfaction. The "eyes" that watch are thus "mirrored" in the eyes that are delineated, but this "mirroring" is less an autobiographical confession than a reiteration of its deferral.

His body is watched by the narrator for signs, but the signs appear illegible. Although his teachers read his body as so many signs of impertinence, the narrator recapitulates these signs as arbitrary and confounding in the extreme: body parts appear to diverge and signify in stray and confounding directions, as if the center of this body does not hold: "He stood through [the inquisition] smiling, his pale lips parted over his white teeth. (His lips were continually twitching, and he had a habit of raising his eyebrows that was contemptuous and irritating to the last degree)" (150). At once voluntary and involuntary ("lips…twitching," "raising eyebrows," and, then, "fingers toyed with the buttons of his overcoat, and an occasional jerking of the other hand which held his hat"), like the oxymoron of a deliberate hysteria, Paul's body fractures in defense against the watching of his inquisitors. His features are thus both defense and anxiety, animated by a policing gaze that cannot fully control the body it seeks to regulate. Suggesting that the divergently signifying features are a kind of decoy and protection against an onslaught of inquisition, the narrator describes Paul's face as a kind of strategic battle: "his set smile did not desert him…" (151). As a tactical response to the regulatory law, Paul's gestures form against and through that law, complying with and escaping the norm at every opportunity: "Paul was always smiling, always glancing about him, seeming to feel that people might be watching him and trying to detect something" (151).

Like the gendered surface of Cather's own narrative, Paul's presentation is maddening precisely for the expectations that it defies. In describing Paul's "conscious expression" as "as afar as possible from boyish mirthfulness" (151), Cather suggests that the expression might correspond with boyish sadness or, equally, possible, with feminine guile. The latter reading gains some further credibility when that "expression" is said to be "usually attributed to insolence or 'smartness'"(151). Paul offers his enigmatic features in the place of a verbal response when the inquisitors seek to extract from him some confession of transgression. Asked whether a particular remark to a woman was polite or impolite, Paul refuses the choice, occupying the suspended zone of the law, neither conformity nor infraction.

"When he was told he could go, he bowed gracefully and went out. His bow was a like a repetition of the scandalous red carnation." His bow is scandalous, perhaps because it is after all a certain defiant raising of the ass, invitation to sodomy, that takes place precisely through the very "polite" convention of deferring to the law. What repeats here is a gesture that both covers and defers some allegedly criminal sexuality, that takes place against and through the law that produces that criminality.

When Paul flees to New York and takes up briefly with a young man from Yale—a certain sign of transient homosexuality even then—he occupies a room which remains imperfect until he has flowers brought up. This repetition of the scandalous red carnation appears momentarily free from the ban of suspension.

The flowers thus ready the scene for Paul's version of the mirror stage: "He spent nearly an hour in dressing, watching every stage of his toilet carefully in the mirror. Everything was quite perfect; he was exactly the kind of boy he had always wanted to be" (167). That Paul now assumes the place of the one who *watches* himself constitutes a displacement of the persecutorial "watchers" who hounded him in and from Pittsburgh. His pleasure is split between the watching and the mirror, the body idealized, projected, and bound within the circle of his own, projective desire. But the fantasy of radical self-origination cannot only be sustained at the price of debt, becoming an outlaw, and finally finding himself on the run. At the end of the story, carnations reappear, "their red glory over" (174), and Paul recognizes the "losing game...this revolt against the homilies by which the world is run." Here the homiletic utterance that concludes "Tommy the Unsentimental," that symbolic muttering to the effect that women just can't do without men because they sure do like 'em, carries the force of a prohibition, at once casual and deadly, that culminates in Paul's death. Before his jump in front of the train, however, the watching function is retaken by hounding and persecutorial figures; the consequent anxiety twists his body into diverging parts, as if his lips were seeking to abandon his teeth: "He stood watching the approaching locomotive, his teeth chattering, his lips drawn away from them in a frightened smile; once or twice he glanced nervously sidewise, as though he were being watched" (174).

Paul watches the persecutorial watcher, and in jumping before the train, destroys the "picture making mechanism," "the disturbing visions" at the same time that he releases his body into an orgiastic flight and relaxation: "He felt something strike his chest,—his body was being thrown swiftly through the air, on and on, immeasurably far and fast, while his limbs gently relaxed."

Released from prohibitive scrutiny, the body frees itself only through its own dissolution. The final figure of "Paul dropped back into the immense design of things" confirms the ultimate force of the law, but this force unwittingly sustains the eroticism it seeks to foreclose: is this his death or his erotic release? "Paul dropped back": ambiguously dropped by another and by himself, his agency arrested and perhaps, finally, yielded.

6

PASSING, QUEERING: NELLA LARSEN'S
PSYCHOANALYTIC CHALLENGE

> Can identity be viewed other than as a by-product of a manhandling
> of life, one that, in fact, refers no more to a consistent pattern of
> sameness than to an inconsequential process of otherness?
> —Trinh T. Minh-ha

A number of theoretical questions have been raised by the effort to
think the relationship between feminism, psychoanalysis, and race studies.
For the most part, psychoanalysis has been used by feminist theorists to
theorize sexual difference as a distinct and fundamental set of linguistic
and cultural relations. The philosopher Luce Irigaray has claimed that the
question of sexual difference is *the* question for our time.[1] This privileging
of sexual difference implies not only that sexual difference should be
understood as more fundamental than other forms of difference, but that
other forms of difference might be *derived* from sexual difference. This
view also presumes that sexual difference constitutes an autonomous
sphere of relations or disjunctions, and is not to be understood as articulated through or *as* other vectors of power.

What would it mean, on the other hand, to consider the assumption of
sexual positions, the disjunctive ordering of the human as "masculine" or
"feminine" as taking place not only through a heterosexualizing symbolic
with its taboo on homosexuality, but through a complex set of racial
injunctions which operate in part through the taboo on miscegenation.
Further, how might we understand homosexuality and miscegenation to
converge at and as the constitutive outside of a normative heterosexuality
that is at once the regulation of a racially pure reproduction? To coin
Marx, then, let us remember that the reproduction of the species will be
articulated as the reproduction *of* relations of reproduction, that is, as the
cathected site of a racialized version of the species in pursuit of hegemony through perpetuity, that requires and produces a normative heterosexuality in its service.[2] Conversely, the reproduction of heterosexuality will

take different forms depending on how race and the reproduction of race are understood. And though there are clearly good historical reasons for keeping "race" and "sexuality" and "sexual difference" as separate analytic spheres, there are also quite pressing and significant historical reasons for asking how and where we might read not only their convergence, but the sites at which the one cannot be constituted save through the other. This is something other than juxtaposing distinct spheres of power, subordination, agency, historicity, and something other than a list of attributes separated by those proverbial commas (gender, sexuality, race, class), that usually mean that we have not yet figured out how to think the relations we seek to mark. Is there a way, then, to read Nella Larsen's text as engaging psychoanalytic assumptions not to affirm the primacy of sexual difference, but to articulate the convergent modalities of power by which sexual difference is articulated and assumed?

Consider, if you will, the following scene from Nella Larsen's *Passing*[3] in which Irene descends the stairs of her home to find Clare, in her desirable way, standing in the living room. At the moment Irene lights upon Clare, Brian, Irene's husband, appears to have found Clare as well. Irene thus finds Clare, finds her beautiful, but at the same time finds Brian finding Clare beautiful as well. The doubling will prove to be important. The narrative voice is sympathetic to Irene, but exceeds her perspective on those occasions on which Irene finds speaking to be impossible.

> She remembered her own little choked exclamation of admiration, when, on coming downstairs a few minutes later than she had intended, she had rushed into the living room where Brian was waiting and had found Clare there too. Clare, exquisite, golden, fragrant, flaunting, in a stately gown of shining black taffeta, whose long, full skirt lay in graceful folds about her slim golden feet; her glistening hair drawn smoothly back into a small twist at the nape of her neck; her eyes sparkling like dark jewels [233].

Irene's exclamation of admiration is never voiced, choked back it seems, retained, preserved as a kind of seeing that does not make its way into speech. She would have spoken, but the choking appears to stifle her voice; what she finds is Brian waiting, Brian finding Clare as well, and Clare herself. The grammar of the description fails to settle the question of who desires whom: "she had rushed into the living room where Brian was waiting and had found Clare there too": is it Irene who finds Clare, or Brian, or do they find her together? And what is it that they find in her, such that they no longer find each other, but mirror each other's desire as each turns toward Clare. Irene will stifle the words which would convey her admiration. Indeed, the exclamation is choked, deprived of air; the exclamation fills the throat and thwarts her speaking. The narrator emerges to speak the words Irene might have spoken: "exquisite, golden, fragrant, flaunting." The narrator thus states what remains caught in Irene's throat, which suggests that Larsen's narrator serves the function of exposing more than Irene herself can risk. In most cases where Irene finds herself unable to speak, the narrator supplies the words. But when it comes to explaining exactly how Clare dies at the end of the novel, the narrator proves as speechless as Irene.

The question of what can and cannot be spoken, what can and cannot be publicly exposed, is raised throughout the text, and it is linked with the larger question of the dangers of public exposure of both color and desire. Significantly, it is precisely what Irene describes as Clare's flaunting that Irene admires, even as Irene knows that Clare, who passes as white, not only flaunts but hides—indeed, is always hiding *in* that very flaunting. Clare's disavowal of her color compels Irene to take her distance from Clare, to refuse to respond to her letters, to try to close her out of her life. And though Irene voices a moral objection to Clare's passing as white, it is clear that Irene engages many of the same social conventions of passing as Clare. Indeed, when they both meet after a long separation, they are both in a rooftop cafe passing as white. And yet, according to Irene, Clare goes too far, passes as white not merely on occasion, but in her life, and in her marriage. Clare embodies a certain kind of sexual daring that Irene defends herself against, for the marriage cannot hold Clare, and Irene finds herself drawn by Clare, wanting to be her, but also wanting her. It is this risk-taking, articulated at once as a racial crossing and sexual infidelity, that alternately entrances Irene and fuels her moral condemnation of Clare with renewed ferocity.

After Irene convinces herself that Brian and Clare are having an affair, Irene watches Clare work her seduction and betrayal on an otherwise unremarkable Dave Freeland at a party. The seduction works through putting into question both the sanctity of marriage and the clarity of racial demarcations:

> Scraps of their conversation, in Clare's husky voice, floated over to her: "…always admired you…so much about you long ago…everybody says so…no one but you…" And more of the same. The man hung rapt on her words, though he was the husband of Felise Freeland, and the author of novels that revealed a man of perception and a devastating irony. And he fell for such pishposh! And all because Clare had a trick of sliding down ivory lids over astonishing black eyes and then lifting them suddenly and turning on a caressing smile [254].

Here it is the trick of passing itself that appears to eroticize Clare, the covering over of astonishing black by ivory, the sudden concession of the secret, the magical transformation of a smile into a caress. It is the changeability itself, the dream of a metamorphosis, where that changeableness signifies a certain freedom, a class mobility afforded by whiteness that constitutes the power of that seduction. This time Irene's own vision of Clare is followed not only by a choking of speech, but by a rage that leads to the shattering of her tea cup, and the interruption of chatter. The tea spreads on the carpet like rage, like blood, figured as dark color itself suddenly uncontained by the strictures of whiteness: "Rage boiled up in her./There was a slight crash. On the floor at her feet lay the shattered cup. Dark stains dotted the bright rug. Spread. The chatter stopped. Went on. Before her. Zulena gathered up the white fragments" (254).

This shattering prefigures the violence that ends the story, in which Clare is discovered by Bellew, her white racist husband, in the company of African-Americans, her color "outed," which initiates her swift and quite literal demise: with Irene ambiguously positioned next to Clare with a hand on her arm, Clare falls from the window, and dies on the street below. Whether she jumped or was pushed remains ambiguous: "What happened next, Irene Redfield never afterwards allowed herself to remember. Never clearly. One moment Clare had been there, a vital glowing thing, like a flame of red and gold. The next she was gone" (271).

Prior to this moment, Bellew climbs the stairs to the Harlem apartment where the salon is taking place, and discovers Clare there; her being there is sufficient to convince him that she is black. Blackness is not primarily a visual mark in Larsen's story, not only because Irene and Clare are both light-skinned, but because what can be seen, what qualifies as a visible marking, is a matter of being able to read a marked body in relation to unmarked bodies, where unmarked bodies constitute the currency of normative whiteness. Clare passes not only because she is light-skinned, but because she refuses to introduce her blackness into conversation, and so withholds the conversational marker which would counter the hegemonic presumption that she is white. Irene herself appears to "pass" insofar as she enters conversations which presume whiteness as the norm without contesting that assumption. This dissociation from blackness that she performs through silence is reversed at the end of the story in which she is exposed to Bellew's white gaze in clear association with African-Americans. It is only on the condition of an association that conditions a naming that her color becomes legible. He cannot "see" her as black before that association, and he claims to her face with unrestrained racism that he would never associate with blacks. If he associates with her, she cannot be black. But if she associates with blacks, she becomes black, where the sign of blackness is contracted, as it were, through proximity, where "race" itself is figured as a contagion transmissable through proximity. The added presumption is that if he were to associate with blacks, the boundaries of his own whiteness, and surely that of his children, would no longer be easily fixed. Paradoxically, his own racist passion *requires* that association; he cannot be white without blacks and without the constant disavowal of his relation to them. It is only through that disavowal that his whiteness is constituted, and through the institutionalization of that disavowal that his whiteness is perpetually—but anxiously—reconstituted.[4]

Bellew's speech is overdetermined by this anxiety over racial boundaries. Before he knows that Clare is black, he regularly calls her "Nig," and it seems that this term of degradation and disavowal is passed between them as a kind of love toy. She allows herself to be eroticized by it, takes it on, acting as if it were the most impossible appellation for her. That he calls her "Nig" suggests that he knows or that there is a kind of knowingness in the language he speaks. And yet, if he can call her that and remain her husband, he cannot know. In this sense, she defines the fetish, an object of desire about which one says, "I know very well that this cannot be, but I desire this all the same," a formulation which implies its equivalence: "Precisely because this cannot be, I desire it all the more." And yet Clare is a fetish that holds in place both the rendering of Clare's blackness as an exotic source of excitation and the denial of her blackness altogether. Here the "naming" is riddled with the knowledge that he claims not to have; he notes that she is becoming darker all the time; the term of degradation permits him to see and not to see at the same time. The term sustains his desire as a kind of disavowal, one which structures not only the ambivalence in his desire for Clare, but the erotic ambivalence by which he constitutes the fragile boundaries of his own racial identity. To reformulate an earlier claim, then: although he claims that he would never associate with African-Americans, he requires the association and its disavowal for an erotic satisfaction that is indistinguishable from his desire to display his own racial purity.

In fact, it appears that the uncertain border between black and white is precisely what he eroticizes, what he needs in order to make Clare into the exotic object to be dominated.[5] His name, Bellew, like bellow, is itself a howl, the long howl of white male anxiety in the face of the racially ambiguous woman whom he idealizes and loathes. She represents the spectre of a racial ambiguity that must be conquered. But "Bellew" is also the instrument that fans the flame, the illumination that Clare, literally "light," in some sense *is*. Her luminescence is dependent on the life he breathes into her; her evanescence is equally a function of that power. "One moment Clare had been there, a vital glowing thing, like a flame of red and gold. The next she was gone./ There was a gasp of horror, and above it a sound not quite human, like a beast in agony. 'Nig! My God! Nig!'" Bellew bellows, and at that moment Clare vanishes from the window (271). His speech vacillates between degradation and deification, but opens and closes on a note of degradation. The force of that vacillation illuminates, inflames Clare, but also works to extinguish her, to blow her out. Clare exploits Bellew's need to see only what he wants to see, working not so much the appearance of whiteness, but the vacillation between black and white as a kind of erotic lure. His final naming closes down that vacillation, but functions also as a fatal condemnation—or so it seems.

For it is, after all, Irene's hand which is last seen on Clare's arm, and the narrator, who is usually able to say what Irene cannot, appears drawn into Irene's nonnarrativizable trauma, blanking out, withdrawing at the crucial moment when we expect to learn whose agency it was that catapulted Clare from the window and to her death below. That Irene feels guilt over Clare's death is not quite reason enough to believe that Irene pushed her, since one can easily feel guilty about a death one merely wished would happen, even when one knows that one's wish could not be the proximate cause of the death. The gap in the narrative leaves open whether Clare jumped,

Irene pushed, or the force of Bellew's words literally bellowed her out the window. It is, I would suggest, this consequential gap, and the triangulation that surrounds it, that occasions a rethinking of psychoanalysis, in particular, of the social and psychic status of "killing judgments." How are we to explain the chain that leads from judgment to exposure to death, as it operates through the interwoven vectors of sexuality and race?

Clare's fall: is this a joint effort, or is it at least an action whose causes must remain not fully knowable, not fully traceable? This is an action ambiguously executed, in which the agency of Irene and Clare is significantly confused, and this confusion of agency takes place in relation to the violating speech of the white man. We can read this "finale," as Larsen calls it, as rage boiling up, shattering, leaving shards of whiteness, shattering the veneer of whiteness. Even as it appears that Clare's veneer of whiteness is shattered, it is Bellew's as well; indeed, it is the veneer by which the white project of racial purity is sustained. For Bellew thinks that he would never associate with blacks, but he cannot be white without his "Nig," without the lure of an association that he must resist, without the spectre of a racial ambiguity that he must subordinate and deny. Indeed, he reproduces that racial line by which he seeks to secure his whiteness through producing black women as the necessary and impossible object of desire, as the fetish in relation to which his own whiteness is anxiously and persistently secured.

There are clearly risks in trying to think in psychoanalytic terms about Larsen's story, which, after all, published in 1929, belongs to the tradition of the Harlem Renaissance, and ought properly to be read in the context of that cultural and social world. Whereas many critics have read the text as a tragic story of the social position of the mulatto, others have insisted that the story's brilliance is to be found in its psychological complexity. It seems to me that perhaps one need not choose between the historical and social specificity of the novel, as it has been brought to light by Barbara Christian, Gloria Hull, Hazel Carby, Amritjit Singh, and Mary Helen Washington, on the one hand, and the psychological complexity of cross-identification and jealousy in the text as it has been discussed by Claudia Tate, Cheryl Wall, Mary Mabel Youmans, and Deborah McDowell.[6] Both Tate and McDowell suggest that critics have split over whether this story ought to be read as a story about race and, in particular, as part of the tragic genre of the mulatto, or whether it ought to be read as psychologically complex and, as both McDowell and Carby insist, an allegory of the difficulty of representing black women's sexuality precisely when that sexuality has been exoticized or rendered as an icon of primitivism. Indeed, Larsen herself appears to be caught in that very dilemma, withholding a representation of black women's sexuality precisely in order to avert the consequence of its becoming exoticized. It is this withholding that one might read in *Quicksand*, a novella published the year before *Passing*, where Helga's abstinence is directly related to the fear of being depicted as belonging to "the jungle." McDowell writes, "since the beginning of their 130-year history, black women novelists have treated sexuality with caution and reticence. This is clearly linked to the network of social and literary myths perpetuated throughout history about black women's libidinousness."[7]

The conflict between Irene and Clare, one which spans identification, desire, jealousy, and rage, calls to be contextualized within the historically specific constraints of sexuality and race which produced this text in 1929. And though I can only do that in a very crude way here, I would like briefly to sketch a direction for such an analysis. For I would agree with both McDowell and Carby not only that is it unnecessary to choose whether this novella is "about" race or "about" sexuality and sexual conflict, but that the two domains are inextricably linked, such that the text offers a way to read the racialization of sexual conflict.

Claudia Tate argues that "race...is not the novel's foremost concern" and that "the real impetus for the story is Irene's emotional turbulence" (142) and the psychological ambiguity that surrounds Clare's death. Tate distinguishes her own psychological account from those who reduce the novel to a "trite melodrama" (146) of black women passing for white. By underscoring the ambiguity of Clare's death, Tate brings into relief the narrative and psychic complexity of the novella. Following Tate, Cheryl Wall refuses to separate the psychological ambiguity of the story from its racial significance. Agreeing that "Larsen's most striking insights are into psychic dilemmas confronting certain black women," she argues that what appear to be "the tragic mulattoes of literary convention" are also "the means through which the author demonstrates the psychological costs of racism and sexism." For Wall, the figure of Clare never fully exists apart from Irene's own projections of "otherness" (108). Indeed, according to Wall, Irene's erotic relation to Clare participates in a kind of exoticism that is not fully different from Bellew's. Irene sees in Clare's seductive eyes "the unconscious, the unknowable, the erotic, and the passive," where, according to Wall, "[these] symbolize those aspects of the psyche Irene denies within herself" (108-109). Deborah McDowell specifies this account of psychological complexity and projection by underscoring the conflicted homoeroticism between Clare and Irene. McDowell writes, "though, superficially, Irene's is an account of Clare's passing for white and related issues of racial identity and loyalty, underneath the safety of that surface is the more dangerous story—though not named explicitly—of Irene's awakening sexual desire for Clare" (xxvi). Further, McDowell argues that Irene effectively displaces her own desire for Clare in her "imagination of an affair between Clare and Brian" (xxviii), and that in the final scene "Clare's death represents the death of Irene's sexual feelings, for Clare" (xxix).

To understand the muted status of homosexuality within this text—and hence the displacement, jealousy, and murderous wish that follow—it is crucial to situate this repression in terms of the specific social constraints on the depiction of black female sexuality mentioned above. In her essay, "The Quicksands of Representation," Hazel Carby writes,

> Larsen's representation of both race and class are structured through the prism of black female sexuality. Larsen recognized that the repression of the sensual in Afro-American fiction in response to the long history of the exploitation of black sexuality led to the repression of passion and the repression or denial of female sexuality and desire. But, of course, the representation of black female sexuality meant risking its definition as primitive and exotic within a racist society...Racist sexual ideologies proclaimed the black woman to be a rampant sexual being, and in response black women writers either focused on defending their morality or displaced sexuality onto another terrain [174].

McDowell, on the other hand, sees Larsen as resisting the sexual explicitness found in black female blues singers such as Bessie Smith and Ma Rainey (xiii), but nevertheless wrestling with the problem of rendering public a sexuality which thereby became available to an exoticizing exploitation.[8] In a sense, the conflict of lesbian desire in the story can be read in what is almost spoken, in what is withheld from speech, but which always threatens to stop or disrupt speech. And in this sense the muteness of homosexuality converges in the story with the illegibility of Clare's blackness.

To specify this convergence let me turn first to the periodic use of the term "queering" in the story itself, where queering is linked to the eruption of anger into speech such that speech is stifled and broken, and then to the scene in which Clare and Irene first exchange their glances, a reciprocal seeing that verges on threatening absorption. Conversations in *Passing* appear to constitute the painful, if not repressive, surface of social relations. It is what Clare withholds in conversation that permits her to "pass"; and when Irene's conversation falters, the narrator refers to the sudden gap in the surface of language as "queer" or as "queering." At the time, it seems, "queer" did not yet mean homosexual, but it did encompass an array of meanings associated with the deviation from normalcy which might well include the sexual. Its meanings include: of obscure origin, the state of feeling ill or bad, not straight, obscure, perverse, eccentric. As a verb-form, "to queer" has a history of meaning: to quiz or ridicule, to puzzle, but also, to swindle and to cheat. In Larsen's text, the aunts who raise Clare as white forbid her to mention her race; they are described as "queer" (189). When Gertrude, another passing black woman, hears a racial slur against blacks, Larsen writes, "from Gertrude's direction came a queer little suppressed sound, a snort or a giggle" (202)—something queer, something short of proper conversation, passable prose. Brian's longing to travel to Brazil is described as an "old, queer, unhappy restlessness" (208), suggesting a longing to be freed of propriety.

That Larsen links queerness with a potentially problematic eruption of sexuality seems clear: Irene worries about her sons picking up ideas about sex at school; Junior, she remarks, "'picked up some queer ideas about things—some things—from the older boys.' 'Queer ideas?' [Brian] repeated. 'D'you mean ideas about sex, Irene?'"Ye-es. Not quite nice ones, dreadful jokes, and things like that'" (219-220). Sometimes conversation becomes "queer" when anger interrupts the social surface of conversation. Upon becoming convinced that Brian and Clare are having an affair, Irene is described by Larsen this way: "Irene cried out: 'But Brian, I —' and stopped, amazed at the fierce anger that had blazed up in her./ Brian's head came round with a jerk. His brows lifted in an odd surprise./ Her voice, she realized *had* gone queer" (249). As a term for betraying what ought to remain concealed, "queering" works as the exposure within language—an exposure that disrupts the repressive surface of language—of both sexuality and race. After meeting Clare's husband on the street with her black friend Felise, Irene confesses that she has previously "passed" in front of him. Larsen writes, "Felise drawled: 'Aha! Been 'passing' have you? Well, I've queered that'" (259).

In the last instance, queering is what upsets and exposes passing; it is the act by which the racially and sexually repressive surface of conversation is exploded, by rage, by sexuality, by the insistence on color.

Irene and Clare first meet up after years apart in a café where they are both passing as white. And the process by which each comes to recognize the other, and recognize her as black is at once the process of their erotic absorption each into the other's eyes. The narrator reports that Irene found Clare to be "an attractive-looking woman...with those dark, almost black, eyes and that wide mouth like a scarlet flower against the ivory of her skin...a shade too provocative" (177). Irene feels herself stared at by Clare, and clearly stares back, for she notes that Clare "showed [not] the slightest trace of disconcertment at having been detected in her steady scrutiny." Irene then "feel(s) her color heighten under the continued inspection, [and] slid her eyes down. What she wondered could be the reason for such persistent attention? Had she, in her haste in the taxi, put her hat on back-wards?" From the start, then, Irene takes Clare's stare to be a kind of inspec-tion, a threat of exposure which she returns first as scrutiny and distrust only then to find herself thoroughly seduced: "She stole another glance. Still looking. What strange languorous eyes she had!" Irene resists being watched, but then falls into the gaze, averts the recognition at the same time that she "surrenders" to the charm of the smile.

The ambivalence wracks the motion of the narrative. Irene subse-quently tries to move Clare out of her life, refuses to answer her letters, vows not to invite her anywhere, but finds herself caught up by Clare's seduction. Is it that Irene cannot bear the identification with Clare, or is it that she cannot bear her desire for Clare; is it that she identifies with Clare's passing but needs to disavow it not only because she seeks to uphold the "race" that Clare betrays but because her desire for Clare will betray the family that works as the bulwark for that uplifted race? Indeed, this is a moral version of the family which opposes any sign of passion even within the marriage, even any passionate attachment to the children. Irene comes to hate Clare not only because Clare lies, passes, and betrays her race, but because Clare's lying secures a tentative sexual freedom for Clare, and reflects back to Irene the passion that Irene denies herself.

She hates Clare not only because Clare has such passion, but because Clare awakens such passion in Irene, indeed, a passion *for* Clare: "In the look Clare gave Irene, there was something groping, and hopeless, and yet so absolutely determined that it was like an image of the futile searching and firm resolution in Irene's own soul, and increased the feeling of doubt and compunction that had been growing within her about Clare Kendry." She distrusts Clare as she distrusts herself, but this groping is also what draws her in. The next line reads: "She gave in" (231).

When Irene can resist Clare, she does it in the name of "race," where "race" is tied to the DuBoisian notion of uplift and denotes an idea of "progress" that is not only masculinist but which, in Larsen's story, becomes construed as upward class mobility. This moral notion of "race" which, by the way, is often contested by the celebratory rhetoric of "color" in the text, also requires the idealization of bourgeois family life in which women retain their place in the family. The institution of the family also protects black women from a public exposure of sexuality that would be rendered vulnerable to a racist construction and exploitation. The sexuality that might queer the family becomes a kind of danger: Brian's desire to travel, the boys' jokes, all must be unilaterally subdued, kept out of public speech, not merely in the name of race, but in the name of a notion of racial progress that has become linked with class mobility, masculine uplift, and the bourgeois family. Ironically, Du Bois himself came to praise Larsen's *Quicksand* precisely for elevating black fiction beyond the kind of sexual exoticization that patrons such as Carl Van Vechten sought to promote.[9] Without recognizing that Larsen was struggling with the conflict produced, on the one hand, by such exotic and racist renderings and, on the other hand, by the moral injunctions typified by Du Bois, Du Bois himself praises her writings as an example of uplift itself.[10] And yet, one might argue that *Passing* exemplifies precisely the cost of uplift for black women as an ambiguous death/suicide, whereas *Quicksand* exemplifies that cost as a kind of death in marriage, where both stories resolve on the impossibility of sexual freedom for black women.[11]

What becomes psychically repressed in *Passing* is linked to the specificity of the social constraints on black women's sexuality that inform Larsen's text. If, as Carby insists, the prospect of black women's sexual freedom at the time of Larsen's writing rendered them vulnerable to public violations, including rape, because their bodies continued to be sites of conquest within white racism, then the psychic resistance to homosexuality and to a sexual life outside the parameters of the family must be read in part as a resistance to an endangering public exposure.

To the extent that Irene desires Clare, she desires the trespass that Clare performs, and hates her for the disloyalty that that trespass entails. To the extent that Irene herself eroticizes Clare's racial trespass and Clare's clear lack of loyalty for family and its institutions of monogamy, Irene herself is in a double bind: caught between the prospect of becoming free from an ideology of "race" uncritical in its own masculinism and classism, on the one hand, and the violations of white racism that attend the deprivatization of black women's sexuality, on the other. Irene's psychic ambivalence toward Clare, then, needs to be situated in this historical double-bind.[12] At the same time, we can see mapped within Larsen's text the incipient possibility of a solidarity among black women. The identification between Clare and Irene might be read as the unlived political promise of a solidarity yet to come.

McDowell points out that Irene imagines that Brian is with Clare, and that this imagining coincides with the intensification of Irene's desire *for* Clare. Irene passes her desire for Clare through Brian; he becomes the phantasmatic occasion for Irene to consummate her desire for Clare, but also to deflect from the recognition that it is *her* desire which is being articulated through Brian. Brian carries that repudiated homosexuality, and Irene's jealousy, then, can be understood not only as a rivalry with him for Clare, but the painful consequence of a sacrifice of passion that she repeatedly makes, a sacrifice that entails the displacement or rerouting of her desire through Brian. That Brian appears to act on Irene's desire (although this, importantly, is never confirmed and, so, may be nothing other than an imaginary conviction on Irene's part), suggests that part of that jealousy is anger that he occupies a legitimated sexual position from which he can carry out the desire which she invested in him, that he dares to act the desire which she relegated to him to act on. This is not to discount the possibility that Irene also desires Brian, but there is very little evidence of a passionate attachment to him in the text. Indeed, it is against his passion, and in favor of preserving bourgeois ideals that she clamors to keep him. Her jealousy may well be routed along a conventional heterosexual narrative, but—as we saw in Cather—that is not to foreclose the interpretation that a lesbian passion runs that course.

Freud writes of a certain kind of "jealousy" which appears at first to be the desire to have the heterosexual partner whose attention has wandered, but is motivated by a desire to occupy the place of that wandering partner in order to consummate a foreclosed homosexuality. He calls this a "delusional jealousy…what is left of a homosexuality that has run its course, and it rightly takes its position among the classical forms of paranoia. As an attempt at defence against an unduly strong homosexual impulse it may, in a man, be described in the formula: "*I* do not love him, *she* loves him!'"[13] And, in a woman and in *Passing*, the following formula might apply: "I, Irene, do not love her, Clare: he, Brian, does!"

It is precisely here, in accounting for the sacrifice, that one reformulation of psychoanalysis in terms of race becomes necessary. In his essay on narcissism, Freud argues that a boy child begins to love through sacrificing some portion of his own narcissism, that the idealization of the mother is nothing other than that narcissism transferred outward, that the mother stands for that lost narcissism, promises the return of that narcissism, and never delivers on that promise. For as long as she remains the idealized object of love, she carries his narcissism, she is his displaced narcissism, and, insofar as *she carries it*, she is perceived to *withhold it from him*. Idealization, then, is always at the expense of the ego who idealizes. The ego-ideal is produced as a consequence of being severed from the ego, where the ego is understood to sacrifice some part of its narcissism in the formation and externalization of this ideal.

The love of the ideal will thus always be ambivalent, for the ideal deprecates the ego as it compels its love. For the moment, I would like to detach the logic of this explanation from the drama between boy child and mother which is Freud's focus (not to discount that focus, but to bring into relief other possible foci), and underscore the consequence of ambivalence in the process of idealization. The one I idealize is the one who carries for me the self-love that I myself have invested in that one. And accordingly, I hate that one, for he/she has taken my place even as I yielded my place to him/her, and yet I require that one, for he/she represents the promise of the return of my own self-love. Self-love, self-esteem is thus preserved and vanquished at the site of the ideal.

How can this analysis be related to the questions concerning the racialization of sexuality I have tried to pose? The ego-ideal and its derivative, the super-ego, are regulatory mechanisms by which social ideals are psychically sustained. In this way, the social regulation of the psyche can be read as the juncture of racial and gendered prohibitions and regulations and their forced psychic appropriations. Freud argues speculatively that this ego-ideal lays the groundwork for the super-ego, and that the super-ego is lived as the psychic activity of "watching" and, from the perspective that is the ego, the experience of "being watched": "it (the super-ego) constantly watches the real ego and measures it by that (ego-) ideal." Hence, the super-ego stands for the measure, the law, the norm, one which is embodied by a fabrication, a figure of a being whose sole feature it is to watch, to watch in order to judge, as a kind of persistent scrutiny, detection, effort to expose, that hounds the ego and reminds it of its failures. The ego thus designates the psychic experience of being seen, and the super-ego, that of seeing, watching, exposing the ego. Now, this watching agency is not the same as the idealization which is the ego-ideal; it stands back both from the ego-ideal and the ego, and measures the latter against the former and always, always finds it wanting. The super-ego is not only the measure of the ego, the interiorized judge, but the activity of prohibition, the psychic agency of regulation, what Freud calls *conscience.*[14]

For Freud, this superego represents a norm, a standard, an ideal which is in part socially received; it is the psychic agency by which social regulation proceeds. But it is not just any norm; it is the set of norms by which the sexes are differentiated and installed. The super-ego thus first arises, says Freud, as a prohibition that regulates sexuality in the service of producing socially ideal "men" and "women." This is the point at which Lacan intervened in order to develop his notion of the symbolic, the set of laws conveyed by language itself which compel conformity to notions of "masculinity" and "femininity." And many psychoanalytic feminists have taken this claim as a point of departure for their own work. They have claimed in various ways that sexual difference is as primary as language, that there is no speaking, no writing, without the presupposition of sexual difference. And this has led to a second claim which I want to contest, namely, that sexual difference is more primary or more fundamental than other kinds of differences, including racial difference. It is this assertion of the priority of sexual difference over racial difference that has marked so much psychoanalytic feminism as white, for the assumption here is not only that sexual difference is more fundamental, but that there is a relationship called "sexual difference" that is itself unmarked by race. That whiteness is not understood by such a perspective as a racial category is clear; it is yet another power that need not speak its name. Hence, to claim that sexual difference is more fundamental than racial difference is effectively to assume that sexual difference is white sexual difference, and that whiteness is not a form of racial difference.

Within Lacanian terms, the ideals or norms that are conveyed in language are the ideals or norms that govern sexual difference, and that go under the name of the symbolic. But what requires radical rethinking is what social relations compose this domain of the symbolic, what convergent set of historical formations of racialized gender, of gendered race, of the sexualization of racial ideals, or the racialization of gender norms, makes up both the social regulation of sexuality and its psychic articulations. If, as Norma Alarcón has insisted, women of color are "multiply interpellated," called by many names, constituted in and by that multiple calling, then this implies that the symbolic domain, the domain of socially instituted norms, is composed of *racializing norms*, and that they exist not merely alongside gender norms, but are articulated through one another.[15] Hence, it is no longer possible to make sexual difference prior to racial difference or, for that matter, to make them into fully separable axes of social regulation and power.

In some ways, this is precisely the challenge to psychoanalysis that Nella Larsen offers in *Passing*. And here is where I would follow Barbara Christian's advice to consider literary narrative as a place where theory takes place,[16] and would simply add that I take Larsen's *Passing* to be in part a theorization of desire, displacement, and jealous rage that has significant implications for rewriting psychoanalytic theory in ways that explicitly come to terms with race. If the watching agency described by Freud is figured as a watching judge, a judge who embodies a set of ideals, and if those ideals are to some large degree socially instituted and maintained, then this watching agency is the means by which social norms sear the psyche, expose it to a condemnation that can lead to suicide. Indeed, Freud remarked that the superego, if left fully unrestrained, will fully deprive the ego of its desire, a deprivation which is psychic death, and which Freud claims leads to suicide. If we rethink Freud's "super-ego" as the psychic force of social regulation, and we rethink social regulation in terms which include vectors of power such as gender and race, then it should be possible to articulate the psyche politically in ways which have consequences for social survival.

For Clare, it seems, cannot survive, and her death marks the success of a certain symbolic ordering of gender, sexuality and race, as it marks as well the sites of potential resistance. It may be that as Zulena, Irene's black servant, picks up the shattered whiteness of the broken tea cup, she opens the question of what will be made of such shards. We might read a text such as Toni Morrison's *Sula* as the piecing together of the shattered whiteness that composes the remains of both Clare and Irene in Nella Larsen's text, rewriting Clare as Sula, and Irene as Nel, refiguring that lethal identification between them as the promise of connection in Nel's final call: "girl, girl, girlgirlgirl."[17]

At the close of Larsen's *Passing*, it is Bellew who climbs the stairs and "sees" Clare, takes the measure of her blackness against the ideal of whiteness and finds her wanting. Although Clare has said that she longs for the exposure in order to become free of him, she is also attached to him and his norm for her economic well-being, and it is no accident—even if it is figured as one—that the exposure of her color leads straightway to her death, the literalization of a "social death." Irene, as well, does not want Clare free, not only because Irene might lose Brian, but because she must halt Clare's sexual freedom to halt her own. Claudia Tate argues that the final action is importantly ambiguous, that it constitutes a "psychological death" for Irene just as it literalizes death for Clare. Irene appears to offer a helping hand to Clare who somehow passes out the window to her death. Here, as Henry Louis Gates, Jr. suggests, passing carries the double meaning of crossing the color line and crossing over into death: passing as a kind of passing on.[18]

If Irene turns on Clare to contain Clare's sexuality, as she has turned on and extinguished her own passion, she does this under the eyes of the bellowing white man; his speech, his exposure, his watching divides them against each other. In this sense, Bellew speaks the force of the regulatory norm of whiteness, but Irene identifies with that condemnatory judgment. Clare is the promise of freedom at too high a price, both to Irene and to herself. It is not precisely Clare's race that is "exposed," but blackness itself is produced as marked and marred, a public sign of particularity in the service of the dissimulated universality of whiteness. If Clare betrays Bellew, it is in part because she turns the power of dissimulation against her white husband, and her betrayal of him, at once a sexual betrayal, undermines the reproductive aspirations of white racial purity, exposing the tenuous borders that that purity requires. If Bellew anxiously reproduces white racial purity, he produces the prohibition against miscegenation by which that purity is guaranteed, a prohibition that requires strictures of heterosexuality, sexual fidelity, and monogamy. And if Irene seeks to sustain the black family at the expense of passion and in the name of uplift, she does it in part to avert the position for black women outside the family, that of being sexually degraded and endangered by the very terms of white masculinism that Bellew represents (for instance, she tells Clare not to come to the dance for the Negro Welfare Fund alone, that she'll be taken as a prostitute). Bellew's watching, the power of exposure that he wields, is a historically entrenched social power of the white male gaze, but one whose masculinity is enacted and guaranteed through heterosexuality as a ritual of racial purification. His masculinity cannot be secured except through a consecration of his whiteness. And whereas Bellew requires the spectre of the black woman as an object of desire, he must destroy this spectre to avoid the kind of association that might destabilize the territorial boundaries of his own whiteness. This ritualistic expulsion is dramatized quite clearly at the end of *Passing* when Bellew's exposing and endangering gaze and Clare's fall to death are simultaneous with Irene's offer of an apparently helping hand. Fearing the loss of her husband and fearing her own desire, Irene is positioned at the social site of contradiction: both options threaten to jettison her into a public sphere in which she might become subject, as it were, to the same bad winds. But Irene fails to realize that Clare is as constrained as she is, that Clare's freedom could not be acquired at the expense of Irene, that they do not ultimately enslave each other, but that they are both caught in the vacillating breath of that symbolic bellowing: "Nig! My God! Nig!"

If Bellew's bellowing can be read as a symbolic racialization, a way in which both Irene and Clare are interpellated by a set of symbolic norms governing black female sexuality, then the symbolic is not merely organized by "phallic power," but by a "phallicism" that is centrally sustained by racial anxiety and sexualized rituals of racial purification. Irene's self-sacrifice might be understood then as an effort to avoid becoming the object of that kind of sexual violence, as one that makes her cling to an arid family life and destroy whatever emergence of passion might call that safety into question. Her jealousy must then be read as a psychic event orchestrated within and by this social map of power. Her passion for Clare had to be destroyed only because she could not find a viable place for her own sexuality to live. Trapped by a promise of safety through class mobility, Irene accepted the terms of power which threatened her, becoming its instrument in the end. More troubling than a scene in which the white man finds and scorns his "Other" in the black women, this drama displays in all its painfulness the ways in which the interpellation of the white norm is reiterated and executed by those whom it would— and does—vanquish. This is a performative enactment of "race" that mobilizes every character in its sweep.

And yet, the story reoccupies symbolic power to expose that symbolic force in return, and in the course of that exposure began to further a powerful tradition of words, one which promised to sustain the lives and passions of precisely those who could not survive within the story itself. Tragically, the logic of "passing" and "exposure" came to afflict and, indeed, to end Nella Larsen's own authorial career, for when she published a short story, "Sanctuary," in 1930, she was accused of plagiarism, that is, exposed as "passing" as the true originator of the work.[19] Her response to this condemning exposure was to recede into an anonymity from which she did not emerge. Irene slipped into such a living death, as did Helga in *Quicksand*. Perhaps the alternative would have meant a turning of that queering rage no longer against herself or Clare, but against the regulatory norms that force such a turn: against both the passionless promise of that bourgeois family and the bellowing of racism in its social and psychic reverberations, most especially, in the deathly rituals it engages.

7

ARGUING WITH THE REAL

What is refused in the symbolic order returns in the real.
—Jacques Lacan, *Les Psychoses*

She grounds predication without strictly speaking being marked by
it; she is not determined through the application of such or such
quality. She subsists "within herself" beneath discourse. As that
which has also been called prime matter.
—Luce Irigaray, *Marine Lover*

Counter to the notion that performativity is the efficacious expression of a human will in language, this text seeks to recast performativity as a specific modality of power as discourse. For discourse to materialize a set of *effects*, "discourse" itself must be understood as complex and convergent chains in which "effects" are vectors of power. In this sense, what is constituted in discourse is not fixed in or by discourse, but becomes the condition and occasion for a further action. This does not mean that *any* action is possible on the basis of a discursive effect. On the contrary, certain reiterative chains of discursive production are barely legible as reiterations, for the effects they have materialized are those without which no bearing in discourse can be taken. The power of discourse to materialize its effects is thus consonant with the power of discourse to circumscribe the domain of intelligibility. Hence, the reading of "performativity" as willful and arbitrary choice misses the point that the historicity of discourse and, in particular, the historicity of norms (the "chains" of iteration invoked and dissimulated in the imperative utterance) constitute the power of discourse to enact what it names. To think of "sex" as an imperative in this way means that a subject is addressed and produced by such a norm, and that this norm—and the regulatory power of which it is a token—materializes bodies as an effect of that injunction. And yet, this "materialization," while far from artificial, is not fully stable. For the imperative to be or get "sexed" requires a differentiated production and regulation of masculine and feminine identification that does not fully hold and cannot be fully exhaustive. And further, this imperative, this injunction, requires and institutes a "constitutive outside"—the unspeakable, the unviable, the nonnarrativizable that secures and, hence, fails to secure the very borders of materiality. The normative force of performativity—its power to establish what qualifies as "being"—works not only through reiteration, but through exclusion as well. And in the case of bodies, those exclusions haunt signification as its abject borders or as that which is strictly foreclosed: the unlivable, the nonnarrativizable, the traumatic.

The political terms that are meant to establish a sure or coherent identity are troubled by this failure of discursive performativity to finally and fully establish the identity to which it refers. Iterability underscores the non-self-identical status of such terms; the constitutive outside means that identity always requires precisely that which it cannot abide. Within feminist debate, an increasing problem has been to reconcile the apparent need to formulate a politics which assumes the category of "women" with the demand, often politically articulated, to problematize the category, interrogate its incoherence, its internal dissonance, its constitutive exclusions. The terms of identity have in recent years appeared to promise, and to promise in different ways, a full recognition. Within psychoanalytic terms, the *impossibility* of an identity category to fulfill that promise is a consequence of a set of exclusions which found the very subjects whose identities such categories are supposed to phenomenalize and represent. To the extent that we understand identity-claims as rallying points for political mobilization, they appear to hold out the promise of unity, solidarity, universality. As a corollary, then, one might understand the resentment and rancor against identity as signs of a dissension and dissatisfaction that follow the failure of that promise to deliver.

The recent work of Slavoj Žižek underscores the *phantasmatic* promise of identity as a rallying point within political discourse as well as the inevitability of disappointment. In this respect, his work opens a way to rethink identity-claims as phantasmatic sites, impossible sites, and, hence, as alternately compelling and disappointing.[1]

Žižek works between the Althusserian notion of ideology and the Lacanian symbolic, foregrounding the symbolic law and the real, and backgrounding the imaginary. He also makes clear that he is opposed to poststructuralist accounts of discursivity and proposes to rethink the Lacanian symbolic in terms of ideology. In this chapter, I will employ the term "ideology" in the effort to restate Žižek's position, but I will try to make plain where I think a rewriting of his theory makes a move toward poststructuralism possible, and where I understand a critical rethinking of the "feminine" in relation to discourse and the category of the real is needed. If some of the previous chapters have argued that psychoanalysis might be brought into a productive relation with contemporary discourses which seek to elaborate the complexity of gender, race, and sexuality, then this chapter might be read as an effort to underscore the limitations of psychoanalysis when its founding prohibitions and their heterosexualizing injunctions are taken to be invariant. Central to the task will be the retheorization of what must be excluded from discourse in order for political signifiers to become rallying points, sites of phantasmatic investment and expectation. My questions, then: How might those ostensibly constitutive exclusions be rendered less permanent, more dynamic? How might the excluded return, not as psychosis or the figure of the psychotic within politics, but as that which has been rendered mute, foreclosed from the domain of political signification? How and where is social content attributed to the site of the "real," and then positioned as the unspeakable? Is there not a difference between a theory that asserts that, in principle, every discourse operates through exclusion and a theory that attributes to that "outside" specific social and sexual positions? To the extent that a specific use of psychoanalysis works to foreclose certain social and sexual positions from the domain of intelligibility—and for all time—psychoanalysis appears to work in the service of the normativizing law that it interrogates. How might such socially saturated domains of exclusion be recast from their status as "constitutive" to beings who might be said to matter?

POLITICS OF THE SIGN

Opposed to what he calls "discourse theory," which appears to be a position attributed to a poststructuralism that includes Foucault and Derrida, Žižek at once underscores the centrality of discourse in political mobilization and the limits to any act of discursive constitution. Žižek is surely right that the subject is not a unilateral effect of prior discourses, and that the process of subjectivation outlined by Foucault is in need of a psychoanalytic rethinking. Following Lacan, Žižek argues that the "subject" is produced in language through an act of foreclosure (*Verwerfung*). What is refused or repudiated in the formation of the subject continues to determine that subject. What remains outside this subject, set outside by the act of foreclosure which founds the subject, persists as a kind of defining negativity.[2] The subject is, as a result, never coherent and never self-identical precisely because it is founded and, indeed, continually refounded, through a set of defining foreclosures and repressions[3] that constitute the discontinuity and incompletion of the subject.

Žižek is surely right that any theory of the discursive constitution of the subject must take into account the domain of foreclosure, of what must be repudiated for the subject itself to emerge. But how and to what end does he appropriate the Lacanian notion of the real to designate what remains unsymbolizable, foreclosed from symbolization? Consider the rhetorical difficulty of circumscribing within symbolic discourse the limits of what is and is not symbolizable. On the one hand, the limits to symbolization are necessary to symbolization itself, which produces through exclusion its provisional systematicity. On the other hand, how those limits are set by theory remains problematic, not only because there is always a question of what constitutes the authority of the one who writes those limits, but because the setting of those limits is linked to the contingent regulation of what will and will not qualify as a discursively intelligible way of being.

The production of the *un*symbolizable, the unspeakable, the illegible is also always a strategy of social abjection. Is it even possible to distinguish between the socially contingent rules of subject-formation, understood as regulatory productions of the subject through exclusion and foreclosure, and a set of "laws" or "structures" that constitute the invariant mechanisms of foreclosure through which *any* subject comes into being? To the extent that the law or regulatory mechanism of foreclosure in this latter instance is conceived as ahistorical and universalistic, this law is exempted from the discursive and social rearticulations that it initiates. This exemption is, I would argue, highly consequential insofar as this law is understood to be that which produces and normativizes sexed positionalities in their intelligibility. To the extent that this law engages the traumatic production of a sexual antagonism in its symbolic normativity, it can do this only by barring from cultural intelligibility—and rendering culturally abject—cultural organizations of sexuality that exceed the structuring purview of that law. The risk, of course, is that contingent regulatory mechanisms of subject-production may be reified as universal laws, exempted from the very process of discursive rearticulation that they occasion.

The use of psychoanalysis that remains most persuasive in Žižek's analysis, however, is the linking of political signifiers, rallying points for mobilization and politicization, like "women," "democracy," "freedom," with the notion of phantasmatic investment and phantasmatic promise. His theory makes clear the relationship between *identification* with political signifiers and their capacity both to unify the ideological field and to constitute the constituencies they claim to represent. Political signifiers, especially those that designate subject positions, are not descriptive; that is, they do not represent pregiven constituencies, but are empty signs which come to bear phantasmatic investments of various kinds. No signifier can be radically representative, for every signifier is the site of a perpetual *méconnaisance*; it produces the expectation of a unity, a full and final recognition that can never be achieved. Paradoxically, the failure of such signifiers—"women" is the one that comes to mind—fully to describe the constituency they name is precisely what constitutes these signifiers as sites of phantasmatic investment and discursive rearticulation. It is what opens the signifier to new meanings and new possibilities for political resignification. It is this open-ended and performative function of the signifier that seems to me to be crucial to a radical democratic notion of futurity.

Toward the end of this chapter, I will suggest a way in which the phantasmatic investment in the political signifier needs to be thought in relation to the historicity of such signifiers. I will also offer an argument concerning the status of performativity in both Ernesto Laclau and Žižek, namely, that performativity, if rethought through the Derridean notion of citationality, offers a formulation of the performative character of political signifiers that a radical democratic theory may find valuable.

DISCOURSE AND THE QUESTION OF CONTINGENCY

Crucial to Žižek's effort to work the Althusserian theory through Lacan is the psychoanalytic insight that any effort of discursive interpellation or constitution is subject to failure, haunted by contingency, to the extent that discourse itself invariably fails to totalize the social field. Indeed, any attempt to totalize the social field is to be read as a symptom, the effect and remainder of a trauma that itself cannot be directly symbolized in language. This trauma subsists as the permanent possibility of disrupting and rendering contingent any discursive formation that lays claim to a coherent or seamless account of reality. It persists as the real, where the real is always that which any account of "reality" fails to include. The real constitutes the contingency or lack in any discursive formation. As such, it stands theoretically as a counter both to Foucaultian linguisticism, construed as a kind of discursive monism whereby language effectively brings into being that which it names and to Habermasian rationalism which presumes a transparency of intention in the speech act that is itself symptomatic of a refusal of the psyche, the unconscious, that which resists and yet structures language prior to and beyond any "intention."

In Žižek's view, every discursive formation must be understood in relation to that which it cannot accommodate within its own discursive or symbolic terms. This traumatic "outside" poses the threat of psychosis and becomes itself the excluded and threatening possibility that motivates and, eventually, thwarts the linguistic urge to intelligibility. His position is explicitly linked with the critical reformulation of Althusser proposed by Ernesto Laclau and Chantal Mouffe in *Hegemony and Socialist Strategy*,[4] in particular, with their notion that every ideological formation is constituted through and against a constitutive antagonism and is, therefore, to be understood as an effort to cover over or "suture" a set of contingent relations. Because this ideological suturing is never complete, that is, because it can never establish itself as a *necessary or comprehensive* set of connections, it is marked by a failure of complete determination, a constitutive contingency, that emerges within the ideological field as its permanent (and promising) instability.

Against a causal theory of historical events or social relations, the theory of radical democracy insists that political signifiers are contingently related, and that hegemony consists in the perpetual rearticulation of these contingently related political signifiers, the weaving together of a social fabric that has no necessary ground, but that consistently produces the "effect" of its own necessity through the process of rearticulation. Ideology, then, might be construed as a linking together of political signifiers such that their unity effects the appearance of necessity, but where that contingency is apparent in the nonidentity of those signifiers; the radical democratic reformulation of ideology (still and always itself ideological) consists in the demand that these signifiers be perpetually rearticulated in relation to one another. What is here understood as constitutive antagonism, the nonclosure of definition, is assured by a contingency that underwrites every discursive formation.

The incompletion of every ideological formulation is central to the radical democratic project's notion of political futurity. The subjection of every ideological formation to a *re*articulation of these linkages constitutes the temporal order of democracy as an incalculable future,[5] leaving open the production of new subject-positions, new political signifiers, and new linkages to become the rallying points for politicization.

For Laclau and Mouffe, this politicization will be in the service of radical democracy to the extent that the constitutive exclusions that stabilize the discursive domain of the political—those positions that have been excluded from representability and from considerations of justice or equality—are established in relation to the existing polity as what calls to be included within its terms, i.e., a set of *future* possibilities for inclusion, what Mouffe refers to as part of the not-yet-assimilable *horizon* of community.[6] The ideal of a radical inclusivity is impossible, but this very impossibility nevertheless governs the political field as an idealization of the future that motivates the expansion, linking, and perpetual production of political subject-positions and signifiers.

What appears to guarantee this mobilizing incompleteness of the political field is a contingency that remains constitutive throughout any and all signifying practices. This notion of contingency is directly linked to the notion of "constitutive antagonisms," a notion developed by Laclau and Mouffe in *Hegemony and Socialist Strategy*, and further elaborated in the first chapter of Laclau's *Reflections on the Revolution of Our Time*.[7] In this last work, Laclau distinguishes between the status of *contradictory* social relations and *antagonistic* social relations: those relations that negate one by virtue of a logical necessity and those relations, considered contingent and based in power, that are in a kind of social tension whose consequences cannot be predicted. In this essay, Laclau makes the strong claim that there are relations of production that exceed those that characterize the worker's structural position or "identity" and which preclude the possibility of an immanent or causal account of how social relations will proceed. He remarks that "this constitutive outside is inherent to any antagonistic relationship" (9). Here it seems that what assures that any social description or prediction will be non-totalizing and non-predictive are other *social* relationships that constitute the "outside" to identity: "…antagonism does not occur *within* the relations of production, but between the latter and the social agent's identity outside them" (15). In other words, any attempt to circumscribe an identity in terms of relations of production, and solely within those terms, performs an exclusion and, hence, produces a constitutive outside, understood on the model of the Derridean "supplément," that denies the claim to positivity and comprehensiveness implied by that prior objectivation. In Laclau's terms, "the antagonizing force *denies* my identity in the strictest sense" (18).

The question, then, is whether the contingency or negativity enacted by such antagonizing forces is part of social relations or whether it belongs to the real, the foreclosure of which constitutes the very possibility of the social and the symbolic. In the above, it seems, Laclau links the notions of antagonism and contingency to that *within* the social field which exceeds any positive or objectivist determination or prediction, a supplement within the social but "outside" of posited identity. In Žižek, it seems, this contingency is linked to the Lacanian real in such a way that it is permanently outside the social as such. And within the same essay as above, Laclau also argues for the notion of the "lack" in accounting for the production of identifications (44).[8] If the "outside" is, as Laclau insists, linked to the Derridean logic of the supplement (Laclau, *NRRT*, 84 n. 5), then it is unclear what moves must be taken to make it compatible with the Lacanian notion of the "lack"; indeed, in what follows, I will attempt to read the Lacanian "lack" within Žižek's text according to the logic of the supplement, one which also entails a rethinking of the social specificity of taboo, loss, and sexuality.

Whereas Žižek understands the move from ideology to discourse in Laclau's work to constitute a partial "regression"(Laclau, *NRRT*, 250), and Laclau appears to take issue with Žižek's preservation of Hegel (Žižek, *SO*, xii), they agree that ideology surfaces discursively as an effort to cover over a constitutive "lack" in the subject, a "lack" that is at times rendered equivalent to the notion of "constitutive antagonism" and, at other times, understood as a negativity more fundamental than any given social antagonism, as one that every specific social antagonism presupposes. The suturing together of political signifiers within the ideological domain masks and disarticulates the contingency or "lack" by which it is motivated.[9] This lack or negativity is central to the project of radical democracy precisely because it constitutes within discourse the resistance to all essentialism and all descriptivism. The "subject-position" of women, for instance, is never fixed by the signifier "women"; that term does not describe a preexisting constituency, but is, rather, part of the very production and formulation of that constituency, one that is perpetually renegotiated and rearticulated in relation to other signifiers within the political field. This instability in all discursive fixing is the promise of a teleologically unconstrained futurity for the political signifier. In this sense, the failure of any ideological formation to establish itself as necessary is part of its democratic promise, the ungrounded "ground" of the political signifier as a site of rearticulation.

At stake, then, is how this "contingency" is theorized, a difficult matter in any case for a theory that would account for "contingency" will doubtless also always be formulated through and against that contingency. Indeed, can there be a theory of "contingency" that is not compelled to refuse or cover over that which it seeks to explain?

A number of questions emerge concerning the formulation of this contingency or negativity: To what extent can the Lacanian real be used to stand for this contingency? To what extent does that very substitution saturate this contingency with social significations that become reified *as* the prediscursive? More particularly, in Žižek's work, *which* rendition of the real is appropriated from the Lacanian corpus? If the real is understood as the unsymbolizable threat of castration, an originary trauma motivating the very symbolizations by which it is incessantly covered over, to what extent does this oedipal logic prefigure any and every "lack" in ideological determinations as the lack/loss of the phallus instituted through the oedipal crisis? Does the formulation of the real in terms of the threat of castration establish the oedipally induced sexual differential at a prediscursive level? And is this *fixing* of a set of sexual positionalities under the sign of a "contingency" or "lack" supposed to assure the *unfixity* or instability of any given discursive or ideological formation? By linking this "contingency" with the real, and interpreting the real as the trauma induced through the threat of castration, the Law of the Father, this "law" is posited as accountable for the contingency in all ideological determinations, but is never subject to the same logic of contingency that it secures.

The "Law of the Father" induces trauma and foreclosure through the threat of castration, thereby producing the "lack" against which all symbolization occurs. And yet, this very symbolization of the law as the law of castration is *not* taken as a contingent ideological formulation. As the fixing of contingency in relation to the law of castration, the trauma and "substantial identity"[10] of the real, Žižek's theory thus evacuates the "contingency" of its contingency. Indeed, his theory valorizes a "law" prior to all ideological formations, one with consequential social and political implications for the placing of the masculine within discourse and the symbolic, and the feminine as a "stain," "outside the circuit of discourse" (75).

If symbolization is itself circumscribed through the exclusion and/or abjection of the feminine, and if this exclusion and/or abjection is secured through Žižek's specific appropriation of the Lacanian doctrine of the real, then how is it that what qualifies as "symbolizable" is itself constituted through the *de*symbolization of the feminine as originary trauma? What limits are placed on "women" as a political signifier by a theory that installs its version of signification through the abjection/exclusion of the feminine? And what is the ideological status of a theory that identifies the contingency in all ideological formulations as the "lack" produced by the threat of castration, where that threat and the sexual differential that it institutes are not subject to the discursive rearticulation proper to hegemony? If this law is a necessity, and it is that which secures all contingency in discursive and ideological formulations, then that contingency is legislated in advance as a nonideological necessity and is, therefore, no contingency at all. Indeed, the insistence on the preideological status of the symbolic law constitutes a foreclosure of a contingency in the name of that law, one which, if admitted into discourse and the domain of the symbolizable, might call into question or, at least, occasion a rearticulation of the oedipal scenario and the status of castration. Considering the centrality of that project of rearticulating the oedipal scenario to the various contemporary projects of feminist psychoanalysis (and not only to those "historicizing" feminisms [50] opposed to psychoanalysis), this foreclosure appears to be a consequential ideological move with potentially anti-feminist consequences. A number of significant feminist psychoanalytic reformulations take the contestable centrality of the threat of castration as a point of departure; moreover, they also underscore the role of the *imaginary* in Lacan over and against the almost exclusive focus on the symbolic in relation to the real in Žižek. Considering as well the permutations of oedipal relations in non-heterosexual psychic formations, it seems quite crucial to admit the oedipal scene into a discourse that subjects it to contemporary rearticulations.

Žižek's text appears in some ways to be mindful of these challenges to the real, and we might well ask what it means that the "real" appears within his text as that which needs to be protected or safeguarded from Foucaultian (Žižek, *SO*, 2), feminist (Žižek, *SO*, 50), and poststructuralist (Žižek, *SO*, 72) challenges. If the "real" is itself threatened by these theoretical enterprises, how are we to understand—psychoanalytically—the "defense" of the real? If the "real" is under threat, but is itself understood *as* the threat of castration, to what extent can Žižek's text be read as an effort to protect the "threat" of castration against a set of further "threats"? Do these further threats (Foucault, poststructuralism, feminism) operate within his text as threats to the threat of castration which then operate as tokens of the threat of castration itself, whereby the doctrine of the real becomes the token of a phallus (intoned in the phrase, the "rock of the real" that recurs throughout the text) to be defended against a certain displacement? If the "threat" of castration is to be protected, what then does the threat of castration *secure*? The threat is protected in order to safeguard the law, but if it is in need of protection, the force of that law is already in a crisis that no amount of protection can overcome.

In "The Signification of the Phallus," that threat institutes and sustains the assumption of the masculine sex in relation to the "having" of the phallus, whereby the feminine "sex" is assumed through embodying that threat as the "being" of the phallus, posing as the "loss" with which the masculine is perpetually threatened. To what extent is the stability and fixity of this differential threatened by those positions which take issue with the Žižekian real?

Further, it seems crucial to ask about the rhetorical status of the Žižekian text which reports and asserts the workings of the symbolic law. Significantly, Lacan's own textuality is not considered in the often brilliant appropriations to be found in Žižek's work. Here it is a question of writing *in language* of a foreclosure that institutes language itself: How to write in it and of it, and how to write in such a way that what escapes the full force of foreclosure and what constitutes its displacements can be read in the gaps, fissures, and metonymic movements of the text? Considering the persistence of this linguistic and hermeneutic preoccupation in Lacan's own theoretical writing, it makes sense to ask of Žižek: What is the relation of the textual propositions in *Sublime Object* to the law that it enunciates and "defends"? Is the textual defense of originary foreclosure, designated by the real, itself a *re*articulation of the symbolic law; does Žižek's text enact an identification with that law, and speak in and as that law? To what extent can the textuality of *Sublime Object* be read as a kind of writing of and as the law that it defends? Is the "contingency" of language here mastered in and by a textual practice that speaks as the law, whose rhetoricity is domesticated by the declarative mode? And to what extent does this project of mastery reappear in Žižek's explicit account of how political signifiers operate, more specifically, in the rendition of political performativity that is linked with the impossible "X" of desire?

THE ROCK OF THE REAL

Žižek begins his critique of what he calls "poststructuralism" through the invocation of a certain kind of matter, a "rock" or a "kernel" that not only resists symbolization and discourse, but is precisely what poststructuralism, in his account, itself resists and endeavors to "dissolve." This solidity figures the Lacanian real, the outside to discourse construed as symbolization, and so is a figure that fortifies the theoretical defense of that which, for Žižek, must remain unfigurable, and so might be said to perform the impossibility that it seeks to secure. The rock thus figures the unfigurable, and so emerges not only as a catachresis, but as one that is supposed to secure the borders between what he will call sometimes symbolization and sometimes "discourse," on the one hand, and the "real," on the other, where the latter is designated as that for which no symbolization is possible. Significantly, I think, the "real" that is a "rock" or a "kernel" or sometimes a "substance" is also, and sometimes within the same sentence, "a loss" a "negativity"; as a figure it appears to slide from substance to dissolution, thereby conflating the law that institutes the "lack" and the "lack" itself. If the real is the law, it is the solidity of the law, the incontrovertible status of this law and the threat that it delivers;

if it is the loss, then it is the effect of the law and precisely that which ideological determinations seek to cover; if it is the threatening force of the law, it is the trauma.

The evidence for the real consists in the list of examples of displacement and substitution, given within the grammatical form of an apposition, that attempts to show the traumatic origination of all things that signify. This is the trauma, the loss, that signification seeks to cover over only to displace and enact again. For Žižek signification itself initially takes the form of a *promise* and a *return*, the recovery of an unthematizable loss in and by the signifier, which along the way must break that promise and fail to return in order to remain a signifier at all. For the real is the site of the impossible fulfillment of that promise, and the exclusion of the real from signification is its very condition; the signifier that could deliver on the promise to return to the site of barred jouissance would destroy itself as a signifier.

What interests me is the move that Žižek makes from the signifier as an always uncompleted promise to return to the real, itself figured as the "rock" and the "lack"—figured, I would suggest, in and as the vacillation between substance and its dissolution—to the political signifier, the rallying point for phantasmatic investments and expectations. For Žižek, the political signifier is an empty term, a non-representational term whose semantic emptiness becomes the occasion for a set of phantasmatic investments to accrue and which, through being the site of such investments, wields the power to rally and mobilize, indeed, to produce the very political constituency it appears to "represent." For Žižek, then, the political signifier accrues those phantasmatic investments to the extent that it acts as a promise to return to a pleasurable satisfaction that is foreclosed by the onset of language itself; because there can be no return to this fantasized pleasure, and because such a return would entail the breaking of the prohibition that founds both language and the subject, the site of the lost origin is a site of unthematizable trauma. As a result, the promise of the signifier to make such a return is always already a broken one, but one nevertheless structured by that which must remain outside politicization and which must, for Žižek, always remain the same.

How are we to understand this figure of a rock which is at once the law and the loss instituted by that law? The law as rock is to be found in the Hebrew prayer in which God is "my rock and my redeemer," a phrase that suggests that the "rock" is the unnameable Yahweh, the principle of monotheism. But this rock is also the figure that emerges at the conclusion to Freud's "Analysis Terminable and Interminable" to denote the resistance of women patients to the suggestion that they suffer from penis envy. There Freud remarks, "We often feel that, when we have reached the wish for a penis and the masculine protest, we have penetrated all the psychological strata and reached 'bedrock' [*der gewachsener Fels*] and that our task is accomplished. And this is probably correct, for in the psychical field the biological factor is really the rock-bottom."[11] This is, interestingly, a figure of a ground that is nevertheless sedimented through time, and so not a ground, but an effect of a prior process covered over by this ground. As we will see in Žižek, this is a ground that calls to be secured and protected as a ground and that is always positioned in relation to a set of threats; hence, a contingent ground, a kind of property or territory in need of defense.[12]

Žižek identifies a number of positions that appear to destabilize this "rock," the law of castration, the redeemer, and he also offers a list of "examples" in which this figure of the rock, the hard kernel, appears and reappears. What links these examples together? Indeed, what constitutes the exemplary, and what, the law, in this theoretical effort to keep back the forces of poststructuralist "dissolution"? The list is an impressive one: poststructuralists, historicizing feminists, sadomasochistic Foucaultians, and fascists, where the exemplary instance of fascism is understood as anti-Semitic fascism.

Žižek remarks that "the fundamental gesture of poststructuralism is to deconstruct every substantial identity, to denounce behind its solid consistency an interplay of symbolic overdetermination—briefly, to dissolve the substantial identity into a network of non-substantial, differential relations; the notion of symptom is the necessary counterpoint to it, the substance of enjoyment, the real kernel around which this signifying interplay is structured" (Žižek, *SO*, 73).

Earlier, Žižek invokes this resistant kernel in relation to "the Marxist-feminist criticism of psychoanalysis" and in particular "the idea that its insistence on the crucial role of the Oedipus and the nuclear family triangle transforms a historically conditioned form of patriarchal family into a feature of the universal human condition" (50). Žižek then asks the following question, but asks it through a figure which makes the rock of the real speak: "Is not this effort to historicize the family triangle precisely an attempt to *elude* the 'hard kernel' which announces itself through the 'patriarchal family'—[then in caps] the Real of the Law, the rock of castration?" If the real of the law is precisely what cannot speak, the traumatic site foreclosed from symbolization, then it is with some interest that the real speaks here, qualified here as the real of the law, and that it is Žižek who, it seems, receives the word from the rock, and brings it down the mountain to us. Here it seems that "the real of the law" is the threatening force of the law, the law itself, but not the loss that the law forcibly institutes, for the loss could not be figured as a substance, since the loss will be defined as that which is always and only surreptitiously covered over by an appearance of substance, the loss being that which produces the desire to cover over that gap through signifying effects which carry the desire for substance which, within the social field, is never achieved. The figure of substance, then, appears misplaced here, unless we take it as a figure for incontrovertibility, specifically, the unquestionable status of the law, where that law is understood as the law of castration.

It is, then, clear why this kernel emerges centrally as a sexual antagonism that is constitutive of the family prior to any and all historical or social specificities. In reference to the patriarchal family, Žižek cautions as well against an over-rapid universalization that overrides specific determinations; his language returns most avidly to the dangers, the threats, of an "over-rapid historicization (that) makes us blind to the real kernel which returns as the same through diverse historicizations/symbolizations."

In the paragraph that follows, he offers another example of the same effort at over-rapid historicization, one that also seeks to elude the "real" of the law which, in the above, is rendered equivalent through apposition to "the rock of castration." This example is "concentration camps," and within the formulation of this example yet another string of examples emerges meant to demonstrate the same principle of equivalence: "All the different efforts to attach this phenomenon to a concrete image ('Holocaust,' 'Gulag'...) [the three dots implying a proliferation of equivalent 'examples,' but also an indifference to the specificity of the example, since the example is only interesting as 'proof' of the law], to reduce it to a product of a concrete social order (Fascism, Stalinism...)—what are they if not so many attempts to elude the fact that we are dealing here with the 'real' of our civilization which returns as the same traumatic kernel in all social systems?" (50).

The effect of this citation is to claim that each of these social formations: the family, concentration camps, the Gulag, instantiate the same trauma, and that what is historically textured about each of these sites of trauma is itself indifferent to and ontologically distinct from the lost and hidden referent that is their traumatic status. They are by virtue of this "same traumatic kernel" equivalent to one another as traumas, and what is historical and what is traumatic are made absolutely distinct; indeed, the historical becomes what is most indifferent to the question of trauma, and the political or historical effort to understand the institution of the family or the formation of concentration camps or Gulags cannot account for the "traumatic" character of these formations; and, indeed, what is properly traumatic about them does not belong to their social formation. This is, I take it, what Laclau refers to as the *contingency* in all social determinations, the lack which prevents the totalization of any given social form. But insofar as the real secures this lack, it postures as a self-identical principle that reduces any and all qualitative differences among social formations (identities, communities, practices, etc.) to a formal equivalence.

Here it seems crucial to ask whether the notion of a lack taken from psychoanalysis as that which secures the contingency of *any* and *all* social formations is itself a presocial principle universalized at the cost of every consideration of power, sociality, culture, politics, which regulates the relative closure and openness of social practices. Can Žižekian psychoanalysis respond to the pressure to theorize the historical specificity of trauma, to provide texture for the specific exclusions, annihilations, and unthinkable losses that structure the social phenomena mentioned above? It is unclear whether the examples are merely illustrative in this context, or whether they are the means by which the law orders and subordinates a set of phenomena to reflect back its own enduring continuity. Do the examples demonstrate the law, or do they become "examples" to the extent that they are ordered and rendered equivalent by the very law that then, as an *après-coup* effect, reads back the examples it itself has produced as signs of the law's own persistence? If the priority and the universality of the law are produced as the effects of these examples, then this law is fundamentally dependent on these examples, at which point the law is to be understood as an *effect* of the list of examples even as the examples are claimed to be indifferent and equivalent "instances" and effects of that law.

Moreover, what counts as an "example" is no indifferent matter, despite the relation of equivalence that is drawn among them. If the trauma is the same, and if it is linked with the threat of castration, and if that threat is made known within the family as an interpellation of sexed positionality (the production of "boy" and "girl" taking place through a differential relation to castration), then it is that sexualized trauma which originates in the family and reappears in the Gulag, in concentration camps, in political horror shows of various kinds.

In "Beyond Discourse-Analysis," Žižek circumscribes this trauma further as that which is symptomatized in the asymmetrical relation to "existence" (being a subject, having the phallus) for men and women: "It is no accident that the basic proposition of *Hegemony [and Socialist Strategy]*—"Society does not exist"—evokes the Lacanian proposition 'la Femme n'existe pas' ('Woman doesn't exist')." This non-existence is described again in the next sentence as "a certain traumatic impossibility," and here it becomes clear that what is traumatic is the non-existence of woman, that is, the fact of her castration. This is "a certain fissure which *cannot* be symbolized" (249). We might well ask why the conversation about the castration of woman must stop here. Is this a necessary limit to discourse, or is it imposed in order to ward off a threatening set of consequences? And if one raises a question about this necessary limit, does one inadvertently become the threat of castration itself? For if woman did exist, it seems that, by this logic, she could only exist to castrate.

Žižek's interpretation of the Lacanian doctrine of the real has at least three implications that I will for the most part only indicate: first, the real, understood as the threatening force of the law, is the threat of punishment which induces a necessary loss, where that loss, according to the oedipal logic, is figured as the feminine, as that which is outside the circuit of discursive exchange (what Žižek calls "an inert stain...which cannot be included in the circuit of discourse" [75]), and hence is not available as a political signifier. Where feminism is named in the text, it is primarily cast as an effort to "elude" the kernel, symptomatizing a certain resistance to feminine castration. Secondly, whereas Žižek describes the real as the unsymbolizable, and proceeds to invoke the real against those who defend discourse analysis or language-games, a consideration of the real in

Lacan's third seminar, *Les Psychoses*, suggests a slightly different reading. In that text, Lacan repeatedly remarks that, "what is refused in the symbolic order returns in the real" (22), and specifies that that refusal ought to be understood as *Verwerfung* (foreclosure or repudiation) (21). Lacan's formulation remains ambiguous with respect to the location of both the refusal and that which is refused: "what is refused in the symbolic order" suggests that there are a set of signifiers "in" the symbolic order in the mode of refusal or, indeed, refuse. The French makes it clearer, for it is not what is refused *to* that order, but what in that order is refused: "Ce qui est refusé *dans* l'ordre symbolique" (my emphasis). If what is refused *reappears (resurgit* [22] or *reparait* [21]) in the real (*dans le réel*), then it appears first to have appeared in the symbolic prior to its refusal and reappearance in the real.

In a provocative essay by Michael Walsh, "Reading the Real," the process of *Verwerfung* or foreclosure that institutes the real is described as a matter of "the exclusion of fundamental signifiers from the Symbolic ordering of the subject".[13] In other words, these are signifiers that have been part of symbolization and could be again, but have been separated off from symbolization to avert the trauma with which they are invested. Hence, these signifiers are desymbolized, but this process of desymbolization takes place through the production of a hiatus *in* symbolization. Walsh also recalls that the term *Verwerfung* (which Lacan deploys in the third seminar to delineate a psychosis-producing repudiation over and against a neurosis-producing repression [*Verdrängung*]) is used by Freud to describe the Wolf Man's rejection of castration (Walsh, 73). This resistance to symbolic paternity is symptomatized in the repudiation of signifiers that would readmit the symbolic force of that paternity. These are not signifiers that are merely repressed but could be worked through; they are signifiers whose reentry into symbolization would unravel the subject itself.

The notion of foreclosure offered here implies that what is foreclosed is a signifier, namely, that which has been symbolized, and that the mechanism of that repudiation takes place within the symbolic order as a policing of the borders of intelligibility.[14] Which signifiers qualify to unravel the subject and to threaten psychosis remains unfixed in this analysis, suggesting that what constitutes the domain of what the subject can never speak or know and still remain a subject remains variable, that is, remains a domain variably structured by contingent relations of power. Žižek's rendition of the real presupposes that there is an invariant law that operates uniformly in all discursive regimes to produce through prohibition this "lack" that is the trauma induced by the threat of castration, the threat itself. But if we concur that every discursive formation proceeds through constituting an "outside," we are not thereby committed to the *invariant* production of that outside as the trauma of castration (nor to the generalization of castration as the model for all historical trauma). Moreover, it may further the effort to think psychoanalysis's relation to historical trauma and to the limits of symbolizability if we realize that (a) there may be several mechanisms of foreclosure that work to produce the unsymbolizable in any given discursive regime, and (b) the mechanisms of that production are—however inevitable—still and always the historical workings of specific modalities of discourse and power.

Since (c) the resistance to the real is a resistance to the fact of feminine castration or a denial of the structuring power of that threat for men, those who seek to dissolve the real (they are referred to as feminists, post-structuralists, and historicizers of various kinds) tend to undermine the differential force of castration and its permanent status within and as the symbolic. This "law" requires that castration is the "already having happened" for women, the installation of loss in the articulation of the feminine position, whereas castration signifies as what is always almost happening for men, as anxiety and the fear of losing the phallus, where the loss that is feared is structurally emblematized by the feminine and, hence, is a fear of becoming feminine, becoming abjected as the feminine; this possibility of abjection thus governs the articulation of sexual differ-ence, and the real is the permanent structure that differentiates the sexes in relation to the temporal location of this loss. As noted in the chapter "The Lesbian Phallus", the having and the being of the phallus are determined along these lines as an opposition. The masculine anxiety over loss denotes an impossibility of having, an always already having lost the phallus which makes the "having" into an impossible ideal, and approximates the phallus as the deferral of that having, a having to have that is never had. The having of the phallus as a site of anxiety is already the loss that it fears, and it is this recognition of the masculine implication in abjection that the feminine serves to defer.

The threat of a collapse of the masculine into the abjected feminine threatens to dissolve the heterosexual axis of desire; it carries the fear of occupying a site of homosexual abjection. Indeed, we receive in the opening pages of *Sublime Object* a figure for such abjection when Foucault is introduced and discounted as one "so fascinated by marginal lifestyles constructing their own mode of subjectivity" and then, within parenthesis, "(the sadomasochistic homosexual universe, for example: see Foucault, 1984)." The fantasy of a "universe" of sadomasochistic lifestyle may implicate the figure of the sadomasochistic Foucault as part of the global threat which, given to an historicizing trend and a certain attenuated link with poststructuralism, becomes part of this phantasmatic threat to the seemingly treasured real. If this is a text that defends the trauma of the real, defends the threat of psychosis that the real delivers, and if it defends this latter threat over and against a different kind of threat, it seems that the text proliferates this threat by investing it in a variety of social positions, thereby constituting the text itself as that which seeks to "elude" the challenges of "feminism," "Foucault," and "poststructuralism."

What is the "threat," and who is "eluding" it by what means? Does Žižek's text rhetorically perform an inversion of this dynamic such that feminists and poststructuralists are figured in "denial" and "escape," and Žižek, as the bearer and spokesman for the Law? Or is this the invocation of the law in order to keep the sexual differential in its place, one in which women will always be the symptom of man (not existing), and where the Aristophanic myth of the lack as the consequence of a primary severing necessitates heterosexuality as the site of an imaginary completion and return?

To claim that there is an "outside" to the socially intelligible, and that this "outside" will always be that which negatively defines the social is, I think, a point on which we can concur. To delimit that outside through the invocation of a preideological "law," a prediscursive "law" that works invariantly throughout all history, and further, to make that law function to secure a sexual differential that ontologizes subordination, is an "ideological" move in a more ancient sense, one that might only be understood through a rethinking of ideology as "reification." *That there is always an "outside" and, indeed, a "constitutive antagonism" seems right, but to supply the character and content to a law that secures the borders between the "inside" and the "outside" of symbolic intelligibility is to preempt the specific social and historical analysis that is required, to conflate into "one" law the effect of a convergence of many, and to preclude the very possibility of a future rearticulation of that boundary which is central to the democratic project that Žižek, Laclau, and Mouffe promote.*

If, as Žižek argues, "the real itself offers no support for a direct symbolization of it" (97), then what is the rhetorical status of the metatheoretical claim which symbolizes the real for us? Because the real can never be symbolized, this impossibility constitutes the permanent pathos of symbolization. This is not to claim that there is no real, but, rather, that the real cannot be signified, that it stands, as it were, as the resistance at the core of all signification. But to make this claim is to assert a relation of radical incommensurability between the "symbolization" and "the real," and it is unclear that this very assertion is not already implicated in the first term of the relation. As such, it is unclear to what metasymbolizing status that very assertion disingenuously seeks to lay claim. To claim that the real resists symbolization is still to symbolize the real as a kind of resistance. The former claim (the real resists symbolization) can only be true if the latter claim ("the real resists symbolization" is a symbolization) is true, but if the second claim is true, the first is necessarily false. To presume the real in the mode of resistance is still to predicate it in some way and to grant the real its reality apart from any avowed linguistic capacity to do precisely that.

As resistance to symbolization, the "real" functions in an exterior relation to language, as the inverse of mimetic representationalism, that is, as the site where all efforts to represent must founder. The problem here is that there is no way within this framework to politicize the relation between language and the real. What counts as the "real," in the sense of the unsymbolizable, is always relative to a linguistic domain that authorizes and produces that foreclosure, and achieves that effect through producing and policing a set of constitutive exclusions. Even if every discursive formation is produced through exclusion, that is not to claim that all exclusions are equivalent: what is needed is a way to assess politically how the production of cultural unintelligibility is mobilized variably to regulate the political field, i.e., who will count as a "subject," who will be required not to count. To freeze the real as the impossible "outside" to discourse is to institute a permanently unsatisfiable desire for an ever elusive referent: the sublime object of ideology. The fixity and universality of this relation between language and the real produces, however, a prepolitical pathos that precludes the kind of analysis that would take the real/reality distinction as the instrument and effect of contingent relations of power.

PERFORMATIVE SIGNIFIERS, OR CALLING AN AARDVARK "NAPOLEON"

Žižek's use of the Lacanian "real" to establish the permanent recalcitrance of the referent to symbolization implies that all referring ends up phantasmatically producing (and missing) the referent to which it aspires. Žižek seeks recourse to the "agency of the signifier" in Lacan to develop his own theory of the political performative. Exchanging Kripke's notion of the "rigid designator" for the Lacanian notion of a *point de capiton*, Žižek argues that the pure signifier, empty of all meaning, nevertheless postures as a site of radical semantic abundance. This postulation of a semantic excess at the site of a semantic void is the ideological moment, the discursive event that "totalizes an ideology by bringing to a halt the metonymic sliding of its signified" (99). Žižek argues that these terms do not refer, but act rhetorically to produce the phenomenon they enunciate:

> In itself, it is nothing but a "pure difference": its role is purely structural, its nature is purely performative—its signification coincides with its own act of enunciation; in short, it is a "signifier without the signified." The crucial step in the analysis of an ideological edifice is thus to detect, behind the dazzling splendour of the element which holds it together ("God," "Country," "Party," "Class"…), this self-referential, tautological, performative operation [99].

The implication of this anti-descriptivist view of naming entails both the effectivity *and* the radical contingency of naming as an identity-constituting performance. As a consequence, the name mobilizes an identity at the same time that it confirms its fundamental alterability. The name orders and institutes a variety of free-floating signifiers into an "identity"; the name effectively "sutures" the object. As a rallying point or point of temporary closure for a politics based on "subject positions" (what Žižek via Lacan calls a nodal point, or *point de capiton*), the name designates a contingent and open organizing principle for the formation of political groups. It is in this sense that anti-descriptivism provides a linguistic theory for an anti-essentialist identity politics.

If signifiers become politically mobilizing by becoming sites of phantasmatic investment, then with what are they invested? As promissory notes for the real—counterfeit ones—these signifiers become phantasmatic occasions for a return, a return to that which must be foreclosed in order for symbolization to occur, a return to a conjectured jouissance which cannot be named or described within language precisely because language is itself based on its foreclosure. Indeed, language only comes into being through that foreclosure or primary prohibition. Language then operates by means of the *displacement* of the referent, the multiplication of signifiers at the site of the lost referent. Indeed, signification requires this loss of the referent, and only works as signification to the extent that the referent remains irrecoverable. Were the referent to be recovered, this would lead to psychosis and the failure of language.

What Žižek offers us, then, is an account of politicization that holds out the (impossible) promise of a return to the referent within signification, without psychosis and the loss of language itself. Insofar as performatives are their own *referent*, they appear both to signify and to refer and hence to overcome the divide between referent and signification that is produced and sustained at the level of foreclosure. Significantly, this phantasmatic return to the referent is impossible, and as much as a political signifier holds out the promise of this return without psychosis, it cannot make good on its promise. Phantasmatic investment is invariably followed by disappointment or disidentification. It appears to follow that the movement of political organizations in their factionalization are those in which the sign does not rally and unify in the way that Žižek describes. The advent of factionalization consists in the recognition that the unity promised by the signifier was, in fact, phantasmatic, and a *dis*identification occurs. The rallying force of politics is its implicit promise of the possibility of a livable and speakable psychosis. Politics holds out the promise of the manageability of unspeakable loss.

Following Laclau and Mouffe, Žižek views political signifiers as free-floating and discontinuous within the prepoliticized field of ideology. When these political signifiers become politicized and politicizing, they provide contingent but efficacious points of unity for the otherwise disparate or free-floating elements of ideological life. Following Lacan's notion that the name confers legitimacy and duration on the ego (recasting the ego as subject in language), Žižek considers these unifying terms of politics to function on the model of *proper names*: they do not, strictly speaking, describe any given content or objective correlative, but act as rigid designators that institute and maintain the social phenomena to which they appear to refer. In this sense, a political signifier gains its political efficacy, its power to define the political field, through creating and sustaining its constituency. The power of the terms "women" or "democracy" is *not* derived from their ability to describe adequately or comprehensively a political reality that *already* exists; on the contrary, the political signifier becomes politically efficacious by instituting and sustaining a set of connections *as* a political reality. In this sense, the political signifier in Žižek's view operates as a *performative* rather than a *representational* term. Paradoxically, the political efficacy of the signifier does not consist in its representational capacity; the term neither represents nor expresses some already existing subjects or their interests. The signifier's efficacy is confirmed by its capacity to structure and constitute the political field, to create new subject-positions and new interests.

In Laclau's preface to the English translation of Žižek's *Sublime Object*, he argues that Žižek's theory offers a performative theory of names, and that this performativity is crucial to a theory of politics and hegemony. In Žižek's revision of Kripke, to be considered shortly, the name retroactively constitutes that to which it appears to refer. It gathers together into a unity or identity elements that previously coexisted without any such relation. The signifiers of "identity" effectively or rhetorically produce the very social movements that they appear to represent. The signifier does not refer to a pregiven or already constituted identity, a pure referent or essential set of facts that preexist the identity-signifier or act as the measure of its adequacy. An essentialist politics claims that there is a set of necessary features that describe a given identity or constituency and that these features are in some sense fixed and available prior to the signifier that names them. Žižek argues that the name does not *refer* to a pregiven object; Laclau concludes that this non-referentiality implies "the discursive construction of the object itself."

Laclau then draws the conclusion for a radical democratic politics: "the consequences for a theory of hegemony or politics are easy to see." If the name referred to a pregiven set of features presumed to belong prediscursively to a given object, then there could be no "possibility of any discursive hegemonic variation that could open the space for a political construction of social identities. But if the process of naming of objects amounts to the very act of their constitution, then their descriptive features will be fundamentally unstable and open to all kinds of hegemonic rearticulations."

Laclau then concludes this exposition with a significant remark: "The essentially performative character of naming is the precondition for all hegemony and politics"(Žižek, *SO*, "Preface," xiii-xiv).

Whereas Laclau emphasizes the performative possibilities for destabilizing the already established field of social identities, underscoring variation and rearticulation, Žižek's own theory appears to emphasize the rigid and inflexible status of those signifying names. Žižek refers to those *points de capiton* as stable unifying structures of the political field. Laclau emphasizes in Žižek's theory the *performativity* of the signifier, affirming the variability of signification implicit in a performative use of language freed from the fixity of the referent. But Žižek's theory, a cross between Kripke and Lacan, presumes that political signifiers function like proper names, and that proper names operate on the model of rigid designators. An examination of rigid designation, however, suggests that precisely the variation and rearticulation apparently promised by the performativity of the name is rendered impossible. In fact, if performatives operate rigidly, that is, *to constitute that which they enunciate regardless of circumstance*, then such names constitute a functional essentialism at the level of language. Freed from the referent, the proper name as rigid performative is no less fixed. In the end, it is profoundly unclear whether Žižek's effort to understand political signifiers on the model of a performative theory of names can provide for the kind of variation and rearticulation required for an anti-essentialist radical democratic project.

It is of no small significance that proper names are derived from the *paternal* dispensation of its own name, and that the performative power of the paternal signifier to "name" is derived from the function of the patronym. It is important here in Kripke to distinguish between what he calls "rigid designators" and "nonrigid or accidental designators."[15] The latter are designators that refer, but cannot be said to refer in every possible world, because there is some chance that the world in which they occurred could have been significantly different in structure or composition than the ones that constitute the domain of "possible worlds" for us. Rigid designators, on the other hand, are those which refer to a "necessary existent," that is, refer to an object in any case where it could or could have existed" (Kripke, *NN*, 48). When Kripke then maintains that *names* are rigid designators, he means names of persons, and the example he gives is of the *surname* "Nixon." The example of Nixon is then used to support the thesis that "proper names are rigid designators." The next example is "Aristotle," followed by "Hesperus." Hence, not all names will be rigid designators; in fact, those names that *can be substituted for by a set of descriptions* fail to qualify: "If the name *means the same* as that description of cluster of descriptions, it will not be a rigid designator." The discussion continues to link proper names with "individuals" via Strawson (61) and "people" via Nagel (68).

Between the discussion of proper names that refer as rigid designators to individuals and the discussion of terms like "gold" which refer to objects (116-119), Kripke introduces the notion of the primal baptism. And it is in reference to this activity, which forms the paradigm for naming as such, that we begin to see the link, indeed, the "causal link," between rigid designators that refer to individuals and those that refer to objects. In fact, the baptism which is originally reserved for persons is extrapolated from that original context to apply to things. A proper name of a person *comes to refer* first by a preliminary set of descriptions that assist in the *fixing* of the referent, a referent that subsequently comes to refer rigidly and regardless of its descriptive features. It is, however, only after the introduction of proper names referring to persons that we are given the notion of an "initial baptism" (96). Considered critically, this scene of baptism, which will retroactively become the model for all naming as rigid designation, is the fixing of a referent to a person through the inter-pellation of that person into a religious lineage, a "naming" that is at once an inculcation into a patrilineage that traces back to, and reiterates, the original naming that God the father performs on Adam. The "fixing" of the referent is thus a "citation" of an original fixing, a reiteration of the divine process of naming, whereby naming the son inaugurates his exis-tence within the divinely sanctioned community of man.

Significantly, Kripke concedes that this notion of an "initial baptism" takes place at no time and place, and in this sense the fable of initial baptism shares the fictive space of the act of divine naming that it mimes. Kripke also argues that this naming cannot take place in private (in contrast to what we presume to be the solitary irruption of God's act of nomination) but must always have a social or communal character. The name is not fixed in time, but becomes fixed again and again through time, indeed, becomes fixed through its reiteration: "'passed from link to link'" (96) through a "chain of communication" (91). This begins the characterization of Kripke's causal theory of communication.

This also raises the question of the "link" between language users in Kripke's model. Kripke writes, "When the name is 'passed from link to link,' the receiver of the name must, I think, intend when he learns it to use it with the same reference as the man from whom he heard it" (96). This presumption of social agreement thus is inserted as a prerequisite for the proper name to fix its referent in the mode of rigid designation. But what, we might ask, guarantees this homogeneity of social intention? And if there is no guarantee, as Kripke himself appears to know, what is the fiction of homogenous intention from which this theory draws?

Kripke appears to know that there is no guarantee because he offers the example of an improper or catachrestic use of the proper name: "If I hear the name 'Napoleon' and decide it would be a nice name for my pet aardvark, I do not satisfy this condition." This improper usage, however, inheres in the possibility of the proper usage, indeed, remains that over and against and through which the proper reiterates itself as proper. It also signals a departure from the homogeneity of intention that appears to link the community of language users together. And yet, by virtue of the very reiterability of the name—the necessity that the name be reiterated in order to name, to fix its referent—this risk of catachresis is continually reproduced. Hence, the very iterability of the name produces the catachrestic divergence from the chain that the referent is meant to forestall. And this raises the further and consequential question of whether the permanent risk of catachresis does not "unfix" the referent. It also raises, I think, the consequential question of whether the referent is itself always only tenuously fixed by this regulation of its use, that is, by the outlawing of this catachrestic divergence from the chain of normative usage.

Baptism is an act which is "initial" or "primal" only to the extent that it *imitates* the originating Adamic act of naming, and so produces that origin *again* through mimetic reiteration. This character of reiteration appears in Kripke's notion of the "linking" which constitutes the homogeneity of communal intention upon which the causal theory of reference depends. Every language user must learn the right intention from a previous language user, and it is only on the presumption that right intention is rightly passed along this chain that the name continues to function as rigid designator. In other words, the link between acts of baptism, mimetically reiterating the divine performative, is the link between members of community, conceived also as a lineage, in which names are handed down and the uniformity of intention is secured. This latter set of links, understood as the "chain of communication," is not only the teaching of names that happens between members of a linguistic community, but is itself the reiteration of that "initial" baptismal moment conceived as ostensive reference, i.e., "This is Aristotle."

Further, not only is baptism an act of naming in which reference is secured through the extension of the surname to embrace or include the first name, but baptism is itself the action of the surname. The "given" or christian name is offered in the name of the patronym; the baptism fixes the name to the extent that it is brought into the patrilineage of the name. For Kripke, the referent is secured through supposing a communal homogeneity of intention. This is a notion that sustains strong links with the notion of the continuous uniformity of the divine will in the Adamic account of nomination (pre-Babel). But it also appears to follow, then, that the fixing of the referent is the forcible production *of* that fictive homogeneity and, indeed, *of* that community: the agreement by which reference becomes fixed (an agreement which is a continual agreeing again that happens through time) is itself reproduced on the condition that reference is fixed in the same way. And if this reiteration is baptismal, that is, the reiteration of the divine performative and, perhaps also, the extension of the divine will in its uniformity,[16] then it is God the father who patronymically extends his putative kingdom through the reiterative fixing of the referent.

The exclusion of catachresis, that is, the prohibition against naming the aardvark "Napoleon," secures the "chain of communication," and regulates and produces the "uniformity" of intention. Catachresis is thus a perpetual risk that rigid designation seeks to overcome, but always also inadvertently produces, despite its best intentions. The larger question, then, is whether Laclau's notion of "the performativity that is essential to all hegemony and all politics" can be construed as rigid designation, as Žižek via the Lacanian revision would suggest, without at once construing this performativity as catachresis. Is not the defilement of sovereignty, divine and paternal, performed by calling the aardvark "Napoleon" precisely the catachresis by which hegemony ought to proceed?[17]

In Kripke, then, it appears that any use of the rigid designator presupposes that there is a language user who has been correctly initiated into the use of a name, one "initiated" into the lineage of proper intention that, passed down generationally, becomes the historical pact that secures the appropriate fixing of the name. Although the name is said to "fix" its referent without describing the referent, it is clear that the instructions handed down through the chain of communication are presupposed in the act of fixing itself, so that the name remains fixed and fixable to the extent that that instruction in right intention and right usage is in place. To be initiated into that historical chain of language users with the right intention, one must first be baptized into that community, and it is in this sense that the baptism of the language user precedes the baptismal designation of any object. Moreover, to the extent that the language user must be installed in that community of those who use language properly, the language user must be linked relationally to other language users, that is, must be positioned in some line of kinship that secures the social lines of transmission whereby proper linguistic intentions are passed along. The person named thus names objects, and in this way the "initiation" into the community of homogenous intention is extended; if the name fixes the object, it also "initiates" the object into the patronymic lineage of authority. Fixing thus never takes place without the paternal authority to fix, which means that the referent remains secure only to the extent that the patrilineal line of authority is there to secure it.

Here the notion of baptism seems significant, for insofar as a baptism is an initiation into the kingdom of God, and the conferring of a "christian name," it is the extension of divine paternity to the one named. And insofar as the Adamic mode of nomination is the model for baptism itself, then it is God's performativity that is reiterated in the fixing of the referent through rigid designation. If rigid designation requires the patronymic production and transmission of a uniformity of intention, i.e., the intention to use language properly, it can secure the lines of this transmission through time through the production of stable kinship, that is, strict lines of patrilineality (it being God the Father's will which is passed along generationally), and through the exclusion of catachresis.

To the extent that a patrilineal form of kinship is presupposed here, and the patronym itself is the paradigm for the rigid designator, it seems crucial to consider that a rigid designator continues to "fix" a person through time only on the condition that there is no change of name. And yet, if the name is to stay the same and the demands of kinship are to met, then the institution of exogamy is necessitated and, with it, the exchange of women. The patronymic operation secures its inflexibility and perpetuity precisely by requiring that women, in their roles as wives and daughters, relinquish their name and secure perpetuity and rigidity for some other patronym, and daughters-in-law are imported to secure the eternity of this patronym. The exchange of women is thus a prerequisite for the rigid designation of the patronym.

The patronym secures its own rigidity, fixity, and universality within a set of kinship lines that designate wives and daughters as the sites of its self-perpetuation. In the patronymic naming of women, and in the exchange and extension of patronymic authority that *is* the event of marriage, the paternal law "performs" the identity and authority of the patronym. This performative power of the name, therefore, cannot be isolated from the paternal economy within which it operates, and the power-differential between the sexes that it institutes and serves.

How, then, does the above analysis bear on the question of Žižek's appropriation of Kripke, his subjection of the doctrine of rigid designation to the Lacanian *point de capiton*, and the further use of this political performative in the notion of hegemony in Laclau and Mouffe? Although Kripke is an anti-descriptivist in his account of how names refer, he is not for that reason in favor of an account of rigid designation as performativity. Does the theory of performativity based in the Lacanian revision of Kripke reinscribe paternal authority in another register? And what alternatives are available for understanding the operation of performativity in hegemony that do not unwittingly reinscribe the paternal authority of the signifier?

In Žižek's words, "what is overlooked, at least in the standard version of anti-descriptivism, is that this guaranteeing the identity of an object in all counterfactual situations—through a change of all its descriptive features is *the retroactive effect of naming itself*: it is the name itself, the signifier, which supports the identity of the object" (95).[18] Žižek thus redescribes the referential function of the name as *performative*. Further, the name, as performative signifier, marks the impossibility of reference and, equivalently, the referent as the site of an impossible desire. Žižek writes, "That 'surplus' in the object which stays the same in all possible worlds is 'something in it more than itself', that is to say the Lacanian *petit objet a*: we search in vain for it in positive reality because it has no positive consistency—because it is just an objectification of a void, a discontinuity opened in reality by the emergence of the signifier" (95).

To the extent that a term is performative, it does not merely refer, but acts in some way to constitute that which it enunciates. The "referent" of a performative is a kind of *action* which the performative itself calls for and participates in. Rigid designation, on the other hand, presumes the alterity of the referent, and the transparency of its own indexical function. The saying of "This is Aristotle" does not bring Aristotle into being; it is a saying that lays bare through ostensive reference an Aristotle exterior to language. It is in this sense that performativity cannot be equated with rigid designation, despite the fact that both terms imply anti-descriptivism.

In Žižek's revison of rigid designation through Lacan, the referent of rigid designation is permanently lost and, hence, constituted as an impossible object of desire, whereas for Kripke, the referent is permanently secured and satisfaction is at hand. Laclau, on the other hand, appears to consider the name in its performativity to be formative, and to locate the referent as a variable effect of the name; indeed, to recast the "referent" as the signified and thereby to open the term to the kind of variability required for hegemony. It is Kripke's position to argue that the name fixes the referent, and Žižek's to say that the name promises a referent that can never arrive, foreclosed as the unattainable real. But if the question of the "referent" is suspended, then it is no longer a question of in what modality it exists—i.e., in reality (Kripke) or in the real (Žižek)—but rather how the name stabilizes its signified through a set of differential relations with other signifiers within discourse.

If, as Kripke's text unwittingly demonstrates, the referent is secured only on the condition that proper usage is differentiated from improper usage, then the referent is produced in consequence of that distinction, and the instability of that distinguishing border between the proper and the catachrestic calls into question the ostensive function of the proper name. Here it seems that what is called "the referent" depends essentially on those catachrestic acts of speech that either fail to refer or refer in the wrong way. It is in this sense that political signifiers that fail to describe, fail to refer, indicate less the "loss" of the object—a position that nevertheless secures the referent even if as a lost referent—than the loss of the loss, to rework that Hegelian formulation. If referentiality is itself the effect of a policing of the linguistic constraints on proper usage, then the possibility of referentiality is contested by the catachrestic use of speech that insists on using proper names improperly, that expands or defiles the very domain of the proper by calling the aardvark 'Napoleon.'

WHEN THE LOST AND IMPROPER REFERENT SPEAKS

If "women" within political discourse can never fully describe that which it names, that is neither because the category simply refers without describing nor because "women" are the lost referent, that which "does not exist," but because the term marks a dense intersection of social relations that cannot be summarized through the terms of identity.[19] The term will gain and lose its stability to the extent that it remains differentiated and that differentiation serves political goals. To the degree that that differentiation produces the effect of a radical essentialism of gender, the term will work to sever its constitutive connections with other discursive sites of political investment and undercut its own capacity to compel and produce the constituency it names. The constitutive instability of the term, its incapacity ever fully to describe what it names, is produced precisely by what is excluded in order for the determination to take place. That there are always constitutive exclusions that condition the possibility of provisionally fixing a name does not entail a necessary collapse of that constitutive outside with a notion of a lost referent, that "bar" which is the law of castration, emblematized by the woman who does not exist. Such a view not only reifies women as the lost referent, that which cannot exist; and feminism, as the vain effort to resist that particular proclamation of the law (a form of psychosis in speech, a resistance to penis envy). To call into question women as the privileged figure for "the lost referent," however, is precisely to recast that description as a possible signification, and to open the term as a site for a more expansive rearticulation.

Paradoxically, the assertion of the real as the constitutive outside to symbolization is meant to support anti-essentialism, for if all symbolization is predicated on a lack, then there can be no complete or self-identical articulation of a given social identity. And yet, if women are positioned as that which cannot exist, as that which is barred from existence by the law of the father, then there is a conflation of women with that foreclosed existence, that lost referent, that is surely as pernicious as any form of ontological essentialism.

If essentialism is an effort to preclude the possibility of a future for the signifier, then the task is surely to make the signifier into a site for a set of rearticulations that cannot be predicted or controlled, and to provide for a future in which constituencies will form that have not yet had a site for such an articulation or which "are" not prior to the siting of such a site.

Here it is not only expected unity that compels phantasmatic investment in any such signifier, for sometimes it is precisely the sense of futurity opened up by the signifier as a site of rearticulations that is the discursive occasion for hope. Žižek persuasively describes how once the political signifier has temporarily constituted the unity that it promises, that promise proves impossible to fulfill and a *dis*identification ensues, one that can produce factionalization to the point of political immobilization. But does politicization always need to overcome disidentification? What are the possibilities of politicizing *dis*identification, this experience of *misrecognition*, this uneasy sense of standing under a sign to which one does and does not belong? And how are we to interpret this disidentification produced by and through the very signifier that holds out the promise of solidarity? Lauren Berlant writes that "feminists must embrace a policy of female disidentification at the level of female essence."[20] The expectation of a full recognition, she writes, leads to a necessary scene of "monstrous doubling" and "narcissistic horror" (253), a litany of complaint and recrimination in the wake of the failure of the term to reflect the recognition it appears to promise. But if the term cannot offer ultimate recognition—and here Žižek is very right to claim that all such terms rest on a necessary *méconnaisance*—it may be that the affirmation of that slippage, that failure of identification is itself the point of departure for a more democratizing affirmation of internal difference.[21]

To take up the political signifier (which is always a matter of taking up a signifier by which one is oneself already taken up, constituted, initiated) is to be taken into a chain of prior usages, to be installed in the midst of significations that cannot be situated in terms of clear origins or ultimate goals. This means that what is called agency can never be understood as a controlling or original authorship over that signifying chain, and it cannot be the power, once installed and constituted in and by that chain, to set a sure course for its future. But what is here called a "chain" of signification operates through a certain insistent citing of the signifier, an iterable practice whereby the political signifier is perpetually resignified, a repetition compulsion at the level of signification; indeed, an iterable practice that shows that what one takes to be a political signifier is itself the sedimentation of prior signifiers, the effect of their reworking, such that a signifier is political to the extent that it implicitly cites the prior instances of itself, drawing the phantasmatic promise of those prior signifiers, reworking them into the production and promise of "the new," a "new" that is itself only established through recourse to those embedded conventions, past conventions, that have conventionally been invested with the political power to signify the future.

It is in this sense, then, that political signifiers might be avowed as performative, but that performativity might be rethought as the force of citationality. "Agency" would then be the double-movement of being constituted in and by a signifier, where "to be constituted" means "to be compelled to cite or repeat or mime" the signifier itself. Enabled by the very signifier that depends for its continuation on the future of that citational chain, agency is the hiatus in iterability, the compulsion to install an identity through repetition, which requires the very contingency, the undetermined interval, that identity insistently seeks to foreclose. The more insistent the foreclosure, the more exacerbated the temporal nondentity of that which is heralded by the signifier of identity. And yet, the future of the signifier of identity can only be secured through a repetition that fails to repeat loyally, a reciting of the signifier that must commit a disloyalty against identity—a catachresis—in order to secure its future, a disloyalty that works the iterability of the signifier for what remains non-self-identical in any invocation of identity, namely, the iterable or temporal conditions of its own possibility.

For the purposes of political solidarity, however provisional, Žižek calls for a political performative that will halt the disunity and discontinuity of the signified and produce a temporary linguistic unity. The failure of every such unity can be reduced to a "lack" with no historicity, the consequence of a transhistorical "law," but such a reduction will miss the failures and discontinuities produced by social relations that invariably exceed the signifier and whose exclusions are necessary for the stabilization of the signifier. The "failure" of the signifier to produce the unity it appears to name is not the result of an existential void, but the result of that term's incapacity to include the social relations that it provisionally stabilizes through a set of contingent exclusions. This incompleteness will be the result of a specific set of social exclusions that return to haunt the claims of identity defined through negation; these exclusions need to be read and used in the reformulation and expansion of a democratizing reiteration of the term. That there can be no final or complete inclusivity is thus a function of the complexity and historicity of a social field that can never be summarized by any given description, and that, for democratic reasons, ought never to be.

When some set of descriptions is offered to fill out the content of an identity, the result is inevitably fractious. Such inclusionary descriptions produce inadvertently new sites of contest and a host of resistances, disclaimers, and refusals to identify with the terms. As non-referential terms, "women" and "queer" institute provisional identities and, inevitably, a provisional set of exclusions. The descriptivist ideal creates the expectation that a full and final enumeration of features is possible. As a result, it orients identity politics toward a full confession of the contents of any given identity category. When those contents turn out to be illimitable, or limited by a preemptory act of foreclosure, identity politics founders on factionalized disputes over self-definition or on the demand to provide ever more personalized and specified testimonies of self-disclosure that never fully satisfy the ideal under which they labor.

To understand "women" as a permanent site of contest,[22] or as a feminist site of agonistic struggle, is to presume that there can be no closure on the category and that, for politically significant reasons, there ought never to be. That the category can never be descriptive is the very condition of its political efficacy. In this sense, what is lamented as disunity and factionalization from the perspective informed by the descriptivist ideal is *affirmed* by the anti-descriptivist perspective as the open and democratizing potential of the category.

Here the numerous refusals on the part of "women" to accept the descriptions offered in the name of "women" not only attest to the specific violences that a partial concept enforces, but to the constitutive impossibility of an impartial or comprehensive concept or category. The claim to have achieved such an impartial concept or description shores itself up by foreclosing the very political field that it claims to have exhausted. This violence is at once performed and erased by a description that claims finality and all-inclusiveness. To ameliorate and rework this violence, it is necessary to learn a double movement: to invoke the category and, hence, provisionally to institute an identity and at the same time to open the category as a site of permanent political contest. That the term is questionable does not mean that we ought not to use it, but neither does the necessity to use it mean that we ought not perpetually to interrogate the exclusions by which it proceeds, and to do this precisely in order to learn how to live the contingency of the political signifier in a culture of democratic contestation.

8

CRITICALLY QUEER

Discourse is not life; its time is not yours.
　　　　　—Michel Foucault, "Politics and the Study of Discourse"

The risk of offering a final chapter on "queer" is that the term will be taken as the summary moment, but I want to make a case that it is perhaps only the most recent. In fact, the temporality of the term is precisely what concerns me here: how is it that a term that signaled degradation has been turned—"refunctioned" in the Brechtian sense—to signify a new and affirmative set of meanings? Is this a simple reversal of valuations such that "queer" means either a past degradation or a present or future affirmation? Is this a reversal that retains and reiterates the abjected history of the term? When the term has been used as a paralyzing slur, as the mundane interpellation of pathologized sexuality, it has produced the user of the term as the emblem and vehicle of normalization; the occasion of its utterance, as the discursive regulation of the boundaries of sexual legitimacy. Much of the straight world has always needed the queers it has sought to repudiate through the performative force of the term. If the term is now subject to a reappropriation, what are the conditions and limits of that significant reversal? Does the reversal reiterate the logic of repudiation by which it was spawned? Can the term overcome its constitutive history of injury? Does it present the discursive occasion for a powerful and compelling fantasy of historical reparation? When and how does a term like "queer" become subject to an affirmative resignification for some when a term like "nigger," despite some recent efforts at reclamation, appears capable of only reinscribing its pain? How and where does discourse reiterate injury such that the various efforts to recontextualize and resignify a given term meet their limit in this other, more brutal, and relentless form of repetition?[1]

In *On the Genealogy of Morals,* Nietzsche introduces the notion of the "sign-chain" in which one might read a utopian investment in discourse, one that reemerges within Foucault's conception of discursive power.

Nietzsche writes, "the entire history of a 'thing,' an organ, a custom can be a continuous sign-chain of ever new interpretations and adaptations whose causes do not even have to be related to one another but, on the contrary, in some cases succeed and alternate with one another in a purely chance fashion" (77). The "ever new" possibilities of resignification are derived from the postulated historical discontinuity of the term. But is this postulation itself suspect? Can resignifiability be derived from a pure historicity of "signs"? Or must there be a way to think about the constraints on and in resignification that takes account of its propensity to return to the "ever old" in relations of social power? And can Foucault help us here or does he, rather, reiterate Nietzchean hopefulness within the discourse of power? Investing power with a kind of vitalism, Foucault echoes Nietzsche as he refers to power as "ceaseless struggles and confrontations...produced from one moment to the next, at every point, or rather in every relation from one point to another."[2]

Neither power nor discourse are rendered anew at every moment; they are not as weightless as the utopics of radical resignification might imply. And yet how are we to understand their convergent force as an accumulated effect of usage that both constrains and enables their reworking? How is it that the apparently injurious effects of discourse become the painful resources by which a resignifying practice is wrought? Here it is not only a question of how discourse injures bodies, but how certain injuries establish certain bodies at the limits of available ontologies, available schemes of intelligibility. And further, how is it that those who are abjected come to make their claim through and against the discourses that have sought their repudiation?

PERFORMATIVE POWER

Eve Sedgwick's recent reflections on queer performativity ask us not only to consider how a certain theory of speech acts applies to queer practices, but how it is that "queering" persists as a defining moment of performativity.[3] The centrality of the marriage ceremony in J.L. Austin's examples of performativity suggests that the heterosexualization of the social bond is the paradigmatic form for those speech acts which bring about what they name. "I pronounce you..." puts into effect the relation that it names. But from where and when does such a performative draw its force, and what happens to the performative when its purpose is precisely to undo the presumptive force of the heterosexual ceremonial?

Performative acts are forms of authoritative speech: most performatives, for instance, are statements that, in the uttering, also perform a certain action and exercise a binding power.[4] Implicated in a network of authorization and punishment, performatives tend to include legal sentences, baptisms, inaugurations, declarations of ownership, statements which not only perform an action, but confer a binding power on the action performed. If the power of discourse to produce that which it names is linked with the question of performativity, then the performative is one domain in which power acts *as* discourse.

Importantly, however, there is no power, construed as a subject, that acts, but only, to repeat an earlier phrase, a reiterated acting that *is* power in its persistence and instability. This is less an "act," singular and deliberate, than a nexus of power and discourse that repeats or mimes the discursive gestures of power. Hence, the judge who authorizes and installs the situation he names invariably *cites* the law that he applies, and it is the power of this citation that gives the performative its binding or conferring power. And though it may appear that the binding power of his words is derived from the force of his will or from a prior authority, the opposite is more true: it is *through* the citation of the law that the figure of the judge's "will" is produced and that the "priority" of textual authority is established.[5] Indeed, it is through the invocation of convention that the speech act of the judge derives its binding power; that binding power is to be found neither in the subject of the judge nor in his will, but in the citational legacy by which a contemporary "act" emerges in the context of a chain of binding conventions.

Where there is an "I" who utters or speaks and thereby produces an effect in discourse, there is first a discourse which precedes and enables that "I" and forms in language the constraining trajectory of its will. Thus there is no "I" who stands *behind* discourse and executes its volition or will *through* discourse. On the contrary, the "I" only comes into being through being called, named, interpellated, to use the Althusserian term, and this discursive constitution takes place prior to the "I"; it is the transitive invocation of the "I." Indeed, I can only say "I" to the extent that I have first been addressed, and that address has mobilized my place in speech; paradoxically, the discursive condition of social recognition *precedes and conditions* the formation of the subject: recognition is not conferred on a subject, but forms that subject. Further, the impossibility of a full recognition, that is, of ever fully inhabiting the name by which one's social identity is inaugurated and mobilized, implies the instability and incompleteness of subject-formation. The "I" is thus a citation of the place of the "I" in speech, where that place has a certain priority and anonymity with respect to the life it animates: it is the historically revisable possibility of a name that precedes and exceeds me, but without which I cannot speak.

QUEER TROUBLE

The term "queer" emerges as an interpellation that raises the question of the status of force and opposition, of stability and variability, *within* performativity. The term "queer" has operated as one linguistic practice whose purpose has been the shaming of the subject it names or, rather, the producing of a subject *through* that shaming interpellation. "Queer" derives its force precisely through the repeated invocation by which it has become linked to accusation, pathologization, insult. This is an invocation by which a social bond among homophobic communities is formed through time. The interpellation echoes past interpellations, and binds the speakers, as if they spoke in unison across time. In this sense, it is always an imaginary chorus that taunts "queer!" To what extent, then, has the performative "queer" operated alongside, as a deformation of, the "I pronounce you…" of the marriage ceremony? If the performative operates as the sanction that performs the heterosexualization of the social bond, perhaps it also comes into play precisely as the shaming taboo which "queers" those who resist or oppose that social form as well as those who occupy it without hegemonic social sanction.

On that note, let us remember that reiterations are never simply replicas of the same. And the "act" by which a name authorizes or deauthorizes a set of social or sexual relations is, of necessity, *a repetition.* "Could a performative succeed," asks Derrida, "if its formulation did not repeat a 'coded' or iterable utterance…if it were not identifiable in some way as a 'citation'?"[6] If a performative provisionally succeeds (and I will suggest that "success" is always and only provisional), then it is not because an intention successfully governs the action of speech, but only because that action echoes prior actions, and *accumulates the force of authority through the repetition or citation of a prior, authoritative set of practices.* What this means, then, is that a performative "works" to the extent that *it draws on and covers over* the constitutive conventions by which it is mobilized. In this sense, no term or statement can function performatively without the accumulating and dissimulating historicity of force.

This view of performativity implies that discourse has a history[7] that not only precedes but conditions its contemporary usages, and that this history effectively decenters the presentist view of the subject as the exclusive origin or owner of what is said.[8] What it also means is that the terms to which we do, nevertheless, lay claim, the terms through which we insist on politicizing identity and desire, often demand a turn *against* this constitutive historicity. Those of us who have questioned the presentist assumptions in contemporary identity categories are, therefore, sometimes charged with depoliticizing theory. And yet, if the genealogical critique of the subject is the interrogation of those constitutive and exclusionary relations of power through which contemporary discursive resources are formed, then it follows that the critique of the queer subject is crucial to the continuing *democratization* of queer politics. As much as identity terms must be used, as much as "outness" is to be affirmed, these same notions must become subject to a critique of the exclusionary operations of their own production: For whom is outness a historically available and affordable option? Is there an unmarked class character to the demand for universal "outness"? Who is represented by *which* use of the term, and who is excluded? For whom does the term present an impossible conflict between racial, ethnic, or religious affiliation and sexual politics? What kinds of policies are enabled by what kinds of usages, and which are backgrounded or erased from view? In this sense, the genealogical critique of the queer subject will be central to queer politics to the extent that it constitutes a self-critical dimension within activism, a persistent reminder to take the time to consider the exclusionary force of one of activism's most treasured contemporary premises.

As much as it is necessary to assert political demands through recourse to identity categories, and to lay claim to the power to name oneself and determine the conditions under which that name is used, it is also impossible to sustain that kind of mastery over the trajectory of those categories within discourse. This is not an argument *against* using identity categories, but it is a reminder of the risk that attends every such use. The expectation of self-determination that self-naming arouses is paradoxically contested by the historicity of the name itself: by the history of the usages that one never controlled, but that constrain the very usage that now emblematizes autonomy; by the future efforts to deploy the term against the grain of the current ones, and that will exceed the control of those who seek to set the course of the terms in the present.

If the term "queer" is to be a site of collective contestation, the point of departure for a set of historical reflections and futural imaginings, it will have to remain that which is, in the present, never fully owned, but always and only redeployed, twisted, queered from a prior usage and in the direction of urgent and expanding political purposes. This also means that it will doubtless have to be yielded in favor of terms that do that political work more effectively. Such a yielding may well become necessary in order to accommodate—without domesticating—democratizing contestations that have and will redraw the contours of the movement in ways that can never be fully anticipated in advance.

It may be that the conceit of autonomy implied by self-naming is the paradigmatically presentist conceit, that is, the belief that there is a one who arrives in the world, in discourse, without a history, that this one makes oneself in and through the magic of the name, that language expresses a "will" or a "choice" rather than a complex and constitutive history of discourse and power which compose the invariably ambivalent resources through which a queer and queering agency is forged and reworked. To recast queer agency in this chain of historicity is thus to avow a set of constraints on the past and the future that mark at once the *limits* of agency and its most *enabling conditions*. As expansive as the term "queer" is meant to be, it is used in ways that enforce a set of overlapping divisions: in some contexts, the term appeals to a younger generation who want to resist the more institutionalized and reformist politics sometimes signified by "lesbian and gay"; in some contexts, sometimes the same, it has marked a predominantly white movement that has not fully addressed the way in which "queer" plays—or fails to play—within non-white communities; and whereas in some instances it has mobilized a lesbian activism,[9] in others the term represents a false unity of women and men. Indeed, it may be that the critique of the term will initiate a resurgence of both feminist and anti-racist mobilization within lesbian and gay politics or open up new possibilities for coalitional alliances that do not presume that these constituencies are radically distinct from one another. The term will be revised, dispelled, rendered obsolete to the extent that it yields to the demands which resist the term precisely because of the exclusions by which it is mobilized.

We no more create from nothing the political terms that come to represent our "freedom" than we are responsible for the terms that carry the pain of social injury. And yet, neither of those terms are as a result any less necessary to work and rework within political discourse.

In this sense, it remains politically necessary to lay claim to "women," "queer," "gay," and "lesbian," precisely because of the way these terms, as it were, lay their claim on us prior to our full knowing. Laying claim to such terms in reverse will be necessary to refute homophobic deployments of the terms in law, public policy, on the street, in "private" life. But the necessity to mobilize the necessary error of identity (Spivak's term) will always be in tension with the democratic contestation of the term which works against its deployments in racist and misogynist discursive regimes. If "queer" politics postures independently of these other modalities of power, it will lose its democratizing force. The political deconstruction of "queer" ought not to paralyze the use of such terms, but, ideally, to extend its range, to make us consider at what expense and for what purposes the terms are used, and through what relations of power such categories have been wrought. Some recent race theory has underscored the use of "race" in the service of "racism," and proposed a politically informed inquiry into the process of *racialization*, the formation of race.[10] Such an inquiry does not suspend or ban the term, although it does insist that an inquiry into formation is linked to the contemporary question of what is at stake in the term. The point may be taken for queer studies as well, such that "queering" might signal an inquiry into (a) the *formation* of homosexualities (a historical inquiry which cannot take the stability of the term for granted, despite the political pressure to do so) and (b) the *deformative* and *misappropriative* power that the term currently enjoys. At stake in such a history will be the differential formation of homosexuality across racial boundaries, including the question of how racial and reproductive relations become articulated through one another.

One might be tempted to say that identity categories are insufficient because every subject position is the site of converging relations of power that are not univocal. But such a formulation underestimates the radical challenge to the subject that such converging relations imply. For there is no self-identical subject who houses or bears these relations, no site at which such relations converge. This converging and interarticulation *is* the contemporary fate of the subject. In other words, the subject as a self-identical entity is no more.

It is in this sense that the temporary totalization performed by identity categories is a necessary error. And if identity is a necessary error, then the assertion of "queer" will be necessary as a term of affiliation, but it will not fully describe those it purports to represent. As a result, it will be necessary to affirm the contingency of the term: to let it be vanquished by those who are excluded by the term but who justifiably expect representation by it, to let it take on meanings that cannot now be anticipated by a younger generation whose political vocabulary may well carry a very different set of investments. Indeed, the term "queer" itself has been precisely the discursive rallying point for younger lesbians and gay men and, in yet other contexts, for lesbian interventions and, in yet other contexts, for bisexuals and straights for whom the term expresses an affiliation with anti-homophobic politics. That it can become such a discursive site whose uses are not fully constrained in advance ought to be safeguarded not only for the purposes of continuing to democratize queer politics, but also to expose, affirm, and rework the specific historicity of the term.

GENDER PERFORMATIVITY AND DRAG

How, if at all, is the notion of discursive resignification linked to the notion of gender parody or impersonation? First, what is meant by understanding gender as an impersonation? Does this mean that one puts on a mask or persona, that there is a "one" who precedes that "putting on," who is something other than its gender from the start? Or does this miming, this impersonating precede and form the "one," operating as its formative precondition rather than its dispensable artifice?

The construal of gender-as-drag according to the first model appears to be the effect of a number of circumstances. One of them I brought on myself by citing drag as an example of performativity, a move that was taken then, by some, to be *exemplary* of performativity. If drag is performative, that does not mean that all performativity is to be understood as drag. The publication of *Gender Trouble* coincided with a number of publications that did assert that "clothes make the woman," but I never did think that gender was like clothes, or that clothes make the woman. Added to these, however, are the political needs of an emergent queer movement in which the publicization of theatrical agency has become quite central.[11]

The practice by which gendering occurs, the embodying of norms, is a compulsory practice, a forcible production, but not for that reason fully determining. To the extent that gender is an assignment, it is an assignment which is never quite carried out according to expectation, whose addressee never quite inhabits the ideal s/he is compelled to approximate. Moreover, this embodying is a repeated process. And one might construe repetition as precisely that which *undermines* the conceit of voluntarist mastery designated by the subject in language.

As *Paris Is Burning* made clear, drag is not unproblematically subversive. It serves a subversive function to the extent that it reflects the mundane impersonations by which heterosexually ideal genders are performed and naturalized and undermines their power by virtue of effecting that exposure. But there is no guarantee that exposing the naturalized status of heterosexuality will lead to its subversion. Heterosexuality can augment its hegemony *through* its denaturalization, as when we see denaturalizing parodies that reidealize heterosexual norms *without* calling them into question.

On other occasions, though, the transferability of a gender ideal or gender norm calls into question the abjecting power that it sustains. For an occupation or reterritorialization of a term that has been used to abject a population can become the site of resistance, the possibility of an enabling social and political resignification. And this has happened to a certain extent with the notion of "queer." The contemporary redeployment enacts a prohibition and a degradation against itself, spawning a different order of values, a political affirmation from and through the very term which in a prior usage had as it final aim the eradication of precisely such an affirmation.

It may seem, however, that there is a difference between the embodying or performing of gender norms and the performative use of discourse. Are these two different senses of "performativity," or do they converge as modes of citationality in which the compulsory character of certain social imperatives becomes subject to a more promising deregulation? Gender norms operate by requiring the embodiment of certain ideals of femininity and masculinity, ones that are almost always related to the idealization of the heterosexual bond. In this sense, the initiatory performative, "It's a girl!" anticipates the eventual arrival of the sanction, "I pronounce you man and wife." Hence, also, the peculiar pleasure of the cartoon strip in which the infant is first interpellated into discourse with "It's a lesbian!" Far from an essentialist joke, the queer appropriation of the performative mimes and exposes both the binding power of the heterosexualizing law *and its expropriability.*

To the extent that the naming of the "girl" is transitive, that is, initiates the process by which a certain "girling" is compelled, the term or, rather, its symbolic power, governs the formation of a corporeally enacted femininity that never fully approximates the norm. This is a "girl," however, who is compelled to "cite" the norm in order to qualify and remain a viable subject. Femininity is thus not the product of a choice, but the forcible citation of a norm, one whose complex historicity is indissociable from relations of discipline, regulation, punishment. Indeed, there is no "one" who takes on a gender norm. On the contrary, this citation of the gender norm is necessary in order to qualify as a "one," to become viable as a "one," where subject-formation is dependent on the prior operation of legitimating gender norms.

It is in terms of a norm that compels a certain "citation" in order for a viable subject to be produced that the notion of gender performativity calls to be rethought. And precisely in relation to such a compulsory citationality that the theatricality of gender is also to be explained. Theatricality need not be conflated with self-display or self-creation. Within queer politics, indeed, within the very signification that is "queer," we read a resignifying practice in which the desanctioning power of the name "queer" is reversed to sanction a contestation of the terms of sexual legitimacy. Paradoxically, but also with great promise, the subject who is "queered" into public discourse through homophobic interpellations of various kinds *takes up* or *cites* that very term as the discursive basis for an opposition. This kind of citation will emerge as *theatrical* to the extent that it *mimes and renders hyperbolic* the discursive convention that it also *reverses.* The hyperbolic gesture is crucial to the exposure of the homophobic "law" that can no longer control the terms of its own abjecting strategies.

To oppose the theatrical to the political within contemporary queer politics is, I would argue, an impossibility: the hyperbolic "performance" of death in the practice of "die-ins" and the theatrical "outness" by which queer activism has disrupted the closeting distinction between public and private space have proliferated sites of politicization and AIDS awareness throughout the public realm. Indeed, an important set of histories might be told in which the increasing politicization *of* theatricality for queers is at stake (more productive, I think, than an insistence on the two as polar opposites within queerness). Such a history might include traditions of cross-dressing, drag balls, street walking, butch-femme spectacles, the sliding between the "march" (New York City) and the parade (San Francisco); die-ins by ACT UP, kiss-ins by Queer Nation; drag performance benefits for AIDS (by which I would include both Lypsinka's and Liza Minnelli's in which she, finally, does Judy[12]); the convergence of theatrical work with theatrical activism;[13] performing excessive lesbian sexuality and iconography that effectively counters the desexualization of the lesbian; tactical interruptions of public forums by lesbian and gay activists in favor of drawing public attention and outrage to the failure of government funding of AIDS research and outreach.

The increasing theatricalization of political rage in response to the killing inattention of public policy-makers on the issue of AIDS is allegorized in the recontextualization of "queer" from its place within a homophobic strategy of abjection and annihilation to an insistent and public severing of that interpellation from the effect of shame. To the extent that shame is produced as the stigma not only of AIDS, but also of queerness, where the latter is understood through homophobic causalities as the "cause" and "manifestation" of the illness, theatrical rage is part of the public resistance to that interpellation of shame. Mobilized by the injuries of homophobia, theatrical rage reiterates those injuries precisely through an "acting out," one that does not merely repeat or recite those injuries, but that also deploys a hyperbolic display of death and injury to overwhelm the epistemic resistance to AIDS and to the graphics of suffering, or a hyperbolic display of kissing to shatter the epistemic blindness to an increasingly graphic and public homosexuality.

MELANCHOLIA AND THE LIMITS OF PERFORMANCE

The critical potential of "drag" centrally concerns a critique of a prevailing truth-regime of "sex," one that I take to be pervasively heterosexist: the distinction between the "inside" truth of femininity, considered as psychic disposition or ego-core, and the "outside" truth, considered as appearance or presentation, produces a contradictory formation of gender in which no fixed "truth" can be established. Gender is neither a purely psychic truth, conceived as "internal" and "hidden," nor is it reducible to a surface appearance; on the contrary, its undecidability is to be traced as the play *between* psyche and appearance (where the latter domain includes what appears *in words*). Further, this will be a "play" regulated by heterosexist constraints though not, for that reason, fully reducible to them.

In no sense can it be concluded that the part of gender that is performed is therefore the "truth" of gender; performance as bounded "act" is distinguished from performativity insofar as the latter consists in a reiteration of norms which precede, constrain, and exceed the performer and in that sense cannot be taken as the fabrication of the performer's "will" or "choice"; further, what is "performed" works to conceal, if not to disavow, what remains opaque, unconscious, unperformable. The reduction of performativity to performance would be a mistake.

The rejection of an expressive model of drag which holds that some interior truth is exteriorized in performance needs, however, to be referred to a psychoanalytic consideration on the relationship between how gender *appears* and what gender *signifies*. Psychoanalysis insists that the opacity of the unconscious sets limits to the exteriorization of the psyche. It also argues, rightly I think, that what is exteriorized or performed can only be understood through reference to what is barred from the signifier and from the domain of corporeal legibility.

How precisely do repudiated identifications, identifications that do not "show," circumscribe and materialize the identifications that do? Here it seems useful to rethink the notion of gender-as-drag in terms of the analysis of gender melancholia.[14] Given the iconographic figure of the melancholic drag queen, one might consider whether and how these terms work together. Here, one might ask also after the disavowal that occasions performance and that performance might be said to enact, where performance engages "acting out" in the psychoanalytic sense.[15] If melancholia in Freud's sense is the effect of an ungrieved loss (a sustaining of the lost object/Other as a psychic figure with the consequence of heightened identification with that Other, self-beratement, and the acting out of unresolved anger and love),[16] it may be that performance, understood as "acting out," is significantly related to the problem of unacknowledged loss. Where there is an ungrieved loss in drag performance (and I am sure that such a generalization cannot be universalized), perhaps it is a loss that is refused and incorporated in the performed identification, one that reiterates a gendered idealization and its radical uninhabitability. This is neither a territorialization of the feminine by the masculine nor an "envy" of the masculine by the feminine, nor a sign of the essential plasticity of gender. What it does suggest is that gender performance allegorizes a loss it cannot grieve, allegorizes the incorporative fantasy of melancholia whereby an object is phantasmatically taken in or on as a way of refusing to let it go.

The analysis above is a risky one because it suggests that for a "man" performing femininity or for a "woman" performing masculinity (the latter is always, in effect, to perform a little less, given that femininity is often cast as the spectacular gender) there is an attachment to and a loss and refusal of the figure of femininity by the man, or the figure of masculinity by the woman. Thus, it is important to underscore that drag is an effort to negotiate cross-gendered identification, but that cross-gendered identification is not the exemplary paradigm for thinking about homosexuality, although it may be one. In this sense, drag allegorizes some set of melancholic incorporative fantasies that stabilize *gender*. Not only are a vast number of drag performers straight, but it would be a mistake to think that homosexuality is best explained through the performativity that is drag. What does seem useful in this analysis, however, is that drag exposes or allegorizes the mundane psychic and performative practices by which heterosexualized genders form themselves through the renunciation of the *possibility* of homosexuality, a foreclosure that produces a field of heterosexual objects at the same time that it produces a domain of those whom it would be impossible to love. Drag thus allegorizes *heterosexual melancholy*, the melancholy by which a masculine gender is formed from the refusal to grieve the masculine as a possibility of love; a feminine gender is formed (taken on, assumed) through the incorporative fantasy by which the feminine is excluded as a possible object of love, an exclusion never grieved, but "preserved" through the heightening of feminine identification itself. In this sense, the "truest" lesbian melancholic is the strictly straight woman, and the "truest" gay male melancholic is the strictly straight man.

What drag exposes, however, is the "normal" constitution of gender presentation in which the gender performed is in many ways constituted by a set of disavowed attachments or identifications that constitute a different domain of the "unperformable." Indeed, it may well be that what constitutes the *sexually* unperformable is performed instead as *gender iden-tification.*[17] To the extent that homosexual attachments remain unacknowl-edged within normative heterosexuality, they are not merely constituted as desires that emerge and subsequently become prohibited. Rather, these are desires that are proscribed from the start. And when they do emerge on the far side of the censor, they may well carry that mark of impossibili-ty with them, performing, as it were, as the impossible within the possible. As such, they will not be attachments that can be openly grieved. This is, then, less *the refusal* to grieve (a formulation that accents the choice involved) than a preemption of grief performed by the absence of cultural conventions for avowing the loss of homosexual love. And it is this absence that produces a culture of heterosexual melancholy, one that can be read in the hyperbolic identifications by which mundane heterosexual masculinity and femininity confirm themselves. The straight man *becomes* (mimes, cites, appropriates, assumes the status of) the man he "never" loved and "never" grieved; the straight woman *becomes* the woman she "never" loved and "never" grieved. It is in this sense, then, that what is most apparently performed as gender is the sign and symptom of a perva-sive disavowal.

Moreover, it is precisely to counter this pervasive cultural risk of gay melancholia (what the newspapers generalize as "depression") that there has been an insistent publicization and politicization of grief over those who have died from AIDS; the NAMES Project Quilt is exemplary, ritu-alizing and repeating the name itself as a way of publically avowing the limitless loss.[18]

Insofar as grief remains unspeakable, the rage over the loss can redou-ble by virtue of remaining unavowed. And if that very rage over loss is publically proscribed, the melancholic effects of such a proscription can achieve suicidal proportions. The emergence of collective institutions for grieving are thus crucial to survival, to the reassembling of community, the reworking of kinship, the reweaving of sustaining relations. And inso-far as they involve the publicization and dramatization of death, they call to be read as life-affirming rejoinders to the dire psychic consequences of a grieving process culturally thwarted and proscribed.

GENDERED AND SEXUAL PERFORMATIVITY

How then does one link the trope by which discourse is described as "performing" and that theatrical sense of performance in which the hyperbolic status of gender norms seems central? What is "performed" in drag is, of course, *the sign* of gender, a sign that is not the same as the body that it figures, but that cannot be read without it. The sign, understood as a gender imperative—"girl!"—reads less as an assignment than as a command and, as such, produces its own insubordinations. The hyperbolic conformity to the command can reveal the hyperbolic status of the norm itself, indeed, can become the cultural sign by which that cultural imperative might become legible. Insofar as heterosexual gender norms produce inapproximable ideals, heterosexuality can be said to operate through the regulated production of hyperbolic versions of "man" and "woman." These are for the most part compulsory performances, ones which none of us choose, but which each of us is forced to negotiate. I write "forced to negotiate" because the compulsory character of these norms does not always make them efficacious. Such norms are continually haunted by their own inefficacy; hence, the anxiously repeated effort to install and augment their jurisdiction.

The resignification of norms is thus a function of their *inefficacy*, and so the question of subversion, of *working the weakness in the norm*, becomes a matter of inhabiting the practices of its rearticulation. The critical promise of drag does not have to do with the proliferation of genders, as if a sheer increase in numbers would do the job, but rather with the exposure or the failure of heterosexual regimes ever fully to legislate or contain their own ideals. Hence, it is not that drag *opposes* heterosexuality, or that the proliferation of drag will bring down heterosexuality; on the contrary, drag tends to be the allegorization of heterosexuality and its constitutive melancholia. As an allegory that works through the hyperbolic, drag brings into relief what is, after all, determined only in relation to the hyperbolic: the understated, taken-for-granted quality of heterosexual performativity. At its best, then, drag can be read for the way in which hyperbolic norms are dissimulated as the heterosexual mundane. At the same time these same norms, taken not as commands to be obeyed, but as imperatives to be "cited," twisted, queered, brought into relief as heterosexual imperatives, are not, for that reason, necessarily subverted in the process.

It is important to emphasize that although heterosexuality operates in part through the stabilization of gender norms, gender designates a dense site of significations that contain and exceed the heterosexual matrix. Although forms of sexuality do not unilaterally determine gender, a non-causal and non-reductive connection between sexuality and gender is nevertheless crucial to maintain. Precisely because homophobia often operates through the attribution of a damaged, failed, or otherwise abject gender to homosexuals, that is, calling gay men "feminine" or calling lesbians "masculine," and because the homophobic terror over performing homosexual acts, where it exists, is often also a terror over losing proper gender ("no longer being a real or proper man" or "no longer being a real and proper woman"), it seems crucial to retain a theoretical apparatus that will account for how sexuality is regulated through the policing and the shaming of gender.

We might want to claim that certain kinds of sexual practices link people more strongly than gender affiliation,[19] but such claims can only be negotiated, if they can, in relation to specific occasions for affiliation; there is nothing in either sexual practice or in gender to privilege one over the other. Sexual practices, however, will invariably be experienced differentially depending on the relations of gender in which they occur. And there may be forms of "gender" within homosexuality which call for a theorization that moves beyond the categories of "masculine" and "feminine." If we seek to privilege sexual practice as a way of transcending gender, we might ask at what cost the *analytic* separability of the two domains is taken to be a distinction in fact. Is there perhaps a specific gender pain that provokes such fantasies of a sexual practice that would transcend gender difference altogether, in which the marks of masculinity and femininity would no longer be legible? Would this not be a sexual practice paradigmatically fetishistic, trying not to know what it knows, but knowing it all the same? This question is not meant to demean the fetish (where would we be without it?), but it does mean to ask whether it is only according to a logic of the fetish that the radical separability of sexuality and gender can be thought.

In theories such as Catharine MacKinnon's, sexual relations of subordination are understood to establish differential gender categories, such that "men" are those defined in a sexually dominating social position and "women" are those defined in subordination. Her highly deterministic account leaves no room for relations of sexuality to be theorized apart from the rigid framework of gender difference or for kinds of sexual regulation that do not take gender as their primary objects (i.e., the prohibition of sodomy, public sex, consensual homosexuality). Hence, Gayle Rubin's influential distinction between the domains of sexuality and gender in "Thinking Sex" and Sedgwick's reformulation of that position have constituted important theoretical opposition to MacKinnon's deterministic form of structuralism.[20]

My sense is that now this very opposition needs to be rethought in order to muddle the lines between queer theory and feminism.[21] For surely it is as unacceptable to insist that relations of sexual subordination determine gender position as it is to separate radically forms of sexuality from the workings of gender norms. The relation between sexual practice and gender is surely not a structurally determined one, but the destabilizing of the heterosexual presumption of that very structuralism still requires a way to think the two in a dynamic relation to one another.

In psychoanalytic terms, the relation between gender and sexuality is in part negotiated through the question of the relationship between identification and desire. And here it becomes clear why refusing to draw lines of causal implication between these two domains is as important as keeping open an investigation of their complex interimplication. For, if to identify as a woman is not necessarily to desire a man, and if to desire a woman does not necessarily signal the constituting presence of a masculine identification, whatever that is, then the heterosexual matrix proves to be an *imaginary* logic that insistently issues forth its own unmanageability. The heterosexual logic that requires that identification and desire be mutually exclusive is one of the most reductive of heterosexism's psychological instruments: if one identifies *as* a given gender, one must desire a different gender. On the one hand, there is no one femininity with which to identify, which is to say that femininity might itself offer an array of identificatory sites, as the proliferation of lesbian femme possibilities attests. On the other hand, it is hardly descriptive of the complex dynamic exchanges of lesbian and gay relationships to presume that homosexual identifications "mirror" or replicate one another. The vocabulary for describing the difficult play, crossing, and destabilization of masculine and feminine identifications within homosexuality has only begun to emerge within theoretical language: the non-academic language historically embedded in gay communities is here much more instructive. The thought of sexual difference *within* homosexuality has yet to be theorized in its complexity.

For one deciding issue will be whether social strategies of regulation, abjection, and normalization will not continue to relink gender and sexuality such that the oppositional analysis will continue to be under pressure to theorize their interrelations. This will not be the same as reducing gender to prevailing forms of sexual relations such that one "is" the effect of the sexual position one is said to occupy. Resisting such a reduction, it ought to be possible to assert a set of non-causal and non-reductive relations between gender and sexuality, not only to link feminism and queer theory, as one might link two separate enterprises, but to establish their constitutive inter-relationship. Similarly, the inquiry into both homosexuality and gender will need to cede the priority of *both* terms in the service of a more complex mapping of power that interrogates the formation of each in specified racial regimes and geopolitical spatializations. And the task, of course, does not stop here, for no one term can serve as foundational, and the success of any given analysis that centers on any one term may well be the marking of its own limitations as an exclusive point of departure.

The goal of this analysis, then, cannot be pure subversion, as if an undermining were enough to establish and direct political struggle. Rather than denaturalization or proliferation, it seems that the question for thinking discourse and power in terms of the future has several paths to follow: how to think power as resignification together with power as the convergence or interarticulation of relations of regulation, domination, constitution? How to know what might qualify as an affirmative resignification—with all the weight and difficulty of that labor—and how to run the risk of reinstalling the abject at the site of its opposition? But how, also, to rethink the terms that establish and sustain bodies that matter?

The film *Paris Is Burning* has been interesting to read less for the ways in which it deploys denaturalizing strategies to reidealize whiteness and heterosexual gender norms than for the less stabilizing rearticulations of kinship it occasioned. The drag balls themselves at times produce high femininity as a function of whiteness and deflect homosexuality through a transgendering that *reidealizes* certain bourgeois forms of heterosexual exchange. And yet, if those performances are not immediately or obviously subversive, it may be that it is rather in the *reformulation of kinship*, in particular, the redefining of the "house" and its forms of collectivity, mothering, mopping, reading, and becoming legendary, that the appropriation and redeployment of the categories of dominant culture enable the formation of kinship relations that function quite supportively as oppositional discourse. In this sense, it would be interesting to read *Paris Is Burning* against, say, Nancy Chodorow's *The Reproduction of Mothering* and ask what happens to psychoanalysis and kinship as a result. In the former, the categories like "house" and "mother" are derived from that family scene, but also deployed to form alternative households and community. This *resignification* marks the workings of an agency that is (a) not the same as voluntarism, and that (b) though *implicated* in the very relations of power it seeks to rival, is not, as a consequence, reducible to those dominant forms.

Performativity describes this relation of being implicated in that which one opposes, this turning of power against itself to produce alternative modalities of power, to establish a kind of political contestation that is not a "pure" opposition, a "transcendence" of contemporary relations of power, but a difficult labor of forging a future from resources inevitably impure.

How will we know the difference between the power we promote and the power we oppose? Is it, one might rejoin, a matter of "knowing?" For one is, as it were, in power even as one opposes it, formed by it as one reworks it, and it is this simultaneity that is at once the condition of our partiality, the measure of our political unknowingness, and also the condition of action itself. The incalculable effects of action are as much a part of their subversive promise as those that we plan in advance.

The effects of performatives, understood as discursive productions, do not conclude at the terminus of a given statement or utterance, the passing of legislation, the announcement of a birth. The reach of their signifiability cannot be controlled by the one who utters or writes, since such productions are not owned by the one who utters them. They continue to signify in spite of their authors, and sometimes against their authors' most precious intentions.

It is one of the ambivalent implications of the decentering of the subject to have one's writing be the site of a necessary and inevitable expropriation. But this yielding of ownership over what one writes has an important set of political corollaries, for the taking up, reforming, deforming of one's words does open up a difficult future terrain of community, one in which the hope of ever fully recognizing oneself in the terms by which one signifies is sure to be disappointed. This not owning of one's words is there from the start, however, since speaking is always in some ways the speaking of a stranger through and as oneself, the melancholic reiteration of a language that one never chose, that one does not find as an instrument to be used, but that one is, as it were, used by, expropriated in, as the unstable and continuing condition of the "one" and the "we," the ambivalent condition of the power that binds.

NOTES

PREFACE

1. Judith Butler, *Gender Trouble: Feminism and the Subversion of Identity* (New York: Routledge, 1990).

INTRODUCTION

1. Clearly, sex is not the only such norm by which bodies become materialized, and it is unclear whether "sex" can operate as a norm apart from other normative requirements on bodies. This will become clear in later sections of this text.

2. Abjection (in latin, *ab-jicere*) literally means to cast off, away, or out and, hence, presupposes and produces a domain of agency from which it is differentiated. Here the casting away resonates with the psychoanalytic notion of *Verwerfung*, implying a foreclosure which founds the subject and which, accordingly, establishes that foundation as tenuous. Whereas the psychoanalytic notion of *Verwerfung*, translated as "foreclosure," produces sociality through a repudiation of a primary signifier which produces an unconscious or, in Lacan's theory, the register of the real, the notion of *abjection* designates a degraded or cast out status within the terms of sociality. Indeed, what is foreclosed or repudiated *within* psychoanalytic terms is precisely what may not reenter the field of the social without threatening psychosis, that is, the dissolution of the subject itself. I want to propose that certain abject zones within sociality also deliver this threat, constituting zones of uninhabitability which a subject fantasizes as threatening its own integrity with the prospect of a psychotic dissolution ("I would rather die than do or be that!"). See the entry under "Forclusion" in Jean Laplanche and J.-B. Pontalis, *Vocabulaire de la psychanalyse* (Paris: Presses Universitaires de France, 1967) pp. 163-167.

3. See Sherry Ortner, "Is Female to Male as Nature is to Culture?", in *Woman, Culture, and Society*, Michele Rosaldo and Louise Lamphere (Stanford: Stanford University Press, 1974) pp. 67-88.

4. For different but related approaches to this problematic of exclusion, abjection, and the creation of "the human," see Julia Kristeva, *Powers of Horror: An Essay on Abjection*, tr. Leon Roudiez (New York: Columbia University Press, 1982); John Fletcher and Andrew Benjamin, eds., *Abjection, Melancholia and Love: The Work of Julia Kristeva* (New York and London: Routledge, 1990); Jean-François Lyotard, *The Inhuman: Reflections on Time*, tr. Geoffrey Bennington and Rachel Bowlby (Stanford: Stanford University Press, 1991).

5. For a very provocative reading which shows how the problem of linguistic referentiality is linked with the specific problem of referring to bodies, and what might be meant by "reference" in such a case, see Cathy Caruth, "The Claims of Reference," *The Yale Journal of Criticism*, vol. 4, no. 1 (Fall 1990): pp. 193-206.

6. Although Foucault distinguishes between juridical and productive models of power in *The History of Sexuality, Volume One*, tr. Robert Hurley (New York: Vintage, 1978), I have argued that the two models presuppose each other. The production of a subject—its subjection (*assujetissement*)—is one means of its regulation. See my "Sexual Inversions," in Domna Stanton, ed., *Discourses of Sexuality* (Ann Arbor: University of Michigan Press, 1992), pp. 344-361.

7. It is not simply a matter of construing performativity as a repetition of acts, as if "acts" remain intact and self-identical as they are repeated in time, and where "time" is understood as external to the "acts" themselves. On the contrary, an act is itself a repetition, a sedimentation, and congealment of the past which is precisely foreclosed in its act-like status. In this sense an "act" is always a provisional failure of memory. In what follows, I make use of the Lacanian notion that every act is to be construed as a repetition, the repetition of what cannot be recollected, of the irrecoverable, and is thus the haunting spectre of the subject's deconstitution. The Derridean notion of iterability, formulated in response to the theorization of speech acts by John Searle and J.L. Austin, also implies that every act is itself a recitation, the citing of a prior chain of acts which are implied in a present act and which perpetually drain any "present" act of its presentness. See note 9 below for the difference between a repetition in the service of the fantasy of mastery (i.e., a repetition of acts which build the subject, and which are said to be the constructive or constituting acts of a subject) and a notion of repetition-compulsion, taken from Freud, which breaks apart that fantasy of mastery and sets its limits.

8. The notion of temporality ought not to be construed as a simple succession of distinct "moments," all of which are equally distant from one another. Such a spatialized mapping of time substitutes a certain mathematical model for the kind of duration which resists such spatializing metaphors. Efforts to describe or name this temporal span tend to engage spatial mapping, as

philosophers from Bergson through Heidegger have argued. Hence, it is important to underscore the effect of *sedimentation* that the temporality of construction implies. Here what are called "moments" are not distinct and equivalent units of time, for the "past" will be the accumulation and congealing of such "moments" to the point of their indistinguishability. But it will also consist of that which is refused from construction, the domains of the repressed, forgotten, and the irrecoverably foreclosed. That which is not included— exteriorized by boundary—as a phenomenal constituent of the sedimented effect called "construction" will be as crucial to its definition as that which is included; this exteriority is not distinguishable as a "moment." Indeed, the notion of the "moment" may well be nothing other than a retrospective fantasy of mathematical mastery imposed upon the interrupted durations of the past.

To argue that construction is fundamentally a matter of iteration is to make the temporal modality of "construction" into a priority. To the extent that such a theory requires a spatialization of time through the postulation of discrete and bounded moments, this temporal account of construction presupposes a spatialization of temporality itself, what one might, following Heidegger, understand as the reduction of temporality to time.

The Foucaultian emphasis on *convergent* relations of power (which might in a tentative way be contrasted with the Derridean emphasis on iterability) implies a mapping of power relations that in the course of a genealogical process form a constructed effect. The notion of convergence presupposes both motion and space; as a result, it appears to elude the paradox noted above in which the very account of temporality requires the spatialization of the "moment." On the other hand, Foucault's account of convergence does not fully theorize what is at work in the "movement" by which power and discourse are said to converge. In a sense, the "mapping" of power does not fully theorize temporality.

Significantly, the Derridean analysis of iterability is to be distinguished from simple repetition in which the distances between temporal "moments" are treated as uniform in their spatial extension. The "betweenness" that differentiates "moments" of time is not one that can, within Derridean terms, be spatialized or bounded as an identifiable object. It is the nonthematizable différance which erodes and contests any and all claims to discrete identity, including the discrete identity of the "moment." What differentiates moments is not a spatially extended duration, for if it were, it would also count as a "moment," and so fail to account for what falls between moments. This "entre," that which is at once "between" and "outside," is something like non-thematizable space and non-thematizable time as they converge.

Foucault's language of construction includes terms like "augmentation," "proliferation," and "convergence," all of which presume a temporal domain not explicitly theorized. Part of the problem here is that whereas Foucault appears to want his account of genealogical effects to be historically specific, he would favor an account of genealogy over a philosophical account of temporality. In "The Subject and Power" (Hubert Dreyfus and Paul Rabinow, eds., *Michel Foucault: Beyond Structuralism and Hermeneutics* [Chicago: Northwestern University Press, 1983]), Foucault refers to "the diversity of…logical sequence" that characterizes power relations. He would doubtless reject the apparent linearity implied by models of iterability which link them with the linearity of older models of historical sequence. And yet, we do not receive a specification of "sequence": Is it the very notion of "sequence" that varies historically, or are there configurations of sequence that vary, with sequence itself remaining invariant? The specific social formation and figuration of temporality is in some ways unattended by both positions. Here one might consult the work of Pierre Bourdieu to understand the temporality of social construction.

9. See J.L. Austin, *How to Do Things With Words*, J.O. Urmson and Marina Sbisà, eds. (Cambridge, Mass.: Harvard University Press, 1955), and *Philosophical Papers* (Oxford: Oxford University Press, 1961), especially pp. 233-252; Shoshana Felman, *The Literary Speech-Act: Don Juan with J.L. Austin, or Seduction in Two Languages*, tr. Catherine Porter (Ithaca: Cornell University Press, 1983); Barbara Johnson, "Poetry and Performative Language: Mallarmé and Austin," in *The Critical Difference: Essays in the Contemporary Rhetoric of Reading* (Baltimore: Johns Hopkins University Press, 1980), pp. 52-66; Mary Louise Pratt, *A Speech Act Theory of Literary Discourse* (Bloomington: Indiana University Press, 1977); and Ludwig Wittgenstein, *Philosophical Investigations*, tr. G.E.M. Anscombe (New York: Macmillan, 1958), part 1.

10. Jacques Derrida, "Signature, Event, Context," in *Limited, Inc.*, Gerald Graff, ed.; tr. Samuel Weber and Jeffrey Mehlman (Evanston: Northwestern University Press, 1988), p. 18.

11. See Michel Borch-Jacobsen, *The Freudian Subject*, tr. Catherine Porter (Stanford: Stanford University Press, 1988). Whereas Borch-Jacobsen offers an interesting theory of how identification precedes and forms the ego, he tends to assert the priority of identification to any libidinal experience, where I would insist that identification is itself a passionate or libidinal assimilation. See also the useful distinction between an imitative model and a mimetic model of identification in Ruth Leys, "The Real Miss Beauchamp: Gender and the Subject of Imitation" in Judith Butler and Joan Scott, eds., *Feminists Theorize the Political* (New York: Routledge, 1992), pp. 167-214; Kaja Silverman, *Male Subjectivity at the Margins* (New York: Routledge, 1992), pp. 262-270; Mary Ann Doane, "Misrecognition and Identity," in Ron Burnett, ed., *Explorations in Film Theory: Selected Essays from Ciné-Tracts* (Bloomington: Indiana University Press, 1991), pp. 15-25; and Diana Fuss, "Freud's Fallen Women: Identification, Desire, and 'A Case of Homosexuality in a Woman,'" in *The Yale Journal of Criticism*, vol. 6, no. 1, (1993): pp. 1-23.

12. Sigmund Freud, *The Ego and the Id*, James Strachey, ed.; tr. Joan Riviere (New

York: Norton, 1960), p. 16.

12. Nietzsche argues that the ideal of God was produced "[i]n the same measure" as a human sense of failure and wretchedness, and that the production of God was, indeed, the idealization which instituted and reenforced that wretchedness; see Friedrich Nietzsche, *On the Genealogy of Morals*, tr. Walter Kaufmann (New York: Vintage, 1969), section 20. That the symbolic law in Lacan produces "failure" to approximate the sexed ideals embodied and enforced by the law, is usually understood as a promising sign that the law is not fully efficacious, that it does not exhaustively constitute the psyche of any given subject. And yet, to what extent does this conception of the law produce the very failure that it seeks to order, and maintain an ontological distance between the laws and its failed approximations such that the deviant approximations have no power to alter the workings of the law itself?

14. I take seriously the critique of Lacan which underscores the limited and phallogocentric implications of the specular model in "The Mirror Stage" in chapter 2.

15. See Michael Omi and Howard Winant, *Racial Formation in the United States: From 1960s to the 1980s* (New York: Routledge, 1986). See also Anthony Appiah, "The Uncompleted Argument: Du Bois and the Illusion of Race," in Henry Louis Gates, Jr., ed., *"Race", Writing and Difference* (Chicago: University of Chicago Press, 1986), pp. 21-37; Colette Guillaumin, "Race and Nature: The System of Marks," *Feminist Studies*, vol. 8, no.2, (Fall, 1988): pp.25-44; David Lloyd, "Race Under Representation," *Oxford Literary Review* 13 (Spring 1991): pp. 62-94; Sylvia Wynter, "On Disenchanting Discourse: 'Minority' Literary Criticism and Beyond," in Abdul R. JanMohammed and David Lloyd, eds., *The Nature and Context of Minority Discourse* (New York: Oxford University Press, 1990), pp. 432-469.

Again, to claim that race is produced, constructed or even that it has a fictive status is not to suggest that it is artificial or dispensable. Patricia Williams concludes *The Alchemy of Race and Rights* with a phrase which underscores that the rhetorical constructions of race are lived: "A complexity of messages implied in our being" (Cambridge: Harvard University Press, 1991), p. 236. In a postscript entitled "A Word on Categories" she remarks, "While being black has been the most powerful social attribution in my life, it is only one of a number of governing narratives or presiding fictions by which I am constantly reconfiguring myself in the world"(p.256). Here the attribution of being black constitutes not only one of many "presiding fictions," but it is a *mobilizing* fiction, one "by which" her reflexive reconfiguration proceeds. Here the attribution, however fictive, is not only "presiding", that is, a continuous and powerful framework, but it is also, paradoxically and with promise, a *resource*, the means *by which* her transformation becomes possible. I cite these lines here to underscore that calling race a construction or an attribution in no way deprives the term of its force in life; on the contrary, it becomes precisely a presiding and indispensable force within politically saturated discourses in which the term must continually be resignified *against* its racist usages.

16. See Gayatri Chakravorty Spivak, "Scattered Speculations on the Question of Value" and "Subaltern Studies: Deconstructing Historiography," in *In Other Worlds: Essays in Cultural Politics* (New York: Routledge, 1987); and "Can the Subaltern Speak?" in Cary Nelson and Lawrence Goldberg, eds., *Marxism and the Interpretation of Culture* (Urbana: University of Illinois Press, 1988); Tejaswini Niranjana, *History, Post-Structuralism, and the Colonial Context* (Berkeley: University of California Press, 1992); Chandra Talpade Mohanty, "Cartographies of Struggle: Third World Women and the Politics of Feminism" and "Under Western Eyes: Feminist Scholarship and Colonial Discourses" in Chandra Mohanty, Ann Russo, and Lourdes Torres, eds., *Third World Women and the Politics of Feminism* (Bloomington: Indiana University Press, 1991), pp. 1-80; Lisa Lowe, *Critical Terrains: French and British Orientalisms* (Ithaca: Cornell University Press, 1991).

17. Eve Kosofsky Sedgwick, *Epistemology of the Closet*, (Berkeley: University of California Press, 1990).

18. Eve Kosofsky Sedgwick, "Across Gender, Across Sexuality: Willa Cather and Others," *South Atlantic Quarterly*, vol. 88: no. 1 (Winter 1989): pp. 53-72.

19. Foucault argues that psychoanalysis maintains a repressive law which is juridical in form, that is, negative, regulatory, and restrictive. And Foucault asks where the desire said to be "repressed" by the law is not itself the effect, the product, the incited result of that law. Foucault's thinly veiled characterization of "the law of desire" in Lacan fails to take account of the generative effects of that law within psychoanalytic theory. In the following characterization of psychoanalysis, Foucault argues that the same model of power is to be found in psychoanalytic positions that impute a prediscursive status to repressed sexuality and those that understand desire itself as the *effect* of prohibition:

> What distinguishes the analysis made in terms of the repression of instincts from that made in terms of the law of desire is clearly the way in which they each conceive of power. They both rely on a common representation of power which, depending on the use made of it and the position it is accorded with respect to desire, leads to two contrary results: either to the promise of a "liberation," if power is seen as having only an external hold on desire, or, if it is constitutive of desire itself, to the affirmation: you are always-already trapped.

[*The History of Sexuality, Volume One*, pp. 82-83]. Foucault then characterizes the Lacanian law in terms of a juridical performative: "It speaks, and that is the rule" (p. 83), this law is "monotonous...seemingly doomed to repeat itself." Here Foucault presumes that this repetition is a repetition of what is self-identical. Hence, Foucault understands the performative and repetitive workings of the Lacanian law to produce uniform and homogenous subjects; the normalized "subjects" of repression.

But repetition is not subjectivating in Lacan in the way that Foucault implies. In fact, repetition is not only the mark that subjectivation has in some sense *failed* to occur, but that it is itself a further instance of that failing. That which repeats in the subject is that which is radically excluded from the formation of the subject, that which threatens the boundary and the coherence of the subject itself.

In this way, Lacan follows Freud's analysis of repetition compulsion in *Beyond the Pleasure Principle.* In that text, Freud argues that certain forms of repetition compulsion could not be understood in the service of a fantasy of *mastering* traumatic material, but rather were in the service of a death drive which sought to undo or de-cathect the ego itself. In Lacan, repetition is precisely that which undermines the fantasy of mastery associated with the ego, a "resistance of the subject." He describes this effort to regain the fantasized place prior to ego-formation as the aim of repetition, where repetition is the deconstituting of the ego: "Repetition first appears in a form that is not clear, that is not self-evident, like a reproduction, or a making present, *in act.*" That every act is in some sense a repetition of what is *irrecoverable* is made plain in the following: "An act, a true act, always has an element of structure, by the fact of concerning a real that is not self-evidently caught up in it" (cited in Jacques Lacan, *The Four Fundamental Concepts of Psychoanalysis,* ed. Jacques-Alain Miller; tr. Alan Sheridan [New York: Norton, 1978], p. 49.

CHAPTER I : BODIES THAT MATTER

1. Gianni Vattimo, "Au dela du matière et du text," in *Matière et Philosophie* (Paris: Centre Georges Pompidou, 1989), p. 5.

2. For a further discussion on how to make use of poststructuralism to think about the material injuries suffered by women's bodies, see the final section of my "Contingent Foundations: Feminism and the Question of Postmodernism," in Judith Butler and Joan Scott, eds., *Feminists Theorize the Political* (New York: Routledge), 1992, pp. 17-19; see also in that same volume, Sharon Marcus, "Fighting Bodies, Fighting Words: A Theory and Politics of Rape Prevention," pp. 385-403.

3. Jacques Derrida, *Positions,* Alan Bass, ed. (Chicago: University of Chicago, 1978), p. 64. On the following page, he writes: "I will not say whether the concept of matter is metaphysical or nonmetaphysical. This depends upon

the work to which it yields, and you know that I have unceasingly insisted, as concerns the nonideal exteriority of the writing, the gram, the trace, the text, etc. upon the necessity of never separating them from *work*, a value itself to be thought outside its Hegelian affiliations" (p.65).

4. For a compelling analysis of how the form/matter distinction becomes essential to the articulation of a masculinist politics, see Wendy Brown's discussion of Machiavelli in *Manhood and Politics* (Totowa, N. J.: Rowman & Littlefield, 1988), pp. 87-91.

5. See Marx's first thesis on Feuerbach, in which he calls for a materialism which can affirm the practical activity that structures and inheres in the object as part of that object's objectivity and materiality: "The chief defect of all previous materialism (including Feuerbach's) is that the object, actuality, sensuousness is conceived only in the form of the *object or perception* (*Anschauung*), but not as *sensuous human activity, practice* (*Praxis*), not subjectively" (Karl Marx, *Writings of the Young Marx on Philosophy and Society*, tr. Lloyd D. Easton and Kurt H. Guddat [New York: Doubleday, 1967], p. 400). If materialism were to take account of praxis as that which constitutes the very matter of objects, and praxis is understood as socially transformative activity, then such activity is understood as constitutive of materiality itself. The activity proper to *praxis*, however, requires the transformation of some object from a former state to a latter state, usually understood as its transformation from a natural to a social state, but also understood as a transformation of an alienated social state to a non-alienated social state. In either case, according to this new kind of materialism that Marx proposes, the object is not only transformed, but in some significant sense, the object *is* transformative activity itself and, further, its materiality is established through this temporal movement from a prior to a latter state. In other words, the object *materializes* to the extent that it is a site of *temporal transformation*. The materiality of objects, then, is in no sense static, spatial, or given, but is constituted in and as transformative activity. For a fuller elaboration of the temporality of matter, see also Ernst Bloch, *The Principle of Hope*, tr. Neville Plaice, Stephen Plaice, and Paul Knight (Cambridge, Mass.: MIT Press, 1986); Jean-François Lyotard, *The Inhuman: Reflections on Time*, pp. 8-23.

6. Aristotle, "De Anima," *The Basic Works of Aristotle*, tr. Richard McKeon (New York: Random House, 1941), bk.2, ch.1, 412a10, p. 555. Subsequent citations from Aristotle will be from this edition and to standard paragraph numbering only.

7. See Thomas Laqueur, *Making Sex: Body and Gender from the Greeks to Freud* (Cambridge, Mass.: Harvard University Press, 1990), p. 28; G.E.R. Lloyd, *Science, Folklore, Ideology* (Cambridge: Cambridge University Press, 1983). See also Evelyn Fox Keller, *Reflections on Gender and Science* (New Haven: Yale

University Press, 1985); Mary O'Brien, *The Politics of Reproduction* (London: Routledge, 1981).

8. Aristotle, "De Anima," bk.2, ch.1, 412b7-8.

9. Foucault, *The History of Sexuality, Volume One*, p. 152. Original: "Non pas donc 'histoire des mentalités' qui ne tiendrait compte des corps que par la manière dont on les aperçues ou dont on leur a donné sens et valeur; mais 'histoire des corps' et de la manière dont on a *investi* ce qu'il y a de plus *matèrial*, de plus vivant en eux," *Histoire de la sexualité 1: La volonté de savoir* (Paris: Gallimard, 1978), p. 200.

10. Michel Foucault, *Discipline and Punish: The Birth of the Prison* (New York: Pantheon, 1977), p. 30. Original: "L'homme dont on nous parle et qu'on invite à libérer est déjà en lui-même l'effet d'un assujettissement bien plus profond que lui. Une 'âme' l'habite et le porte à l'existence, qui est elle-même une pièce dans la maîtrise que le pouvoir exerce sur le corps. L'âme, effet et instrument d'une anatomie politique; l'âme, prison du corps," Michel Foucault, *Surveillance et punir* (Paris: Gallimard, 1975), p. 34.

11. "What was at issue was not whether the prison environment was too harsh or too aseptic, too primitive or too efficient, but its very materiality as an instrument and vector of power [c'était sa matérialité dans la mesure où elle est instrument et vecteur de pouvoir]," *Discipline and Punish*, p. 30 (*Surveillance et punir*, p. 35).

12. This is not to make "materiality" into the effect of a "discourse" which is its cause; rather, it is to displace the causal relation through a reworking of the notion of "effect." Power is established in and through its effects, where these effects are the dissimulated workings of power itself. There is no "power," taken as a substantive, that has dissimulation as one of its attributes or modes. This dissimulation operates through the constitution and formation of an epistemic field and set of "knowers"; when this field and these subjects are taken for granted as prediscursive givens, the dissimulating effect of power has succeeded. Discourse designates the site at which power is installed as the historically contingent formative power of things within a given epistemic field. The production of material effects is the formative or constitutive workings of power, a production that cannot be construed as a unilateral movement from cause to effect. "Materiality" appears only when its status as contingently constituted through discourse is erased, concealed, covered over. Materiality is the dissimulated effect of power.

Foucault's claim that power is materializing, that it is the production of material effects, is specified in *Discipline and Punish* in the materiality of the body. If "materiality" is an effect of power, a site of transfer between power relations, then insofar as this transfer is the subjection/subjectivation of the body, the principle of this *assujettissement* is "the soul." Taken as a norma-tive/normalizing ideal, the "soul" functions as the formative and regulatory principle of this material body, the proximate instrumentality of its subordi-nation. The soul renders the body uniform; disciplinary regimes train the body through a sustained repetition of rituals of cruelty that produce over the time the gestural stylistics of the imprisoned body. In the *History of Sexuality, Volume One*, "sex" operates to produce a uniform body along differ-ent axes of power, but "sex" as well as "the soul" are understood to subjugate and subjectivate the body, produce an enslavement, as it were, as the very principle of the body's cultural formation. It is in this sense that materializa-tion can be described as the sedimenting effect of a regulated iterability.

13.   ...an ideology always exists in an apparatus, and its practice, or practices. This existence is material.
   Of course, the material existence of the ideology in an apparatus and its practices does not have the same modality as the material existence of a paving-stone or a rifle. But, at the risk of being taken for a Neo-Aristotelian (NB Marx had a very high regard for Aristotle), I shall say that 'matter is dis-cussed in many senses', or rather that it exists in different modalities, all root-ed in the last instance in 'physical' matter

   Louis Althusser, "Ideology and Ideological State Apparatuses (Notes towards an Investigation)" in *Lenin and Philosophy and Other Essays* (New York: Monthly Review Press, 1971), p. 166; first published in *La Pensée*, 1970.

14. See *An Ethics of Sexual Difference*, tr. Carolyn Burke (Ithaca: Cornell University Press, 1993); *Éthique de la différence sexuelle* (Paris: Éditions de Minuit, 1984).

15. Bridget McDonald argues that for Irigaray, "the *entre* is the site of difference where uniformity becomes divided...every *entre* is a shared space where dif-ferentiated poles are not only differentiated, but are also subject to meeting one another in order to exist as differentiated...," "Between Envelopes," unpublished ms.

16. For a discussion of a notion of an "interval" which is neither exclusively space nor time, see Irigaray's reading of Aristotle's *Physics*, "Le Lieu, l'inter-valle," *Éthique de la Différence*, pp. 41-62.

17. This will be related to the occupation of the paternal name in Willa Cather's fiction. See in particular Tommy's occupation of her father's place in Willa Cather's "Tommy the Unsentimental," considered in chapter five of this text.

18. See Elizabeth Spelman, "Woman as Body: Ancient and Contemporary Views," *Feminist Studies* 8:1 (1982): pp. 109-131.

19. See Elizabeth Weed's "The Question of Style," in Carolyn Burke, Naomi Schor, and Margaret Whitford, eds., *Engaging with Irigaray* (New York: Columbia University Press, forthcoming); and Elizabeth Grosz, *Sexual Subversions* (London: Routledge, 1991).

20. This is my translation even though it is clear that Irigaray in the following uses the term for "being" [être] and not for "essence" [*essence*] based on the sense of the subsequent sentence in which the notion of an "essence" remains foreign to the feminine and the final sentence in which the truth of that being is wrought through an oppositional logic: "Elle ne se constitue pas pour autant en *une*. Elle ne se referme pas sur ou dans une vérité ou une essence. L'essence d'une vérité lui reste étrangère. Elle n'a ni n'est un être. Et elle n'oppose pas, à la vérité masculine, une vérité féminine," Luce Irigaray, "Lèvres voilées," *Amante Marine de Friedrich Nietzsche* (Paris: Éditions de Minuit, 1980), p. 92; "She does not set herself up as the *one*, as a (single) female unit. She is not closed up or around one single truth or essence. The essence of a truth remains foreign to her. She neither has nor is a being. And she does not oppose a feminine truth to a masculine truth," *Marine Lover*, tr. Gillian Gill (New York: Columbia University Press, 1991), p. 86.

Given Naomi Schor's reading of "essence" as itself a catachresis, one might ask whether the discourse of essence cannot be redoubled outside of traditional metaphysical proprieties. Then the feminine could well enjoy an essence, but that enjoyment would be at the expense of metaphysics. Naomi Schor, "This Essentialism Which Is Not One: Coming to Grips with Irigaray," *Differences: A Journal of Feminist Cultural Studies* 2:1 (1989): pp. 38-58.

21. Jane Gallop, *Thinking through the Body* (New York: Columbia University Press, 1990).

22. Strictly speaking, matter as *hyle* does not figure centrally in the Platonic corpus. The term *hyle* is for the most part Aristotelian. In the *Metaphysics* (1036a), Aristotle claims that *hyle* can only be known through analogy. It is defined as potency (*dynamis*), and is isolated as one of the four causes; it is also described as the principle of individuation. In Aristotle, it is sometimes identified with the *hypokeimenon* (*Physics*, 1, 192a), but it is not considered a thing. Although Aristotle faults Plato for failing to differentiate between *hyle* and *steresis* (privation), he nevertheless identifies the Platonic notion of the receptacle (*hypodoche*) with *hyle* (*Physics*, 4, 209b). Like Aristotelian *hyle*, the *hypodoche* is indestructible, can only be known by means of "bastard reasoning"(*Timaeus*, 52a-b), and is that for which no definition can be given ["there is no definition of matter, only of *eidos*" *Metaphysics*, 1035b]. In Plato, *hypodoche* takes on the meaning of place or *chora*. It is only once Aristotle supplies an explicit philosophical discourse on matter that Plotinus writes a reconstruction of the Platonic doctrine of matter. This then becomes the occasion for Irigaray's critical citation of Plato/Plotinus in "Une Mère de Glace" in

Speculum of the Other Woman, tr. Gillian Gill (Ithaca: Cornell University Press, 1985), pp. 168-179.

23. Derrida, *Positions*, p. 64.

24. All citations will be to the standard paragraph number and to *Plato: The Collected Dialogues*, Edith Hamilton and Huntington Cairns, eds., Bollingen Series 71. (Princeton: Princeton University Press, 1961).

25. In the *Theatetus* "dechomenon" is described as a "bundle of wax," so Aristotle's choice of the "wax" image in *de Anima* to describe matter might be read as an explicit reworking of the Platonic *dechomenon.*

26. Here *diaschematizomenon* brings together the senses of "to be modelled after a pattern" and "formation," suggesting the strong sense in which schemas are formative. Plato's language prefigures Aristotle's formulation in this specific respect.

27. For a discussion on how *physis* or *phusis* meant genitals, see John J. Winkler's discussion, "*Phusis* and *Natura* Meaning 'Genitals,'" in *The Constraints of Desire: The Anthropology of Sex and Gender in Ancient Greece* (New York: Routledge, 1990), pp. 217-220.

28. This very opposition insists upon the *materiality* of language, what some will call the materiality of the signifier, and is what Derrida proposes to elaborate in "Chora," *Poikilia. Études offertes à Jean-Pierre Vernant* (Paris, EHESS, 1987). To call attention, however, to that word's materiality would not be sufficient, for the point is to gesture toward that which is neither material nor ideal, but which, as the inscriptional space in which that distinction occurs, is neither/nor. It is the neither/nor which enables the logic of either/or, which takes idealism and materialism as its two poles.

   Derrida refers to this inscriptional space as a third gender or genre, which he associates on page 280 of the above text with a "neutral space"; neutral because participating in neither pole of sexual difference, masculine or feminine. Here the receptacle is precisely what destabilizes the distinction between masculine and feminine. Consider the way that this inscriptional space is described, especially how the act of inscription works on it: "in a third genre/gender and in the neuter space of a place without place, a place where everything marks it, but which in itself is not marked." Later, on p. 281, Socrates will be said to resemble Chora inasmuch as he is someone or something. "In every case, he takes his place, which is not a place among others, but perhaps *place itself*, the irreplacable. Irreplaceable, and implacable place…"(my translation).

   The polarity of idealism/materialism has come under question. But that is not to claim that there are no future questions. For what do we make of

Irigaray's claim that for Plato, the inscriptional space is a way of figuring and disfiguring femininity, a way of muting the feminine, and recasting it as mute, passive surface. Recall that for Plato the receptacle receives all things, is that through which a certain penetrative generativity works, but which itself can neither penetrate nor generate. In this sense, the receptacle can be read as a guarantee that there will be no destabilizing mimesis of the masculine, and the feminine will be permanently secured as the infinitely penetrable. This move is repeated in Derrida in his references to "the place without place where everything marks it, but which in itself is not marked." Have we discovered here the unmarked condition of all inscription, that which can have no mark of its own, no proper mark, precisely because it is that which, excluded from the proper, makes the proper possible? Or is this unmarked inscriptional space one whose mark has been erased, and is under compulsion to remain under permanent erasure?

"She (is) nothing other than the sum or the process of that which inscribes itself *'on'* her, 'à son sujet, à meme son sujet,'" but she is not the *subject* or the *present support* of all these interpretations, and she does not reduce to these interpretations. That which exceeds any interpretation, but which is itself not any interpretation. This description does not explain, however, why there is this prohibition against interpretation here. Is this not perhaps a virgin spot in or outside of the territory of metaphysics?

Although here Derrida wants to claim that the receptacle cannot be matter, in *Positions* he confirms that matter can be used "twice," and that in its redoubled effect, it can be precisely that which *exceeds* the form/matter distinction. But here, where matter and mater are linked, where there is a question of a materiality invested with femininity, and then subjected to an erasure, the receptacle cannot be matter, for that would be to reinstall it in the binarism from which it is excluded.

29. See Julia Kristeva, "The Semiotic *Chora* Ordering the Drives," in *Revolution in Poetic Language* (New York: Columbia University Press, 1984); abridged and translated version of *La révolution du langage poétique* (Paris: Éditions du Seuil, 1974).

30. For a very interesting discussion of the topography of reproduction in Plato and for a good example of psychoanalytic and classical thinking, see Page DuBois' *Sowing the Body* (Chicago: University of Chicago Press, 1988).

31. Irigaray makes a similar argument in *La Croyance même* (Paris: Éditions Galilée, 1983) in the course of rereading the *fort-da scene* in Freud's *Beyond the Pleasure Principle.* In that text she offers a brilliant rereading of the action of imaginary mastery effected by the little boy in repeatedly throwing his spool out of the crib and retrieving the spool as a way of rehearsing the departures and returns of his mother. Irigaray charts the scenography of this masterful play and locates the substitute for the maternal in the curtains, the folds of

the bed linen that receive, hide, and return the spool. Like the *chora*, "she"—the dissimulated maternal support for the scene—is the absent but necessary condition for the play of presence and absence: "Elle y était et n'y était pas, elle donnait lieu mais n'avait pas lieu, sauf son ventre et encore...Elle n'y était pas d'ailleurs, sauf dans cette incessante transfusion de vie entre elle et lui, par un fil creux. Elle donne la possibilité de l'entrée en présence mais n'y a pas lieu"(p. 31).

32. *Plotinus' Enneads*, tr. Stephen MacKenna, 2nd ed. (London: Faber & Faber, 1956).

33. Irigaray, "Une Mère de Glace," in *Speculum*, p. 179; original, p. 224.

34. Irigaray makes a similar argument about the *cave* as inscriptional space in *Speculum*. She writes, "The cave is the representation of something always already there, of the original matrix/womb which these men cannot represent...," p. 244; original, p. 302.

35. My thanks to Jen Thomas for helping me to think this through.

36. Naomi Schor, "This Essentialism Which Is Not One: Coming to Grips with Irigaray," p. 48.

37. Luce Irigaray, "When Our Lips Speak Together," *This Sex Which Is Not One*, tr. Catherine Porter with Carolyn Burke (Ithaca: New York, 1985), p. 216; *Ce sexe qui n'en est pas un*, (Paris: Editions de Minuit, 1977), p. 215.

38. *This Sex*, p. 77; *Ce sexe*, p. 75.

39. For readings in feminist ethical philosophy which reformulate Irigaray's position in very interesting ways, see Drucilla Cornell, *Beyond Accommodation: Ethical Feminism, Deconstruction, and the Law* (New York: Routledge, 1991); Gayatri Chakravorty Spivak, "French Feminism Revisited: Ethics and Politics," in *Feminists Theorize the Political*, pp. 54-85.

40. Contiguous relations disrupt the possibility of the enumeration of the sexes, i.e., the first and second sex. Figuring the feminine as/through the contiguous thus implicitly contests the hierarchical binarism of masculine/feminine. This opposition to the quantification of the feminine is an implicit argument with Lacan's *Encore: Le séminaire Livre XX* (Paris: Éditions du Seuil, 1975). It constitutes one sense in which the feminine "is not one." See *Amante marine*, pp. 92-93.

41. Margaret Whitford, *Luce Irigaray: Philosophy in the Feminine* (London: Routledge, 1991), p. 177.

42. Ibid, pp. 180-81.

43. Irigaray, "The Power of Discourse," in *This Sex Which Is Not One*, p. 76.

44. Donna Haraway, responding to an earlier draft of this paper in a hot tub in Santa Cruz, suggested that it is crucial to read Irigaray as reinforcing Plato as the origin of Western representation. Referring to the work of Martin Bernal, Haraway argues that the "West" and its "origins" are constructed through a suppression of cultural heterogeneity, in particular, the suppression of African cultural exchange and influence. Haraway may be right, but Irigaray's point is to expose the violent production of the European "origins" in Greece and so is not incompatible with the view Haraway outlines. My suggestion is that this violence is remaindered within the Platonic doctrine as the "site" of representational inscription and that one way to read Plato and Irigaray for their founding exclusions is by asking, What becomes stored in that receptacle?

45. H. G. Liddell and Robert Scott, *Greek-English Lexicon*, (Oxford: Oxford University Press, 1957).

46. It is important to raise a cautionary note against too quickly reducing sexual positions of active penetration and passive receptivity with masculine and feminine positions within the ancient Greek context. For an important argument against such a conflation, see David Halperin, *One Hundred Years of Homosexuality* (New York: Routledge, 1990), p. 30.

47. What follows may be an overreading, as some of my classicist readers have suggested.

48. Diotima attempts to explain to an apparently witless Socrates that heterosexual procreation not only contains but produces the effects of immortality, thus linking heterosexual procreation with the production of timeless truths. See *The Symposium* 206b-208b. Of course, this speech needs also to be read in the rhetorical context of the dialogue which might be said to assert this heterosexual norm, only later to produce its male homosexual contestation.

49. See Mary Douglas, *Purity and Danger* (London: Routledge & Kegan Paul, 1978); Peter Stallybrass and Allon White, *The Politics and Poetics of Transgression* (Ithaca: Cornell University Press, 1986).

CHAPTER 2: THE LESBIAN PHALLUS AND THE MORPHOLOGICAL IMAGINARY

A version of the first part of this chapter was given as "The Lesbian Phallus: Does Heterosexuality Exist?" at the Modern Language Association Meetings in Chicago, December 1990. An earlier version of this chapter was published as "The Lesbian Phallus and the Morphological Imaginary" in *differences: A Journal of Feminist Cultural Studies*, vol. 4, no. 1 (Spring, 1992), pp. 133-171.

1. Sigmund Freud, "On Narcissism: An Introduction" (1914), *The Standard Edition of the Complete Psychological Works of Sigmund Freud*, vol. 14, tr. and ed. James Strachey (London: Hogarth, 1961), pp. 67-104; original: "Zur Einführung des Narzissmus," *Gesammelte Werke*, vol. 10 (London: Imago, 1946), pp. 137-70. This reference will be given as "1914" in the text.

2. "Einzig in der engen Höhle, des Bachenzahnes weilt die Seele" quoted in Freud, "On Narcissism," p. 82. A better translation would be: "Alone in the narrow hole of the jaw-tooth dwells the soul."

3. Freud, "The Ego and the Id," *The Standard Edition*, *XIX*, pp. 1-66.

4. Freud then supplies a footnote: "I.e., the ego is ultimately derived from bodily sensations, chiefly from those springing from the surface of the body. It may thus be regarded as a mental projection of the surface of the body, besides...representing the superficies of the mental apparatus" (Freud, *XIX*, 26). Although Freud is offering an account of the development of the ego, and claiming that the ego is derived from the projected surface of the body, he is inadvertently establishing the conditions for the articulation of the body *as morphology*.

5. For an extended and informative discussion of this problem in psychological and philosophical literature that bears on psychoanalysis, see Elizabeth Grosz, *Volatile Bodies* (Bloomington: Indiana University Press, 1993).

6. Jacques Lacan, *The Seminar of Jacques Lacan, Book 1: Freud's Papers on Technique, 1953–54*, tr. Alan Sheridan (New York: Norton, 1985) p. 122; original: *Le Séminaire de Jacques Lacan, Livre I: Les écrits techniques de Freud* (Paris: Seuil, 1975), p. 141. Subsequent citations will appear in the text as (*I*), and citations to other seminars will appear in the text by roman numerals as well. A slash ("/") separates English and French pagination respectively.

7. Jane Gallop, *Thinking Through the Body* (New York: Columbia University Press, 1988), p. 126.

8. See Kaja Silverman, "The Lacanian Phallus," *differences: A Journal of Feminist Cultural Studies*, vol. 4; no. 1 (1992), pp. 84-115.

9. This figure of the threatening mouth recalls Freud's description of Irma's mouth in *The Interpretation of Dreams*. Lacan refers to that mouth as "this something which properly speaking is unnameable, the back of this throat,

the complex unlocatable form, which also makes it into the primitive object *par excellence*, the abyss of the feminine organ from which all life emerges, this gulf of the mouth, in which everything is swallowed up, and no less the image of death in which everything comes to its end" (*II*, 164).

10. Jeff Nunokawa, "In Memorium and the Extinction of the Homosexual," *ELH* 58 (Winter 1991): pp. 130-155.

11. Although somaticization is understood as part of symptom-formation, it may be that morphological development and the assumption of sex is the generalized form of the somatic symptom.

    Richard Wollheim offers an extended discussion of the bodily ego in which he maintains that incorporative fantasies are central to corporeal self-representation and to psychic development. Kleinian in approach, Wollheim argues that not only incorporative fantasy, but internalization as well casts doubt on the separability of the subject from its internalized objects. The thesis of the bodily ego is the thesis of this inseparability. See Richard Wollheim, "The Bodily Ego" in Richard Wollheim and James Hopkins, eds., *Philosophical Essays on Freud* (New York and London: Cambridge University Press, 1982), pp. 124-138.

12. See Maurice Merleau-Ponty on "the flesh of the world" and the intertwining of touch, surface, and vision in "The Intertwining—The Chiasm," *The Visible and the Invisible*, tr. Alphonso Lingis; Claude Lefort, ed. (Evanston: Northwestern University Press, 1968), pp. 130-55.

13. See Louis Althusser, "Ideology and Ideological State Apparatuses (Notes towards an Investigation)," p. 166.

14. Julia Kristeva, *Desire in Language: A Semiotic Approach to Literature and Art*, Leon Roudiez, ed.; tr. Thomas Gorz, Alice Jardine, and Leon Roudiez (New York: Columbia University Press, 1980), pp. 134-36.

15. Irigaray prefers to formulate this primary material relation in terms of material contiguity or proximity. See her "The Power of Discourse and the Subordination of the Feminine" in *This Sex Which Is Not One*, p. 75.

16. In "the mirror stage" the imaginary is not yet distinguished from the symbolic as it will be later for Lacan.

17. One might read Monique Wittig's strategy with respect to renaming in *The Lesbian Body* as a reworking of this Lacanian presumption. The name confers morphological distinctness, and names which explicitly disavow the patronymic lineage become the occasions for the disintegration of the (paternal) version of bodily integrity as well as the reintegration and reformation

of other versions of bodily coherence.

18. See Margaret Whitford's recent excellent discussion on Luce Irigaray and the feminine imaginary in her *Luce Irigaray: Philosophy in the Feminine* (London: Routledge, 1991), pp. 53-74.

19. Naomi Schor, "This Essentialism Which Is Not One: Coming to Grips with Irigaray," p. 48.

20. "Il y suffit de comprendre le stade du miroir comme une identification au sens plein que l'analyse donne à ce terme: àsavoir la transformation produite chez le sujet quand il assume une image,—dont la prédestination à cet effet de phase est suffisamment indiquée par l'usage, dans la théorie, du terme antique d'*imago*" (Jacques Lacan, "Le stade du miroir," *Écrits*, p. 90). From the introduction of the *imago*, Lacan then moves to the jubilant assumption by the infant of his [sic] "image spéculaire," an exemplary situation of the symbolic matrix in which the "je" or the subject is said to be precipitated in a primordial form, prior to the dialectic of identification with an other. Failing to distinguish here between the formation of the "je" and the "moi," Lacan proceeds in the next paragraph, with a further elucidation of "cette forme" as that which might rather be designated as the "*je-idéal*," the ego-ideal, a translation which effects the confusing convergence of the *je* with the *moi*. To claim that this form could be termed the "*je-idéal*" is contingent upon the explanatory uses that such a term authorizes. In this case, that provisional translation will put in a known register, "un registre connu," that is, known from Freud, that phantasmatic and primary identification which Lacan describes as "la souche des identifications secondaires…" Here it seems that the social construction of the ego takes place through a dialectic of identifications between an already partially constituted ego and the Other. The mirror-stage is precisely the primary identification, presocial and determined "dans une ligne de fiction," along a line of fiction (imaginary, specular) which precipitates the secondary (social and dialectical) identifications. Later, this will become clear when Lacan argues that the narcissistic relation prefigures and shapes social relations as well as relations to objects (which are also social in the sense of linguistically mediated). In a sense, the mirror-stage *gives form* or *morphe* to the ego through the phantasmatic delineation of a body in control. That primary act of form-giving is then displaced or extrapolated onto the world of other bodies and objects, providing the condition ("la souche": the trunk of a tree which, it appears, has fallen or has been cut down but which serves as fertile ground) of their appearance. This wood fallen or chopped, ready for use, resonates with the meanings of matter as "hyle" considered in chapter one. In this sense, for Lacan, primary identifications are indissociable from matter.

21. Jacques Lacan, "The Mirror Stage," *Écrits: A Selection*, tr. Alan Sheridan, (New

York: Norton, 1977), p. 4; original: "La fonction du stade du miroir s'avère pour nous dès lors comme un cas particulier de la fonction de l'*imago* qui est d'établir une relation de l'organisme à sa réalité—ou, comme on dit, de l'*Innenwelt* à l'*Umwelt*" (*Écrits Vol. I* [Paris: Seuil, 1971], p. 93).

22. Lacan later comes to disjoin the ego from the subject, linking the ego with the register of the imaginary, and the subject with the register of the symbolic. The subject pertains to the symbolic order and that which constitutes the structure/language of the unconscious. In *Seminar I* he writes, "The ego is an imaginary function, but it is not to be confused with the subject." "The unconscious completely eludes that circle of certainties by which man recognizes himself as ego. There is something outside this field which has every right to speak as I...It is precisely what is most misconstrued by the domain of the ego which, in analysis, comes to be formulated as properly speaking the I" (p. 193). In *Seminar II*, he continues: "The ego...is a particular object within the experience of the subject. Literally, the ego is an object—an object which fills a certain function which we here call the imaginary function" (p. 44). And later: "The subject is no one. It is decomposed, in pieces. And it is jammed, sucked in by the image, the deceiving and realised image, of the other, *or equally* [my emphasis], by its own specular image" (p. 54).

23. The identification with this imago is called "anticipatory," a term that Alexandre Kojève reserves for the structure of *desire*. See Alexandre Kojève, *Introduction to the Reading of Hegel*, tr. James Nichols; Allan Bloom, ed. (Ithaca: Cornell University Press, 1980), p. 4. As anticipatory, the *imago* is a futural projection, a proleptic and phantasmatic idealization of bodily control that cannot yet exist and that in some sense can never exist: "this form situates the agency of the ego, before its social determination, in a fictional direction..." The identificatory production of that boundary—the effect of the bounded mirror—establishes the ego as and through a fictional, idealizing, and centering spatial unity. This is the inauguration of the *bodily* ego, the phenomenological access to morphology and to a bounded or discrete sense of the "I." Of course, this constitutes a *méconnaissance* precisely by virtue of the incommensurability that marks the relation between that fictional, projected body and the decentered, disunified bodily matrix from which that idealizing gaze emerges. To reparaphrase Freud along Lacanian lines, then, the ego first and foremost misrecognizes itself outside itself in the *imago* as a bodily ego.

This image not only *constitutes* the ego, but constitutes the ego as *imaginary* (Lacan refers time and again to the "imaginary origin of the ego's function," i.e., the ego *as* a consequence of primary and secondary identifications constituted in the imaginary). In other words, the ego is an imaginary production, one which takes place foremost through the projection/production of a bodily ego, and which is necessary for the functioning of the subject, but which is equally and significantly *tenuous* as well. The loss of control that in the infant characterizes undeveloped motor control persists within the adult as that excessive domain of sexuality that is stilled and deferred through the invocation of the "ego-ideal" as a center of control. Hence, every effort to inhabit fully an identification with the *imago* (where "identification with" converges ambiguously with "production of") fails because the sexuality temporarily harnessed and bounded by that ego (one might say "jammed" by that ego) cannot be fully or decisively constrained by it. What is left outside the mirror frame, as it were, is precisely the unconscious that comes to call into question the representational status of what is shown *in* the mirror. In this sense, the ego is produced through *exclusion*, as any boundary is, and what is excluded is nevertheless negatively and vitally constitutive of what "appears" bounded within the mirror.

24. Note the precedent for the formulation of the ego as estranged object in Jean-Paul Sartre, *The Transcendence of the Ego*, tr. and intro., Forest Williams and Robert Kirkpatrick (New York: Noonday, 1957).

25. Jacques Lacan, "The Meaning of the Phallus," *Feminine Sexuality: Jacques Lacan and the École Freudienne*, tr. Jacqueline Rose, Juliet Mitchell, ed. (New York: Norton, 1985), p. 82. Further citations in the text will be to "Rose."

26. For a fine analysis of how phallomorphism works in Lacan, and for an eluci-dation of Irigaray's trenchant critique of that phallomorphism, see Whitford, *Luce Irigaray: Philosophy in the Feminine*, pp. 58–74 and 150–152. Whitford reads Lacan's essay on the mirror stage through Irigaray's critique, and argues not only that the mirror stage is itself dependent upon the prior presumption of the maternal as ground, but that the phallomorphism that the essay articu-lates authorizes a "male imaginary [in which] male narcissism is extrapo-late[d] to the transcendental" (p. 152). Whitford also traces Irigaray's efforts to establish a female imaginary over and against the male imaginary in Lacan. Although I am clearly in some sympathy with the project of deautho-rizing the male imaginary, my own strategy will be to show that the phallus can attach to a variety of organs, and that the efficacious disjoining of phallus from penis constitutes both a narcissistic wound to phallomorphism and the production of an anti-heterosexist sexual imaginary. The implications of my strategy would seem to call into question the integrity of either a masculine or a feminine imaginary.

27. "...le stade du miroir est un drame dont la poussée interne se précipite de l'insuffisance à l'anticipation—et qui pour le sujet, pris au leurre de l'identi-fication spatiale, machine les fantasmes qui se succèdent d'une image morcelée du corps à une forme que nous appellerons orthopédique de sa totalité,—et àl'armure enfin assumée d'une identité aliénante, qui va mar-quer de sa structure rigide tout son développement mental" (Lacan, *Écrits I*, pp. 93-94). It is interesting that the piecemeal character of the body is phan-tasmatically overcome through the taking on of a kind of armor or orthope-

dic support, suggesting that the artificial extension of the body is integral to its maturation and enhanced sense of control. The protective and expansive figural possibilities of armor and orthopedics suggest that insofar as a certain phallic potency is the effect of the transfigured body in the mirror, this potency is purchased through artificial methods of phallic enhancement, a thesis with obvious consequences for the lesbian phallus.

28. "In Freudian doctrine, the phallus is not a fantasy, if what is understood by that is an imaginary effect...." (Rose, p. 79).

29. "Le phallus ici s'éclaire de sa fonction. Le phallus dans la doctrine freudienne n'est pas un fantasme, s'il faut entendre par là un effet imaginaire. Il n'est pas non plus comme tel un objet (partiel, interne, bon, mauvais etc...) pour autant que ce terme tend à apprécier la réalité intéressée dans une relation. Il est encore moins l'organe, pénis ou clitoris, qu'il symbolise. Et ce n'est pas sans raison que Freud en a pris la référence au simulacre qu'il était pour les Anciens."
"Car le phallus est un signifiant..."(*Écrits*, p. 690).

30. Clearly, Lacan also repudiates the clitoris as an organ that might be identified with the phallus. But note that the penis and the clitoris are always symbolized differently; the clitoris is symbolized as penis envy (not having), whereas the penis is symbolized as the castration complex (having with the fear of losing) (Rose, p. 75). Hence, the phallus symbolizes the clitoris as not having the penis, whereas the phallus symbolizes the penis through the threat of castration, understood as a kind of dispossession. To have a penis is to have that which the phallus *is* not, but which, precisely by virtue of this not-being, constitutes the occasion for the phallus to signify (in this sense, the phallus requires and reproduces the diminution of the penis in order to signify—almost a kind of master-slave dialectic between them).
   Not to have the penis is already to have lost it and, hence, to be the occasion for the phallus to signify its power to castrate; the clitoris will signify as penis-envy, as a lack which, through its envy, will wield the power to dispossess. To "be" the phallus, as women are said to be, is to be both dispossessed and dispossessing. Women "are" the phallus in the sense that they absently reflect its power; this is the signifying function of the lack. And those female body parts which are not the penis fail, therefore, to have the phallus, and so are precisely a set of "lacks." Those body parts fail to phenomenalize precisely because they cannot properly wield the phallus. Hence, the very description of how the phallus symbolizes (i.e., as penis-envy *or* castration) makes implicit recourse to differentially marked body parts, which implies that the phallus does not symbolize penis and clitoris in the same way. The clitoris can never be said, within this view, to be an example of "having" the phallus.

31. In the following chapter, "Phantasmatic Identification and the Assumption of

Sex," I attempt to argue that the assumption of sexed positions within the symbolic operates through the threat of castration, a threat addressed to a male body, a body marked as male prior to its "assumption" of masculinity, and that the female body must be understood as the embodiment of this threat and, obversely, the guarantee that the threat will not be realized. This oedipal scenario which Lacan understands as central to the assumption of binary sex is itself founded on the threatening power of the threat, the unbearability of demasculinized manhood and phallicized femininity. Implicit to these two figures, I argue, is the spectre of homosexual abjection, one which is clearly culturally produced, circulated, contested, and contingent.

32. See Maria Torok, "The Meaning of Penis-Envy in Women," tr. Nicholas Rand, in *differences: A Journal of Feminist Cultural Studies*, vol. 4, no.1 (Spring, 1992): pp. 1-39. Torok argues that penis-envy in women is a "mask" which symptomatizes the prohibition on masturbation and effects a deflection from the orgasmic pleasures of masturbation. Inasmuch as penis-envy is a modality of desire for which no satisfaction can be gained, it masks the ostensibly more prior desire for auto-erotic pleasures. According to Torok's highly normative theory of female sexual development, the masturbatory orgasmic pleasures experienced and then prohibited (by the mother's intervention) produce first a penis-envy which cannot be satisfied and then a renunciation of that desire in order to rediscover and reexperience masturbatory orgasm in the context of adult heterosexual relations. Torok thus reduces penis-envy to a mask and prohibition which presumes that female sexual pleasure is not only centered in auto-eroticism, but that this pleasure is primarily *unmediated* by sexual difference. She also reduces all possibilities of cross-gendered phantasmatic identification to a deflection from the masturbatory heterosexual nexus, such that the primary prohibition is against unmediated self-love. Freud's own theory of narcissism argues that auto-eroticism is always modeled on imaginary object-relations, and that the Other structures the masturbatory scene phantasmatically. In Torok, we witness the theoretical installation of the Bad Mother whose primary task is to prohibit masturbatory pleasures and who must be overcome (the mother figured, as in Lacan, as obstruction) in order to rediscover masturbatory sexual happiness with a man. The mother thus acts as a prohibition that must be overcome in order for heterosexuality to be achieved and the return to self and wholeness that that purportedly implies for a woman. This developmental celebration of heterosexuality thus works through the implicit foreclosure of homosexuality or the abbreviation and rerouting of female homosexuality as masturbatory pleasure. Penis-envy would characterize a lesbian sexuality that is, as it were, stalled between the irrecoverable memory of masturbatory bliss and the heterosexual recovery of that pleasure. In other words, if penis-envy is in part code for lesbian pleasure, or for other forms of female sexual pleasure that are, as it were, stopped along the heterosexual developmental trajectory, then lesbianism is "envy" and, hence, both a deflection from pleasure and

infinitely unsatisfying. In short, there can be lesbian pleasure for Torok, for if the lesbian is "envious", she embodies and enacts the very prohibition on pleasure that, it seems, only heterosexual union can lift. That this essay is found useful by some feminists continues to surprise and alarm me.

33. For a very interesting account of castration anxiety in lesbian subjectivity, see Teresa de Lauretis's recent work on the mannish lesbian, especially her discussion of Radclyffe Hall "before the mirror" in her forthcoming book, *Practices of Love* (Bloomington: Indiana University Press).

34. Here it will probably be clear that I am in agreement with Derrida's critique of Lévi-Strauss's atemporalized notion of structure. In "Structure, Sign, and Play," Derrida asks what gives structure its structurality, that is, the quality of being a structure, suggesting that that status is endowed or derived and, hence, nonoriginary. A structure "is" a structure to the extent that it persists as one. But how to understand how the manner of that persistence inheres in the structure itself? A structure does not remain self-identical through time, but "is" to the extent that it is reiterated. Its iterability is thus the condition of its identity, but because iterability presupposes an interval, a difference, between terms, identity, constituted through this discontinuous temporality, is conditioned and contested by this difference from itself. This is a difference constitutive of identity—as well as the principle of its impossibility. As such, it is difference as différance, a deferral of any resolution into self-identity.

CHAPTER 3: PHANTASMATIC IDENTIFICATION AND THE ASSUMPTION OF SEX

A portion of this essay was first presented at the American Philosophical Association, Central Division, April 1991; sections of the first portion of the essay appeared in a shorter version in Elizabeth Wright,ed. *Feminism and Psychoanalysis: A Critical Dictionary* (London; Basil Blackwell, 1992).

1. Here one might follow a Wittgensteinian way of thinking and consider that it is very possible to assert that sexuality is constrained, and to understand the sense of that claim without taking the added and unnecessary step of then offering a metaphysics of constraint to secure the meaningfulness of the claim.

2. I use the term "phantasmatic" to recall the use of that term by Jean Laplanche and J.-B Pontalis in which the identificatory locations of the subject are labile, explained in endnote 7 below. I retain the term "fantasy" and "fantasize" for those active imaginings which presuppose a relative locatedness of the subject in relation to regulatory schemes.

3. Clearly, it is this already circulating trope of homosexuality as a kind of social and psychic death that is exploited and strengthened in homophobic discourses which understand AIDS to be the result of homosexuality (rendered as definitionally unsafe, as danger itself) rather than the result of the exchange of fluids. Here it seems that James Miller's *The Passion of Michel Foucault* (New York: Simon and Schuster, 1992) exploits the trope of homosexuality as itself a death wish and fails to make an adequate distinction between homosexual practices that constitute safe sex and those which do not. Although Miller declines to draw a strict causal link between homosexuality and death, it is precisely the metaphorical nexus of the two that focuses his analysis and which has occasioned the appearance of "level-headed" reviews in which a certain heterosexual prurience becomes free to express itself under the rubric of sober criticism. For one of the few counter-examples to this trend, see the review of Miller's book by Wendy Brown in *differences: A Journal of Feminist Criticism* (Fall 1993; forthcoming).

Significantly, Miller conflates three separate concepts: (1) a popular notion of the "death wish," understood as a desire to die, with (2) the psychoanalytic notion of a "death drive," understood as a *conservative*, regressive, and repetitive tendency by which an organism strives toward equilibrium (difficult to reconcile with the orgiastic excesses of self-obliteration without an extended argument, of which there is none), and (3) the notion introduced by Georges Bataille of "the death of the subject" and Foucault's "the death of the author." Miller appears not to understand that this last concept is not the same as the death of the biological organism, but operates for Bataille, as it does for Foucault, as a vitalistic and life-affirming possibility. If "the subject" in its conceit of self-mastery *resists* and domesticates life through its insistence on instrumental control, the subject is *itself* a sign of death. The decentered or vanquished subject initiates the possibility of a heightened eroticism and an affirmation of life beyond the hermetic and closed circuit of the subject. Just as, for Foucault, the death of the author is in some ways the beginning of a conception of writing as that which precedes and mobilizes the one who writes, connecting the one who writes with a language which "writes" the one, so "the death of the subject" in Bataille is in some ways the beginning of a life-enhancing eroticism. For Foucault's explicit linking of sadomasochistic choreography and the affirmation of life through erotic relationality, see "Interview with Foucault," *Salmagundi* (Winter 1982–83), p. 12.

4. Jacques Lacan, "The Meaning of the Phallus," p. 75. Original: "Il y a là une antimonie interne à l'assomption par l'homme (*Mensch*) de son sexe; pouquoi doit-il n'en assumer les attributs qu'à travers une menace, voire sous l'aspect d'une privation?" (*Ecrits, II*, p. 103-4).

5. Note the theological roots of "assume" in the notion of "assumption" (*assomption*) in which the Virgin is said to be "assumed" into heaven. This absorption into the divine kingdom becomes the figure in Lacan for the way in which

sex is acquired. The agency of "assumption" clearly comes from the law. Significantly, though, this assumption of sex is figured through the upward travel of the Virgin, a figure of chaste ascension, thus installing a prohibition on female sexuality at the moment of ascending to "sex." Hence, taking on a sex is at once the regulation of a sexuality and, more specifically, the splitting of feminine sexuality into the idealized and the defiled.

6. See the important use of the notion of identificatory "failure" in Jacqueline Rose, *Sexuality and the Field of Vision* (London: Verso, 1986), pp. 90-91; Mary Ann Doane, "Commentary: Post-Utopian Difference" in Elizabeth Weed, ed., *Coming to Terms: Feminism, Theory, Politics* (New York: Routledge, 1989), p. 76.; Teresa de Lauretis, "Freud, Sexuality, Perversion," in Domna Stanton, ed., *Discourses of Sexuality* (Ann Arbor: University of Michigan Press, 1993), p. 217.

7. See Laplanche and Pontalis, "Fantasy and the Origins of Sexuality," in Victor Burgin, James Donald, Cora Kaplan, eds., *Formations of Fantasy* (London: Methuen, 1986). Fantasy in this sense is to be understood not as an activity *of* an already formed subject, but of the staging and dispersion of the subject into a variety of identificatory positions. The scene of fantasy is derived from the impossibility of a return to primary satisfactions; hence, fantasy rehearses that desire and its impossibility, and remains structured by a prohibition upon the possibility of a return to origins. The essay offers itself as an account of the "origin" of fantasy, but it suffers under the same prohibition. Thus, the effort to describe *theoretically* the origins of fantasy is always also a *fantasy* of origin.

   The notion of "original fantasy" which Laplanche and Pontalis describe is not *an object* of desire, but the stage or setting for desire:

   > In fantasy the subject does not pursue the object or its sign: he appears caught up himself in the sequence of images. He forms no representation of the desired object, but is himself represented as participating in the scene although, in the earliest forms of fantasy, he cannot be assigned any fixed place in it (hence, the danger, in treatment of interpretations which claim to do so). As a result, the subject, although always present in the fantasy, may be so in a desubjectivized form, that is to say, in the very syntax of the sequence in question. On the other hand, to the extent that desire is not purely an upsurge of drives, but is articulated into the fantasy, the latter is a favoured spot for the most primitive defensive reactions, such as turning against one-self, or into an opposite, projection, negation: these defenses are even indissolubly linked with the primary function of fantasy, to be a setting for desire, in so far as desire itself originates as prohibition, and the conflict may be an original conflict. (pp. 26-27)

   Earlier Laplanche and Pontalis argue that fantasy emerges on the condition that an original object is lost, and that this emergence of fantasy coincides with the emergence of auto-eroticism. Fantasy originates, then, as an effort both *to cover* and *to contain* the separation from an original object. As a consequence, fantasy is the dissimulation of that loss, the imaginary recovery and articulation of that lost object. Significantly, fantasy emerges as a *scene* in which the recovery installs and distributes the "subject" in the position of both desire and its object. In this way, fantasy seeks to override the distinction between a desiring subject and its object by staging an imaginary scene in which both positions are appropriated and inhabited by the subject. This activity of "appropriating" and "inhabiting," what we might call the dissimulation of the subject in fantasy, effects a reconfiguration of the subject itself. The idea of a subject which opposes the object of its desire, which encounters that object in its alterity, is itself the effect of this phantasmatic scene. The subject only becomes individuated through loss. This loss is never fully encountered precisely because fantasy emerges to take up the position of the lost object, to expand the imaginary circuit of the subject to inhabit and incorporate that loss. The subject thus emerges in its individuation, as a consequence of separation, *as a scene*, in the mode of displacement. Precisely because that separation is a nonthematizable trauma, it initiates a subject in its separateness only through a fantasy which scatters that subject, simultaneously extending the domain of its auto-eroticism. Insofar as fantasy orchestrates the subject's love affair *with itself*, recovering and negating the alterity of the lost object through installing it as a further instance of the subject, fantasy delimits an auto-erotic project of incorporation.

8. For a reading of Lacan which argues that prohibition or, more precisely, *the bar* is foundational, see Jean-Luc Nancy and Philippe Lacoue-Labarthe, *The Title of the Letter: A Reading of Lacan*, trs. Francois Raffoul and David Pettigrew (Albany: SUNY Press, 1992).

9. This is a problem that I pursue in relation to both psychoanalysis and Foucault in "Subjection and Resistance: Between Freud and Foucault," in John Rajchman, ed., *The Question of Identity* (New York: Routledge, forthcoming 1994).

10. Kaja Silverman offers an innovative alternative to the heterosexist implications of universalizing the Law of the Father, thus suggesting that the symbolic is capable of a rearticulation that is not governed by the phallus. She argues in favor of a distinction between the symbolic law and the Law of the Father. Drawing on Gayle Rubin's "The Traffic in Women," Silverman argues that the prohibition on incest ought not to be conflated with the Name of the Father: "Neither Lévi-Strauss, Freud, Lacan, nor Mitchell...adduces any structural imperative, analogous to the incest prohibition itself, which dictates that it be women rather than men—or both women and men—that circulate [as gifts of exchange], nor can such an imperative be found. We must consequently pry loose the incest prohibition from the Name-of-the-Father so as to insist, despite the paucity of historical

evidence for doing so, that the Law of Kinship Structure is not necessarily phallic" (Kaja Silverman, *Male Subjectivity at the Margins* p. 37). In seeking to ascertain a way to account for symbolic rearticulations that do not recapitulate compulsory heterosexuality (and the exchange of women) as the premise of cultural intelligibility, I am in clear sympathy with Silverman's project. And it may be that the rearticulation of the phallus in lesbian domains constitutes the "inversion" of the *de*constitution of the phallus that she describes in gay male fantasy. I am not sure, however, that saying "no" to the phallus and, hence, to what symbolizes power (p. 389) within what she calls, following Jacques Rancière, "the dominant fiction," is not itself a reformulation of power, power as resistance. I do agree with Silverman, however, that there is no necessary reason for the phallus to continue to signify power, and would only add that that signifying linkage may well be undone in part through the kinds of rearticulations that proliferate and diffuse the signifying sites of the phallus.

11. One might consider in this connection the parable by Franz Kafka, "An Imperial Message," in which the source of the law is finally untraceable, and in which the injunction of the law becomes increasingly illegible (Franz Kafka, *Parables and Paradoxes* [New York: Schocken, 1958], pp. 13-16).

12. Michel Foucault, "End of the Monarchy of Sex," in Sylvere Lotringer, ed., *Foucault Live*, tr. John Johnston (New York: Semiotext(e), 1989), p. 147.

13. See my "The Force of Fantasy: Mapplethorpe, Feminism, and Discursive Excess" *Differences*, 2:2 (1990), for an account of how the eroticization of the law makes it available to a reverse-discourse in the Foucaultian sense.

14. Sigmund Freud, "Observations of Transference-Love" (1915), *Standard Edition*, vol. 12; "Contributions to the Psychology of Love" (1910), tr. Joan Riviere, *Sexuality and the Psychology of Love* (New York: Collier, 1963), pp. 49-58.

15. Leo Bersani, *The Freudian Body: Psychoanalysis and Art* (New York: Columbia University Press, 1986), p. 64-66, 112-113.

16. For an account of how subaltern "positions" are at once productions and effacements, see Gayatri Chakravorty Spivak, "Subaltern Studies: Deconstructing Historiography," in Ranajit Guha and Gayatri Chakravorty Spivak, eds., *Selected Subaltern Studies* (London: Oxford University Press, 1988), pp. 17-19.

17. See Gloria Anzaldúa, *Borderlands/La Frontera* (San Francisco: Spinsters, Aunt Lute, 1987), pp. 77-91.

18. The question of how race is lived as sexuality echoes the phrasing of Paul Gilroy who argues that "race" is not a monolith but is lived in differential modalities of class. See Paul Gilroy, "'Race,' Class, and Agency," in *"There Ain't No Black in the Union Jack": The Cultural Politics of Race and Nation* (London: Hutchinson, 1987), pp. 15-42. See also Abdul JanMohammed, "Sexuality on/of the Racial Border: Foucault, Wright and the Articulation of 'Racialized Sexuality,'" in *Discourses of Sexuality*, pp. 94-116; M. Jacqui Alexander, "Redrafting Morality: The Postcolonial State and the Sexual Offences Bill of Trinidad and Tobago" and Chandra Talpade Mohanty, "Under Western Eyes: Feminist Scholarship and Colonial Discourses," in Chandra Talpade Mohanty, Ann Russo, Lourdes Torres, eds., *Third World Women and the Politics of Feminism* (Bloomington: Indiana University Press, 1991), pp. 133-52 and pp. 51-80; Frantz Fanon, *Black Skin, White Masks* (New York: Grove Press, 1967); Rey Chow, *Woman and Chinese Modernity: The Politics of Reading Between East and West* (Minnesota: University of Minnesota Press, 1991); Lisa Lowe, *Critical Terrains: French and British Orientalisms* (Ithaca: Cornell University Press, 1991); Walter L. Williams, *The Spirit and the Flesh: Sexual Diversity in American Indian Culture* (Boston: Beacon Press, 1986).

19. Significantly, it is less often individual authors or works that succeed in this kind of complex work, but rather volumes which promote the consideration of different perspectives in a dynamic relationship to one another. For an excellent example of this kind of collective authorial event, see Toni Morrison, ed., *Race-ing Justice, En-gendering Power: Essays on Anita Hill, Clarence Thomas, and the Construction of Social Reality* (New York: Pantheon, 1992).

CHAPTER 4: GENDER IS BURNING: QUESTIONS OF APPROPRIATION AND SUBVERSION

1. Louis Althusser, "Ideology and Ideological State Apparatuses," pp. 170-177; see also "Freud and Lacan," in *Lenin*, pp. 189-220.

2. Gloria Anzaldúa writes, "that focal point or fulcrum, that juncture where the mestiza stands, is where phenomena tend to collide" (p. 79) and, later, "the work of *mestiza* consciousness is to break down the subject-object duality that keeps her a prisoner," "La conciencia de la mestiza," *Borderlands/La Frontera*, p. 80.

3. See Marjorie Garber, *Vested Interests: Cross-Dressing and Cultural Anxiety* (New York: Routledge, 1992), p. 40.

4. bell hooks, "Is Paris Burning?" *Z*, Sisters of the Yam column (June 1991): p. 61.

5. Whereas I accept the psychoanalytic formulation that both the object and aim of love are formed *in part* by those objects and aims that are repudiated, I consider it a cynical and homophobic use of that insight to claim that homosexuality is nothing other than repudiated heterosexuality. Given the culturally repudiated status of homosexuality as a form of love, the argument that seeks to reduce homosexuality to the inversion or deflection of heterosexuality functions to reconsolidate heterosexual hegemony. This is also why the analysis of homosexual melancholy cannot be regarded as symmetrical to the analysis of heterosexual melancholy. The latter is culturally enforced in a way that the former clearly is not, except within separatist communities which cannot wield the same power of prohibition as communities of compulsory heterosexism.

6. Kobena Mercer has offered rich work on this question and its relation to a psychoanalytic notion of "ambivalence." See "Looking for Trouble," reprinted in Henry Abelove, Michèle Barale, and David M. Halperin, eds., *The Lesbian and Gay Studies Reader* (New York: Routledge, 1993), pp. 350-59. Originally published in *Transition* 51 (1991); "Skin Head Sex Thing: Racial Difference and the Homoerotic Imaginary" in Bad Object-Choices, ed., *How Do I Look? Queer Film and Video* (Seattle: Bay Press, 1991), pp. 169-210; "Engendered Species," *Artforum* vol. 30, no. 10 (Summer 1992): pp. 74-78. See also on the relationship between psychoanalysis, race, and ambivalence, Homi Bhabha, "Of Mimicry and Man: The Ambivalence of Colonial Discourse" in *October* 28 (Spring 1984): pp. 125-133.

7. See Linda Singer, *Erotic Welfare: Sexual Theory and Politics in the Age of Epidemic* (New York: Routledge, 1992).

8. For an argument against the construal of the Lacanian symbolic as static and immutable, see Teresa Brennan, *History After Lacan* (London: Routledge, 1993).

CHAPTER 5: "DANGEROUS CROSSING": WILLA CATHER'S MASCULINE NAMES

I would like to express my appreciation to Eve Kosofsky Sedgwick and Michael Moon for introducing me to the work of Willa Cather and to the possibilities of a queer reading of her texts. I am particularly grateful to the seminar on Literary Theory at Tulane University in May of 1991 that Eve Sedgwick invited me to teach, and which I had the good fortune to do with Michael Moon. I would also like to thank the audience at the Center for Literary and Cultural Studies at Harvard University in the spring of 1993 for their numerous and helpful suggestions on this chapter.

1. Sharon O'Brien, *Willa Cather: The Emerging Voice* (New York: Ballantine, 1987),

pp. 13-32. For an interesting rejoinder which focuses on Cather's enduring hostility to women, see Jeane Harris, "A Code of Her Own: Attitudes toward Women in Willa Cather's Short Fiction" *Modern Fiction Studies*, vol. 36, no. 1 (Spring 1990): pp. 81-89.

2. Hermione Lee, *Willa Cather: Double Lives* (New York: Vintage, 1989), pp. 10-15.

3. Eve Kosofsky Sedgwick, "Across Gender, Across Sexuality: Willa Cather and Others," *The South Atlantic Quarterly*, vol. 88, no. 1 (Winter 1989): pp. 53-72.

4. Eve Kosofsky Sedgwick, *Epistemology of the Closet*; see especially the discussion of the pluralization and specification of "ignorances" (p. 8) and the phenomenological description of gay and lesbian youth as "a gap in the discursive fabric of the given" (p. 43).

5. Adrienne Rich, "For Julia in Nebraska," in *A Wild Patience Has Taken Me This Far* (New York: Norton, 1981), p. 17.

6. Willa Cather, *My Ántonia* (Boston: Houghton Mifflin, 1988).

7. "Tommy the Unsentimental" in *Willa Cather: 24 Stories*, Sharon O'Brien, ed., (New York: Penguin, 1987), pp. 62-71.

8. See also on "bohemia" Sedgwick, *Epistemology of the Closet*, pp. 193-95, and Richard Miller, *Bohemia: The Protoculture Then and Now* (Chicago: Nelson-Hall, 1977), cited in Sedgwick.

9. I am indebted to Karin Cope's reading of Gertrude Stein on the question of the limitations of nomination for the articulation of sexuality. See her "'Publicity Is our Pride': The Passionate Grammar of Gertrude Stein" *Pretext* (Summer 1993), and *Gertrude Stein and the Love of Error* (Minneapolis: University of Minnesota Press, forthcoming).

10. It appears that Cather is here miming Shakespeare. Not only did she call herself "Will" and "William" when she was a young woman, but in these texts she invokes the abbreviated "W" as Shakespeare himself was wont to do. See Phyllis C. Robinson, *Willa: The Life of Willa Cather* (New York: Doubleday, 1983), pp. 31-32. See also Joel Fineman, "Shakespeare's *Will*: The Temporality of Rape," *Representations* no. 20 (Fall 1987): pp. 25-76.

11. In a letter dated 1908 to Willa Cather, Sarah Orne Jewett objected to what she understood as Cather's narrative device of writing as a man and about male protagonists, especially in Cather's story "On the Gulls' Road" (1908): "The lover is as well done as he could be when a woman writes in the man's

character,—it must always, I believe, be something of a masquerade. And you could almost have done it yourself—a woman could love her in that same protecting way—a woman could even care enough to wish to take her away from such a life, by some means or other. But oh, how close—how tender— how true the feeling is! The sea air blows through the very letters on the page" (*Letters of Sarah Orne Jewett*, Annie Fields, ed. [Boston: Houghton-Mifflin, 1911], pp. 246-47).

Sarah Orne Jewett's own fiction, particularly "Martha's Lady" (1897) and *The Country of the Pointed Firs* (1896), concern questions of gender and sexuality similar to Cather's own. And the relation between the anonymous narrator of Cather's *My Ántonia* and Jim Burden parallels the narrator who receives the story and the teller of the story in Jewett's *The Country of the Pointed Firs*. Both Jewett's novel and Cather's "Tommy the Unsentimental" (published the same year) interrogate the narrative and erotic dynamics of gift-giving and sacrifice.

12. Slavoj Žižek, *The Sublime Object of Ideology* (London: Verso, 1989), pp. 87-102.

13. See Sedgwick on "sentimentality" in *The Epistemology of the Closet*, pp. 193-99. See also O'Brien's argument that Cather mimes and subverts sentimental fiction by publishing this story in *Home Monthly* magazine, conforming to a formula acceptable to its editors, but only to mock sentimental conventions in the process, in *Willa Cather: The Emerging Voice*, pp. 228-231.

14. See note 11 above.

15. Charlotte Brontë evidently used "Shirley" as a woman's name for the first time in her novel *Shirley* (1849). Cather appears to be continuing and reversing that "coining" in this story, first, by establishing "Tommy" as a girl's name and, second, by establishing Shirley as a patronym. This citation of Brontë suggests that the name is not mimetically related to gender, but functions as an inversion of gendered expectations.

16. *Oxford English Dictionary*, second edition.

17. For a discussion of the signature as a line of credit, see Derrida's reading of Nietzsche's *Ecce Homo* on the temporality of the signature in Jacques Derrida, "Otobiographies: The Teaching of Nietzsche and the Politics of the Proper Name," in Peggy Kamuf ed., *The Ear of the Other*, tr. Avital Ronell (Lincoln: University of Nebraska[!] Press, 1985), pp. 1-40.

18. Havelock Ellis evidently linked blindness to sexual inversion in the 1890s and Cather may have known of his theory. He also claimed that blind people were prone to sexual "shyness" and "modesty," suggesting a link between inhibited desire and failing eyesight. See Havelock Ellis, *Studies in the Psychology of Sex, Vol. I* (Philadelphia: Davis Co., 1928), p. 77; see also *Studies in*

the Psychology of Sex, Vol. II, part 6, "The Theory of Sexual Inversion" (Philadelphia: Davis. Co., 1928), pp. 317-318.

19. Public debates on the appropriateness of women riding bicycles were highly publicized throughout the 1890s in the press, raising the question of whether too much bicycling was harmful to women's health and whether it might not excite women's sexuality in untoward ways. For a discussion of this literature which links the bicycle controversy to larger fears about women's growing independence during the time of "The New Woman," see Patricia Marks, *Bicycles, Bangs, and Bloomers: The New Woman in the Popular Press* (Lexington: Kentucky University Press, 1990), pp. 174-203; see also Virgil Albertini, "Willa Cather and the Bicycle," *The Platte Valley Review*, Vol. 15 no. 1 (Spring 1987): pp. 12-22.

20. "Paul's Case," Willa Cather, *Five Stories* (New York: Vintage, 1956), p. 149.

21. Cather's misogyny effectively renders "Tommy the Unsentimental" implausible as a narrative of love and loss. That Jessica is degraded from the start makes the final "sacrifice" appear superfluous. In this respect it seems especially useful to consider Toni Morrison's acute criticism of Cather's *Sapphira and the Slave Girl*. Morrison argues that the credibility of Cather's narrative is undermined by a recurring and aggrandizing racism. The relation between Sapphira, the slave-mistress, and Nancy, daughter of a devoted slave, lacks plausibility, and the relation between Nancy and her own mother is never credibly represented, because Cather, like Sapphira, has produced the slave girl in the service of her own gratification. Such a displacement resonates with the displacements of Cather's cross-gendered narrations as well, raising the question of the extent to which fictional displacement can be read as a strategy of repudiation. See Toni Morrison, *Playing in the Dark: Whiteness and the Literary Imagination* (Cambridge: Harvard University Press, 1992), pp. 18-28.

22. Willa Cather, "Tom Outland's Story," *Five Stories*, p. 66.

23. For a list of Cather's early pseudonymous names, see O'Brien, *Willa Cather*, p. 230.

CHAPTER 6: PASSING, QUEERING: NELLA LARSEN'S PSYCHOANALYTIC CHALLENGE

The following is a revised version of a lecture given at the University of Santa Cruz in October 1992 as part of a conference on "Psychoanalysis in African-American Contexts: Feminist Reconfigurations" sponsored by Elizabeth Abel, Barbara Christian, and Helene Moglen.

1. See Luce Irigaray, *Éthique de la différence sexuelle*, p. 13.

2. Freud's *Totem and Taboo* attests to the inseparability of the discourse of species reproduction and the discourse of race. In that text, one might consider the twin uses of "development" as (a) the movement toward an advanced state of culture and (b) the "achievement" of genital sexuality within monogamous heterosexuality.

3. *Passing,* in *An Intimation of Things Distant: The Collected Fiction of Nella Larsen,* Charles Larson, ed., forward by Marita Golden (New York: Anchor Books, 1992), pp. 163-276.

4. This suggests one sense in which "race" might be construed as performative. Bellew produces his whiteness through a ritualized production of its sexual barriers. This anxious repetition accumulates the force of the material effect of a circumscribed whiteness, but its boundary concedes its tenuous status precisely because it requires the "blackness" that it excludes. In this sense, a dominant "race" is constructed (in the sense of *materialized*) through reiteration and exclusion.

5. This is like the colonized subject who must resemble the colonizer to a certain degree, but who is prohibited from resembling the colonizer too well. For a fuller description of this dynamic, see Homi Bhabha, "Of Mimicry and Man," p. 126.

6. Where references in the text are made to the following authors, they are to the following studies unless otherwise indicated: Houston A. Baker, Jr., *Modernism and the Harlem Renaissance* (Chicago: Chicago University Press, 1987); Robert Bone, *The Negro Novel in America* (New Haven: Yale University Press, 1958); Hazel Carby, *Reconstructing Womanhood: The Emergence of the Afro-American Woman Novelist* (London and New York: Oxford University Press, 1987); Barbara Christian, *Black Women Novelists: The Development of a Tradition 1892–1976* (Westport, Ct.: Greenwood Press, 1980) and "Trajectories of Self-Definition: Placing Contemporary Afro-American Women's Fiction," in Marjorie Pryse and Hortense J. Spillers, eds., *Conjuring: Black Women, Fiction, and Literary Tradition* (Bloomington: Indiana University Press, 1985), pp. 233-48; Henry Louis Gates, Jr., *Figures in Black: Words, Signs, and the "Racial" Self* (New York and London: Oxford University Press, 1987); Nathan Huggins, *Harlem Renaissance* (New York and London: Oxford University Press, 1971); Gloria Hull, *Color, Sex, and Poetry: Three Women Writers of the Harlem Renaissance* (Bloomington: Indiana University Press, 1987); Deborah E. McDowell, "Introduction" in *Quicksand and Passing* (New Brunswick: Rutgers University Press, 1986); Jacquelyn Y. McLendon, "Self-Representation as Art in the Novels of Nella Larsen," in Janice Morgan and Colette T. Hall, eds., *Redefining Autobiography in Twentieth-Century Fiction* (New York: Garland, 1991); Hiroko Sato, "Under the Harlem Shadow: A Study of Jessie Faucet and Nella Larsen," in Arno Bontemps, ed., *The Harlem Renaissance Remembered*

(New York: Dodd, 1972), pp. 63-89; Amritjit Singh, *The Novels of the Harlem Renaissance* (State College: Pennsylvania State University Press, 1976); Claudia Tate, "Nella Larsen's *Passing*: A Problem of Interpretation," *Black American Literature Forum* 14:4 (1980): pp. 142-46; Hortense Thornton, "Sexism as Quagmire: Nella Larsen's *Quicksand*," *CLA Journal* 16 (1973): pp. 285-301; Cheryl Wall, "Passing for What? Aspects of Identity in Nella Larsen's Novels," *Black American Literature Forum*, vol. 20, nos. 1-2 (1986), pp. 97-111; Mary Helen Washington, *Invented Lives: Narratives of Black Women 1860–1960* (New York: Anchor-Doubleday, 1987).

7. Deborah E. McDowell, "'That nameless...shameful impulse': Sexuality in Nella Larsen's *Quicksand* and *Passing*," in Joel Weixlmann and Houston A. Baker, Jr., eds., *Black Feminist Criticism and Critical Theory: Studies in Black American Literature*, vol. 3 (Greenwood, Fla.: Penkevill Publishing Company, 1988), p. 141. Reprinted in part as "Introduction" to *Quicksand and Passing*. All further citations to McDowell in the text are to this essay.

8. Jewelle Gomez suggests that black lesbian sexuality very often thrived behind the church pew. See Jewelle Gomez, "A Cultural Legacy Denied and Discovered: Black Lesbians in Fiction by Women," *Home Girls: A Black Feminist Anthology* (Latham, NY: Kitchen Table Press, 1983), pp. 120-21.

9. For an analysis of the racist implications of such patronage, see Bruce Kellner, "'Refined Racism': White Patronage in the Harlem Renaissance," in *The Harlem Renaissance Reconsidered*, pp. 93-106.

10. McDowell writes, "Reviewing Claude McKay's *Home to Harlem* and Larsen's *Quicksand* together for *The Crisis*, for example, Du Bois praised Larsen's novel as 'a fine, thoughtful and courageous piece of work,' but criticized McKay's as so 'nauseating' in its emphasis on 'drunkenness, fighting, and sexual promiscuity' that it made him feel...like taking a bath." She cites "Rpt. in *Voices of a Black Nation: Political Journalism in the Harlem Renaissance*, Theodore G. Vincent, ed., (San Francisco: Ramparts Press, 1973), p. 359," in McDowell, p. 164.

11. Indeed, it is the ways in which Helga Crane consistently uses the language of the "primitive" and the "jungle" to describe sexual feeling that places her in a tragic alliance with Du Bois.

12. For an effort to reconcile psychoanalytic conflict and the problematic of incest and the specific history of the African-American family post-slavery, see Hortense J. Spillers, "'The Permanent Obliquity of the In(pha)llibly Straight': In the Time of the Daughters and the Fathers," in Cheryl Wall, ed., *Changing Our Own Words* (New Brunswick: Rutgers, 1989), pp. 127-149.

13. Sigmund Freud, "Some Neurotic Mechanisms in Jealousy, Paranoia and Homosexuality," *SE*, Vol. 18, 1922, p. 225.

14. Significantly, Freud argues that conscience is the sublimation of homosexual libido, that the homosexual desires which are prohibited are not thoroughly destroyed; they are satisfied by the prohibition itself. In this way, the pangs of conscience are nothing other than the displaced satisfactions of homosexual desire. The guilt about such desire is, oddly, the very way in which that desire is preserved.

    This consideration of guilt as a way of locking up or safeguarding desire may well have implications for the theme of white guilt. For the question there is whether white guilt is itself the satisfaction of racist passion, whether the reliving of racism that white guilt constantly performs is not itself the very satisfaction of racism that white guilt ostensibly abhors. For white guilt—when it is not lost to self-pity—produces a paralytic moralizing that *requires* racism to sustain its own sanctimonious posturing; precisely because white moralizing is itself nourished by racist passions, it can never be the basis on which to build and affirm a community across difference; rooted in the desire to be exempted from white racism, to produce oneself as the exemption, this strategy virtually requires that the white community remain mired in racism; hatred is merely transferred outward, and thereby preserved, but it is not overcome.

15. Norma Alarcón, "The Theoretical Subject(s) of *This Bridge Called My Back* and Anglo-American Feminism," in Gloria Anzaldúa, ed., *Making Face, Making Soul: Haciendo Caras* (San Francisco: Aunt Lute, 1990), pp. 356-69.

16. Barbara Christian, "The Race for Theory" in *The Nature and Context of Minority Discourse* (New York: Oxford University Press, 1990), pp. 37-49.

17. Toni Morrison, *Sula* (New York: Knopf, 1973), p. 174.

18. Henry Louis Gates, Jr., *Figures*, p. 202.

19. I am thankful to Barbara Christian for pointing out to me the link between the theme of "passing" and the accusation of plagiarism against Larsen.

CHAPTER 7: ARGUING WITH THE REAL

1. Slavoj Žižek, *The Sublime Object of Ideology*. Cited in the text as *SO*.

2. It is at the theorization of this "negativity" that Žižek rightly links the Lacanian notion of the "lack" to the Hegelian notion of "negativity."

3. Freud distinguishes between repression (*Verdrängung*) and foreclosure (*Verwerfung*) to distinguish between a negation proper to neurosis and that proper to psychosis. This distinction will be discussed further on this essay in conjunction with the real which, Lacan argues, is produced through foreclosure.

4. See Ernesto Laclau and Chantal Mouffe, *Hegemony and Socialist Strategy* (London: Verso, 1985).

5. The non-teleologically constrained notion of futurity opened up by the necessary incompleteness of any discursive formation within the political field links the project of radical democracy with Derrida's work. Later the question will be taken up, whether and how Žižek's strong criticisms of deconstruction and Derrida in particular, situate his theory in relation to futurity. My argument will be that the grounding of "contingency" in the Lacanian notion of the real produces the social field as a permanent stasis, and that this position aligns him more closely with the Althusserian doctrine of "permanent ideology" than with the notion of incalculable futurity found in the work of Derrida, Drucilla Cornell, and some aspects of the Laclau/Mouffe version of radical democracy.

6. See Chantal Mouffe, "Feminism, Citizenship, and Radical Democratic Politics," in *Feminists Theorize the Political,* pp. 369-84.

7. See Laclau's illuminating essay, "New Reflections on the Revolution of our Time," in the book with the same name (London: Verso, 1991). Cited in the text as *NRRT.*

8. Laclau writes, "the hegemonic relationship can be thought only by assuming the category of *lack* as a point of departure." See "Psychoanalysis and Marxism" in *New Reflections on the Revolution of our Time,* pp. 93-96.

9. Here it seems that Žižek and Laclau also converge at the Hegelian assumption that lack produces the desire and/or tendency toward the effect of being or substance. Consider the unproblematized status of "tending" in the following claim by Laclau: "...we find the paradox dominating the whole of social action: freedom exists because society does not achieve constitution as a structural objective order; but any social action *tends towards* the constitution of that impossible object, and thus towards the elimination of the conditions of liberty itself" (44).

10. Žižek, *Sublime Object,* p. 72.

11. Sigmund Freud, "Analysis Terminable and Interminable," in *Therapy and Technique,* tr. Joan Riviere (New York: MacMillan, 1963), p. 271; *Gesammelte*

Werke, Vol. 16. I thank Karin Cope for drawing my attention to this citation.

12. Interestingly, as a figure within the metaphysics of substance, it is one which is used also by Husserl to describe the noematic nucleus of the object of cognition, i.e., that which remains self-identical in an object *regardless of its change of attributes*. In Laclau, this Husserlian take on the kernel/nucleus is evident in descriptions like the following: "The spatialization of the event's temporality takes place through repetition, through the reduction of its variation to an invariable nucleus which is an internal moment of the pre-given structure"(*NRRT*, p. 41). If what is being described is a noematic nucleus that subsists despite and through its possible imaginary variations, on the model of Husserl's *Ideas*, this use of the "nucleus" appears to support the anti-descriptivist position that Laclau and Žižek want to oppose.

    In the third seminar *Les Psychoses*, Lacan refers to psychosis as a "kernel of inertia" (p. 32). This "kernel" (*le noyau*) figures a recalcitrance to the Name of the Father, a repudiation which remains linked to the very symbolizing process it refuses. It might be of interest to consult Nicolas Abraham and Maria Torok's *L'Écorce et le noyau* (Paris: Flammarion, 1987) for the contestation of the primacy of that substantial truth and the theorization of psychosis exclusively in relation to symbolic paternity.

13. Michael Walsh, "Reading the Real," in Patrick Colm Hogan and Lalita Pandit eds., *Criticism and Lacan* (Athens: University of Georgia Press, 1990), pp. 64-86.

14. Žižek argues that "the Real is [language's] inherent limit, the unfathomable fold which prevents it from achieving its identity with itself. Therein consists the fundamental paradox of the relation between the Symbolic and the Real: the bar which separates them is *strictly internal to the Symbolic*." In the explication of this "bar," he continues, "this is what Lacan means when he says that "Woman doesn't exist": Woman qua object is nothing but the materialization of a certain bar in the symbolic universe—witness Don Giovanni." Slavoj Žižek, *For They Know Not What They Do* (London: Verso, 1991), p. 112. See also by the same author, *Looking Awry: An Introduction to Jacques Lacan through Popular Culture* (Boston: MIT Press, 1991), pp. 1-66.

15. Saul Kripke, *Naming and Necessity* (Cambridge, Mass.: Harvard University Press, 1980), p. 45. Cited in the text as *NN*.

16. Although a baptism is the conferring of the personal or "christian" name at birth, as opposed to the surname, it is also, by virtue of being the "christian" name, the initiation or, literally, the immersion into the church and its authority. Hobbes describes baptism as "the sacrament of allegiance of them that are to be received into the kingdom of God" (cited in the *OED* as "*Leviathan*, 499"). Interestingly, the giving of the first name is the initiation

into the order of divine paternity. Adam's naming is at once a blessing and an initiation into the kingdom of God of all things named in Genesis, and baptism is the continuation of the Adamic naming of persons who thereby become initiated into that divine lineage. My thanks to Lisa Lowe for a timely intervention on this matter.

17. Catachresis might be thought in terms of what Lacan refers to as "neologism" in the language of psychosis. Insofar as the catachresis of naming the aardvark Napoleon constitutes within discourse a resistance to symbolic paternity, it might be understood as a politically enabling deployment of psychotic speech. The "neologism" in Lacan is the index of psychosis because a word is coined to cover over a signifier that is excluded; both catachresis and neologism might be construed as a linguistic modality of suturing.

18. In *Naming and Necessity*, Kripke maintained that to the extent that names function as rigid designators, they could never be understood as synonymous or identical with a description or set of descriptions offered about the person who is named. A name refers rigidly, that is, universally and without exception, to a person no matter in what way the descriptions of that person may change or, to use the language, in all counterfactual situations. The account of rigid designation presupposes that names at some point in time became attached to persons. And yet, it appears that they can be attached to persons only on the condition that persons are first identified on the basis of descriptive features. Are there self-identical persons who can be said to exist prior to the fact of their being named? Does the name refer to, and presuppose, the self-identity of persons apart from any description? Or does the name constitute the self-identity of persons?

In the primal baptism, the name thus functions as a kind of permanent label or tag. Kripke concedes that in this first moment, in ascertaining, as it were, where precisely to place this tag, the one with the tag in hand (a fictional one? not already named? the unnameable one? Yahweh?), who does the naming, needs recourse to some preliminary descriptions. Hence, in the baptismal moment, there must be a descriptive basis for the act of naming. And he concedes that persons are bearers of some definite descriptions, like gene sequences, that do guarantee their identity through time and circumstance. And yet, whatever provisional descriptions are consulted in order to fix the name to the person and whatever essential attributes might be found to constitute persons, neither the descriptions nor the attributes are synonymous with the name. Hence, even if descriptions are invoked in naming, in the primal baptism, those descriptions do not function as rigid designators: that is the sole function of the name. The cluster of descriptions that constitute the person prior to the name do not guarantee the identity of the person across possible worlds; only the name, in its function as rigid designator, can provide that guarantee.

19. Gayatri Spivak refers to the category of "woman" as a mistake in relation to linguistic propriety in her "Nietzsche and the Displacement of Women," in Mark Krupnick, ed., *Displacement* (Bloomington: University of Indiana Press, 1983), pp. 169-96. Although her later theory of strategic essentialism, one on which she herself has recently cast doubt, works in a slightly different register, she appears to underscore the use of impossible totalizations as terms of political analysis and mobilization.

20. Lauren Berlant, "The Female Complaint," *Social Text* 19/20 (Fall, 1988), pp. 237-59.

21. On the political benefits of disidentification, see Michel Pêcheux, *Language, Semiotics, Ideology* (Boston: St. Martin's Press, 1975); "Ideology: Fortress or Paradoxical Space," in Sakari Hanninnen and Leena Paldan, eds., *Rethinking Ideology: A Marxist Debate* (New York: International Press, 1983); and chapter three in Rosemary Hennessy, *Materialist Feminism and the Politics of Feminism* (New York: Routledge, 1992).

22. See Denise Riley, *Am I that Name?* (New York: MacMillan, 1989).

CHAPTER 8: CRITICALLY QUEER

This essay was originally published in *GLQ*, vol. 1, no. 1 (Fall 1993). I thank David Halperin and Carolyn Dinshaw for their useful editorial suggestions. This chapter is an altered version of that essay.

1. This is a question that pertains most urgently to recent questions of "hate speech."

2. Foucault, *History of Sexuality, Volume One*, pp. 92-3.

3. See Eve Kosofsky Sedgwick's "Queer Performativity" in *GLQ*, vol. 1, no. 1 (Spring 1993). I am indebted to her provocative work and for prompting me to rethink the relationship between gender and performativity.

4. It is, of course, never quite right to say that language or discourse "performs," since it is unclear that language is primarily constituted as a set of "acts". After all, this description of an "act" cannot be sustained through the trope that established the act as a singular event, for the act will turn out to refer to prior acts and to a reiteration of "acts" that is perhaps more suitably described as a citational chain. Paul de Man points out in "Rhetoric of Persuasion" that the distinction between constative and performative utterances is confounded by the fictional status of both: "...the possibility for language to perform is just as fictional as the possibility for language to assert" (p. 129). Further, he writes,

"considered as persuasion, rhetoric is performative, but considered as a system of tropes, it deconstructs its own performance" (pp. 130-131, in *Allegories of Reading* [New Haven: Yale University Press, 1987]).

5. In what follows, that set of performatives that Austin terms illocutionary will be at issue, those in which the binding power of the act *appears* to be derived from the intention or will of the speaker. In "Signature, Event, Context," Derrida argues that the binding power that Austin attributes to the speaker's intention in such illocutionary acts is more properly attributable to a citational force of the speaking, the iterability that establishes the authority of the speech act, but which establishes the non-singular character of that act. In this sense, every "act" is an echo or citational chain, and it is its citationality that constitutes its performative force.

6. "Signature, Event, Context," p. 18.

7. The historicity of discourse implies the way in which history is constitutive of discourse itself. It is not simply that discourses are located *in* histories, but that they have their own constitutive historical character. Historicity is a term which directly implies the constitutive character of history in discursive practice, that is, a condition in which a "practice" could not exist apart from the sedimentation of conventions by which it is produced and becomes legible.

8. My understanding of the charge of presentism is that an inquiry is presentist to the extent that it (a) universalizes a set of claims regardless of historical and cultural challenges to that universalization or (b) takes a historically specific set of terms and universalizes them falsely. It may be that both gestures in a given instance are the same. It would, however, be a mistake to claim that all conceptual language or philosophical language is "presentist," a claim which would be tantamount to prescribing that all philosophy become history. My understanding of Foucault's notion of genealogy is that it is a specifically philosophical exercise in exposing and tracing the installation and operation of false universals. My thanks to Mary Poovey and Joan W. Scott for explaining this concept to me.

9. See Cherry Smyth, *Lesbians Talk Queer Notions* (London: Scarlet Press, 1992).

10. See Omi and Winant, *Racial Formation in the United States: From the 1960s to the 1980s.*

11. Theatricality is not for that reason fully intentional, but I might have made that reading possible through my reference to gender as "intentional and non-referential" in "Performative Acts and Gender Constitution," an essay published in Sue-Ellen Case, ed., *Performing Feminisms* (Baltimore: Johns

Hopkins University, 1991), pp. 270-82. I use the term "intentional" in a specifically phenomenological sense. "Intentionality" within phenomenology does not mean voluntary or deliberate, but is, rather, a way of characterizing consciousness (or language) as *having an object*, more specifically, as directed toward an object which may or may not exist. In this sense, an act of consciousness may intend (posit, constitute, apprehend) an *imaginary* object. Gender, in its ideality, might be construed as an intentional object, an ideal which is constituted but which does not exist. In this sense, gender would be like "the feminine" as it is discussed as an impossibility by Drucilla Cornell in *Beyond Accommodation* (New York: Routledge, 1992).

12. See David Román, "'It's My Party and I'll Die If I Want To!': Gay Men, AIDS, and the Circulation of Camp in U.S. Theatre," *Theatre Journal* 44 (1992): pp. 305-327; see also by Román, "Performing All Our Lives: AIDS, Performance, Community," in Janelle Reinelt and Joseph Roach, eds., *Critical Theory and Performance* (Ann Arbor: University of Michigan Press, 1992).

13. See Larry Kramer, *Reports from the Holocaust: The Making of an AIDS Activist* (New York: St. Martin's Press, 1989); Douglas Crimp and Adam Rolston, eds., *AIDSDEMOGRAPHICS* (Seattle: Bay Press, 1990); and Doug Sadownick, "ACT UP Makes a Spectacle of AIDS," *High Performance* 13 (1990): pp. 26-31. My thanks to David Román for directing me to this last essay.

14. *Gender Trouble*, pp. 57-65. See also my "Melancholy Genders, Refused Identifications," in *Psychoanalytic Dialogues* (forthcoming).

15. I thank Laura Mulvey for asking me to consider the relation between performativity and disavowal, and Wendy Brown for encouraging me to think about the relation between melancholia and drag and for asking whether the denaturalization of gender norms is the same as their subversion. I also thank Mandy Merck for numerous enlightening questions that led to these speculations, including the suggestion that if disavowal conditions performativity, then perhaps gender itself might be understood on the model of the fetish.

16. See "Freud and the Melancholia of Gender," in *Gender Trouble*.

17. This is not to suggest that an exclusionary matrix rigorously distinguishes between how one identifies and how one desires; it is quite possible to have overlapping identification and desire in heterosexual or homosexual exchange, or in a bisexual history of sexual practice. Further, "masculinity" and "femininity" do not exhaust the terms for either eroticized identification or desire.

18. See Douglas Crimp, "Mourning and Militancy," *October* 51 (Winter 1989): pp. 97-107.

19. See Sedgwick, "Across Gender, Across Sexuality: Willa Cather and Others."

20. See Gayle Rubin, "Thinking Sex: Notes for a Radical Theory of the Politics of Sexuality," in Carole S. Vance, ed., *Pleasure and Danger* (New York: Routledge, 1984), pp. 267-319; Eve Kosofsky Sedgwick, *Epistemology of the Closet*, pp. 27-39.

21. Toward the end of the short theoretical conclusion of "Thinking Sex," Rubin returns to feminism in a gestural way, suggesting that "in the long run, feminism's critique of gender hierarchy must be incorporated into a radical theory of sex, and the critique of sexual oppression should enrich feminism. But an autonomous theory and politics specific to sexuality must be developed" (309).

INDEX OF NAMES

Abraham, Karl, 80
Abraham, Nicolas, 279
ACT UP, 233
Alarcón, Norma, 182, 277
Alexander, M. Jacqui, 270
Althusser, Louis, 35, 69, 121, 122, 188, 190, 191, 225, 252, 258, 270
Andrews, Julie, 126
Anzaldúa, Gloria, 124, 269, 270, 277
Appiah, Anthony, 247
Aristotle, 17, 31-35, 40, 42, 250-254
Austin, J.L., 224, 244, 246, 280

Barrie, J.M., 154
Bataille, Georges, 266
Bergson, Henri-Louis, 244
Berlant, Lauren, 219, 281
Bernal, Martin, 257
Bersani, Leo, 113, 269
Bhabha, Homi, 271, 275
Bloch, Ernst, 250
Borch-Jacobsen, Michel, 246
Bourdieu, Pierre, 246
Brennan, Teresa, 271
Brecht, Bertolt, 223
Brontë, Charlotte, 154, 272

Brown, Wendy, 250, 266
Busch, Wilhelm, 58, 61
Butler, Judith, ix, 243, 246, 249, 268, 269, 283

Carby, Hazel, 173-175, 178, 275
Caruth, Cathy, 244
Cather, Willa, 16, 19, 20, 124, 138-140, 143-145, 148-152, 154, 155, 157-160, 162-164, 179, 248, 252, 256, 270, 271-274
Chodorow, Nancy, 241
Chow, Rey, 117, 270
Christian, Barbara, 173, 182, 274, 275, 277
Cope, Karin, 272
Cornell, Drucilla, 256, 278, 283
Crimp, Douglas, 283

de Beauvoir, Simone, 4
de Lauretis, Teresa, 265, 267
de Man, Paul, 281
Deleuze, Gilles, 4
Derrida, Jacques, 1, 13, 30, 38, 39, 41, 189, 191, 194, 226, 246-248, 252, 254-256, 264, 273, 278, 282
Diotima, 257

Doane, Mary Ann, 246, 265
Douglas, Mary, 257
DuBois, Page, 255
Du Bois, W. E. B., 178, 279

Ellis, Havelock, 273

Fanon, Frantz, 117, 270
Felman, Shoshana, 246
Feuerbach, Ludwig, 250
Fineman, Joel, 272
Foucault, Michel, 9, 10, 17, 22,
    32-35, 93, 109, 189, 192,
    197, 200, 206, 223, 224, 244,
    245, 246, 248, 249, 251, 266,
    268-270, 281, 282
Fox Keller, Evelyn, 250
Freud, Sigmund, 13, 16, 17, 55,
    57-65, 71-74, 82, 83, 90, 91,
    105, 110, 180-182, 200, 204,
    234, 244, 246, 249, 250, 255,
    256, 259-262, 264, 267, 269,
    273, 275, 276, 278, 283
Frye, Marilyn, 126
Fuss, Diana, 246

Gallop, Jane, 38, 57, 82, 253, 258
Garber, Marjorie, 270
Garland, Judy, *x*, 233
Gates, Henry Louis, Jr., 183,
    247, 275, 277
Gilroy, Paul, 270
Gomez, Jewelle, 276
Gramsci, Antonio, 114, 132
Grosz, Elizabeth, 253, 258
Guillaumin, Colette, 247

Habermas, Jürgen, 192
Hall, Radclyffe, 265
Halperin, David, 257
Haraway, Donna, 1, 257
Harris, Jeane, 272
Hegel, Georg Wilhelm
    Friedrich,
    113, 116, 194, 217, 277
Heidegger, Martin, 245
Hoffman, Dustin, 126
Holophernes, 102
hooks, bell, 126, 133-136, 270
Huggins, Nathan, 275
Hull, Gloria, 173, 275
Husserl, Edmund, 279

Irigaray, Luce, 17, 27, 32, 35-39,
    41-51, 54, 73, 124, 167, 187,
    252-257, 259, 260, 262, 274
Irma (Freud's case), 258

JanMohammed, Abdul R., 117,
    247, 268
Jewett, Sarah Orne, 272, 273
Johnson, Barbara, 246
Jones, Ernest, 81

Kafka, Franz, 147, 269
Kant, Immanuel, 66
Kellner, Bruce, 276
Klein, Melanie, 81, 259
Kojève, Alexandre, 261
Kramer, Larry, 283
Kripke, Saul, 153, 206, 210-214,
    216, 217, 279, 280
Kristeva, Julia, 41, 69, 70, 244,
    255, 259

Lacan, Jacques, 12, 14, 17, 20, 22, 55, 57-60, 63, 65, 69-85, 87-90, 95-98, 100, 101, 103, 106-108, 110, 111, 122, 130, 138, 140, 152, 153, 181, 182, 187-191, 194-198, 202, 204, 206, 208, 209, 211, 214, 216, 243, 244, 247-249, 256-264, 266, 268, 270, 271, 277-279, 280

Laclau, Ernesto, 21, 191-194, 202, 207, 209, 210-212, 216, 217, 278, 279

Lacoue-Labarthe, Philippe, 268

Laplanche, Jean, 243, 265, 267

Laqueur, Thomas, 250

Larsen, Nella, 16, 18, 20, 112, 122, 167-170, 172-179, 182, 183, 185, 274-276

Lee, Hermione, 272

Lemmon, Jack, 126

Lévi-Strauss, Claude, 265

Leys, Ruth, 246

Livingston, Jennie, 16, 128, 133-136

Lloyd, David, 247

Lowe, Lisa, 117, 248, 270

Lyotard, Jean-Francois, 244

Lypsinka, 233

Machiavelli, Niccolò, 250

McDonald, Bridget, 252

McDowell, Deborah E., 173-175, 179, 275, 276

McKay, Claude, 276

MacKinnon, Catharine, 238

McLendon, Jacquelyn Y., 275

Madonna, 130

Marcus, Sharon, 249

Marks, Patricia, 274

Marx, Karl, 31, 167, 200, 250

Mercer, Kobena, 271

Merleau-Ponty, Maurice, 69, 259

Miller, James, 266

Miller, Richard, 272

Minnelli, Liza, 233

Minh-ha, Trinh T., 167

Mohanty, Chandra Talpade, 17, 248, 270

Morrison, Toni, 183, 270, 274, 277

Mouffe, Chantal, 21, 192, 193, 207, 209, 216, 278

Nagel, Thomas, 212

NAMES Project, 236

Nancy, Jean-Luc, 268

Nietzsche, Friedrich, 14, 38, 87, 121, 223, 224, 247, 273

Ninja, Willi, 130

Niranjana, Tejaswini, 248

Nunokawa, Jeff, 64, 259

O'Brien, Mary, 251

O'Brien, Sharon, 143, 144, 271-274

Omi, Michael, 247, 282

Ortner, Sherry, 243

Pêcheux, Michel, 281

Plato, 16, 17, 32, 35-48, 50, 53-55, 63, 124, 253-257

Plotinus, 42, 43

Pontalis, J.B., 243, 265, 267
Pratt, Mary Louise, 246

Queer Nation, 233

Rainey, Ma, 175
Rancière, Jacques, 269
Raymond, Janice, 126
Rich, Adrienne, 145, 272
Riley, Denise, 281
Robinson, Phyllis C., 272
Román, David, 283
Rose, Jacqueline, 263, 267
Rubin, Gayle, 239, 268, 282

Sadownick, Doug, 283
St. Laurent, Octavia, 135
Sartre, Jean-Paul, 262
Sato, Hiroko, 275
Schor, Naomi, 45, 253, 256, 260
Searle, John, 244
Sedgwick, Eve Kosofsky, 20,
    144, 145, 160, 162, 224, 238,
    248, 271, 272, 273, 281, 282
Shakespeare, William, 272
Silverman, Kaja, 246, 258, 268
Singer, Linda, 271
Singh, Amritjit, 173, 276
Socrates, 254, 257
Smith, Bessie, 175
Smyth, Cherry, 282
Spelman, Elizabeth, 252
Spillers, Hortense J., 275
Spivak, Gayatri Chakravorty, 1,
    27, 29, 117, 122, 229, 248,
    256, 269, 281
Stein, Gertrude, 272

Strawson, P. F., 212

Tate, Claudia, 173, 174, 183, 276
Thornton, Hortense, 276
Torok, Maria, 264, 265, 279

Van Vechten, Carl, 178
Vattimo, Gianni, 27, 249

Wall, Cheryl, 173, 174, 276
Walsh, Michael, 204, 279
Washington, Mary Helen, 173,
    276
Weed, Elizabeth, 253
Whitford, Margaret, 47, 253,
    256, 260, 262
Wilde, Oscar, 152, 158, 160, 163
Williams, Patricia, 123
Williams, Walter, 117, 270
Winant, Howard, 247, 282
Winkler, John J., 254
Wittgenstein, Ludwig, 246, 265
Wittig, Monique, 259
Wolf Man (Freud's case), 204
Wollheim, Richard, 259
Wynter, Sylvia, 247

Xtravaganza, House of, 125, 134
Xtravaganza, Venus, 125, 129-
    133

Yale University, 133, 165
Youmans, Mary Mabel, 173

Žižek, Slavoj, 20, 21, 153, 188-
    192, 194-211, 214, 216-220,
    273, 277, 279